Healing for Hurting Hearts

A Handbook for Counseling Children and Youth in Crisis

Other Books by Phyllis Kilbourn

Healing the Children of War:

A Handbook for Ministry to Children Who Have Suffered Deep Trauma

Children in Crisis: A New Commitment

Street Children: A Guide to Effective Ministry

Sexually Exploited Children: Working to Protect and Heal

Children Affected by HIV/AIDS: Compassionate Care

Shaping the Future: Girls and Our Destiny

Let All the Children Come:

A Handbook for Holistic Ministry to Children with Disabilities

Healing for Hurting Hearts

A Handbook for Counseling Children and Youth in Crisis

Phyllis Kilbourn

PUBLICATIONS
Fort Washington, PA 19034

HEALING FOR HURTING HEARTS
A Handbook for Counseling Children and Youth in Crisis

Copyright © 2013 by Phyllis Kilbourn.

Published by CLC Publications, U.S.A.
PO Box 1449, Fort Washington, PA 19034
ISBN-13 (trade paper): 978-1-61958-084-8
ISBN-13 (e-book): 978-1-61958-085-5

Contents

Foreword

Phyllis Kilbourn's books offer practical, timely and useful information for professional and lay caregivers. This handbook targets those caregivers who work with children who have been traumatized, exploited, neglected or abandoned. It provides helpers with both the tools and understanding they need to support these children through the healing process.

An issue that several authors address throughout the book is the emotional harm that children may incur when they internalize, rather than express, pain. Kilbourn explains that when children (and adults) internalize their pain and trauma, they create a block that prevents them from receiving and giving love. This affects all of a child's relationships—from the caregiver to someone in the child's primary support system—and, ultimately, blocks a child from the ever-present love of God. Children who have lived through trauma need guidance, to first identify their losses and then to understand how those losses have affected their lives, both physically and emotionally. Unfortunately, some helpers see internalized pain as positive, but it is quite the opposite. The chapters on trauma and grief clearly explain the emotional aspects of a child's development when he or she has experienced trauma. These chapters offer practical interventions that facilitate the healing process through the expression of feelings.

To better relate to children in crisis, caregivers will find the chapters on basic counseling skills, play therapy and group counseling helpful. I believe the chapters on stress, burnout and self-care should be required reading for all caregivers. We enter this work because of God's call to serve and because we have a deep desire to facilitate the alleviation of pain, especially in the lives of children. Finding balance is critical for those who are dedicated to serving God and His children.

The book opens with an excellent biblical overview of children throughout Scripture. The concluding sentences of chapter 1 explain the rationale behind this training manual: "We must never forget God perceives them (children) as precious and sees His glory in their potential. We have the honor of extending our love to them as the extension of His love." My prayer for you is that you continue in your call and not forget that "for of such is the kingdom of heaven" (Matt. 19:14 KJV).

Ann Noonan
Executive Director
Agapé Christian Counseling, Inc.

Contributing Authors

Wendy Middaugh Bovard has worked with children in crisis in five African countries and the Caribbean. Dr. Bovard's work has provided her with many opportunities to care for children with disabilities, including HIV/AIDS children in Kenya and former child soldiers in war-torn northern Uganda. She also united children with their families in Rwanda after the genocide, developed the Outdoor Adventure therapy and most recently, provided psychological support to Haitian children after the 2010 earthquake. Currently, she lives and works in Haiti.

Esther Buff, originally from Switzerland, is a missionary with WEC International. She is also the codirector of Lighthouse Children's Ministry, South Africa, where she has served for twenty-six years, mainly among the Setswana-speaking children. Her focus has been on bringing healing and restoration to the hurting hearts of traumatized children. Today, she has the joy of seeing many of the children she has ministered to, now as adults, reaching out to children suffering because of traumatic experiences.

Irma Chon has a Master of Arts in Christian education and church ministries. She is the children's and youth pastor at Cornerstone Christian Fellowship in Hilliard, Ohio, USA, and is actively involved in training global leaders in leading children in prayer. Her passion is to empower families to know God intimately through prayer and to build their homes upon the strong foundation of His Word.

Christa Foster Crawford holds a Juris Doctorate from Harvard Law School and is also completing a Master of Arts in holistic child development from Malaysia Baptist Theological Seminary. She is an adjunct assistant professor on children at risk at Fuller Theological Seminary, and has authored and edited numerous books, chapters and articles on ministering to trafficked and sexually exploited children and women. Since 2001, Christa has lived in Thailand, where she has ministered at both the grassroots and policy levels. She currently serves as an international consultant, providing resources and expert advice on ending human trafficking and sexual exploitation in Thailand and the Greater Mekong Subregion.

Delores Friesen is professor emerita of pastoral counseling at Fresno Pacific University Biblical Seminary in Fresno, California, USA, where she has taught marriage, family and child counseling at the master's level for twenty-five years. She is an ordained minister, licensed therapist and writer. Delores served twelve years as a missionary in Nigeria and Ghana, and in the short term taught peace, conflict transformation, teaching, counseling and HIV/AIDS assignments globally. Her latest publication is *Living More With Less Study/Action Guide*.

Stephanie Goins holds a doctorate in philosophy from the University of Wales and a master's in psychology from the University of West Florida. She currently serves as vice president of programs for Love146, a nonprofit organization that works to abolish child exploitation and trafficking. Stephanie is also the author of numerous publications relating to the issues of children in crisis. From 1990 to 2010, Stephanie's work with Youth With A Mission (YWAM) focused on children in difficult circumstances, discipleship, team building, training and counseling. She has worked in Africa, Europe and the United States.

Leah Herod earned her doctorate in clinical psychology from Auburn University in Alabama and subsequently opened a private practice specializing in behavioral disorders. Her primary focus has been in working with children, although she has also provided parent-training seminars, worked with groups and teams, offered consultation and provided lay-counselor training. Leah has provided counseling services and consultation to countries in the Middle East, Africa, Southeast Asia and South America. Currently, she is a faculty member in the department of counseling at Columbia International University in South Carolina.

Kim Hoover is a child/adolescent psychiatrist in Winston-Salem, North Carolina, USA, with over twenty years of experience working with children and families. She maintains a private practice, as well as serves as medical director of Youth Opportunities, a nonprofit agency providing mental health services for financially needy families. As a volunteer with Crisis Care Training International (CCTI), she serves as a contributing author and a trainer, most recently helping to conduct training seminars in the Philippines.

Phyllis Kilbourn is founder of Rainbows of Hope and CCTI, both global ministries of WEC International to children in crisis. A child advocate, trauma trainer and author/editor of a number of handbooks focused on interventions for children in crisis, Phyllis also served in Liberia and Kenya with WEC International. She holds a doctorate in education from Trinity International University in Illinois.

Marjorie McDermid, a missionary with WEC International to Equatorial Guinea,

West Africa, has worked in various children's ministries. She also served in WEC USA's home office as editor of its mission magazine for twenty-five years. Since 1995, she has been a child advocate, as well as a writer and editor for Rainbows of Hope and CCTI. She is coeditor of *Sexually Exploited Children: Working to Protect and Heal,* a book in this series.

Harvey Payne earned degrees from Lancaster Bible College in Pennsylvania, Denver Seminary in Colorado and a doctorate in clinical psychology from Massachusetts School of Professional Psychology. He completed a post-doctoral fellowship at the Alfred I. du Pont Hospital for Children in Wilmington, Delaware, USA. He specializes in the evaluation and treatment of children, and has provided consultation, program development and staff training for various agencies. He has served internationally as a consultant and is currently dean of the college of counseling at Columbia International University.

Rosemary Sabatino attended Columbia International University, where her focus was education and biblical studies. She currently serves as international coordinator with CCTI, a global ministry of WEC International, to children in crisis. Rosemary has worked with orphaned and abandoned children in Senegal, West Africa, and has organized and helped conduct CCTI seminars both globally and in the United States.

Keith J. White is director of Mill Grove in London, UK, where, with his wife Ruth, he is responsible for the residential community caring for children who have experienced separation and loss. He holds three degrees, one each from Oxford, Edinburgh and Cardiff universities in the UK. He is former president of the UK Social Care Association and chair of the National Council of Voluntary Child Care Organizations. Currently, Keith is an associate lecturer at Spurgeon's College, and visiting lecturer in child theology at the Malaysian Baptist Theological Seminary. He is chair and founder of the Child Theology Movement.

Mary Beth Young is, above all, a sinner saved by grace who was called to social work and missions at a young age. While attending Moody Bible College, the Lord confirmed she would minister in the United States. Mary Beth has a master's degree of social work from the University of North Carolina at Chapel Hill, USA. She also holds a license of clinical social work and has a special interest in ministering to those who have experienced trauma. Since 2008, Mary Beth has been a volunteer with CCTI, teaching CCTI curricula related to trauma, street children, and sexual exploitation/human trafficking in Senegal, Ukraine, Haiti, and in the United States.

Introduction

Of the 2.2 billion children in the world, clearly two-thirds—1.5 billion—are hurting. They are children at risk and children in crisis—precious children—who have been subjected to the traumatic experiences of neglect, abuse, abandonment and/or exploitation. Such trauma inflicts physical, emotional and spiritual wounding that, if unaddressed, leaves scars that can last a lifetime. Long-term wounding can prevent children from fulfilling their God-created purpose, and destroy their ability to have meaningful and healthy relationships, including their relationship with their Creator-Savior. As the eighth title in a series dedicated to informing and resourcing those who work with children of trauma, this book offers a key component to the mission of bringing healing to the children's hurting hearts—instruction on counseling children and youth in crisis.

We began this project with the end in mind: to produce a practical, effective resource that would help workers and caregivers, our target audience, bring healing and hope to the children they service. Throughout the book, we refer to our audience as counselors or lay counselors. However, we have since realized that our task was to provide new tools for the special people, working in many occupations, who are caregivers. *They may be cooks, nurses, doctors, pastors and teachers who need counseling tools to more effectively meet the children's needs. So although we may use the term counselors, this book is for the compassionate caregivers who seek to be at their best in communicating Christ's love and compassion; we are privileged to serve them.*

This service begins in Part I, where we lay a foundation based on the spiritual and emotional needs of traumatized children. What we know and believe about children determines both how we care for them, and the urgency of our calling. We begin first by recognizing the tremendous value God places on all children, and the importance of their understanding that they are unconditionally loved and accepted. Unfortunately, the serious losses produced by traumatic experiences block the child's ability to receive and believe God's love. This part addresses the importance of understanding the emotional needs stemming from these losses so that caregivers can help children to grieve and resolve them.

Part II provides basic counseling principles and strategies. It begins with an overall view of counseling, and the skills needed to minister to children and youth in crisis. Additionally, this part addresses effective how-to strategies for focused play, counseling sexually abused children and conducting group-counseling sessions. This part presents a broad framework for counseling that guides caregivers in ministering to trauma-impacted children and youth.

In addition to attending to the emotional impact of trauma, we must remember that, like all human beings, children are made up of body, mind and spirit. All of their experiences affect them physically, socially, mentally, emotionally and spiritually. Children and youth in crisis suffer significant spiritual harm—it distorts the way they view themselves, others and God. Part III deals with the spiritual aspects of counseling and focuses on three important areas of spiritual-focused counseling: overcoming the barriers of spiritual healing, understanding forgiveness and reconciliation, and healing prayer for children.

Part IV addresses three wider topics that impact the effectiveness of a counseling program:

1) Peace Education and Conflict Resolution. We must ask ourselves the question, "If the community environment is the main source of trauma to the children, what can be done to change or transform the community?" Chapter 11 focuses on prevention and healing by describing resources for peacemaking and reconciliation, as well as detailing some basic mediation and resolution skills.

2) Cross-Cultural Counseling. Chapter 12 helps the lay counselor prepare for working cross-culturally with children.

3) Integrated Child Protection. Child protection is examined in Chapter 13 from two perspectives: (a) protection through engaging in advocacy for children and (b) protection through a children's program that implements policies providing for their safety and protection.

No program designed to bring healing to children in crisis would be complete without speaking to the issues related to providing support to children, parents and caregivers. Part V addresses the need for and implementation of a healthy family lifestyle and godly parental support as significant prevention and intervention strategies the church could employ to mitigate the cause and effect of trauma-related injury to children. In Chapter 15, *Stress, Burnout and Self-Care,* we address the vital need caregivers have to understand the causes of stress and burnout, and self-care practices that alleviate both.

In addition, caregivers will be delighted to find instructions in Chapter 16 on the use of two trauma-recovery tools (included in the accompanying CD) that will assist them in their communication with traumatized children: *There Is Hope* (for one-on-one counseling) and *Tell Me a Story* (for group counseling). These tools are already in use globally to help children process their trauma and, most importantly, in so doing, help bring them into a closer relationship with Jesus.

Finally, in Part VI, Dr. Keith White offers an inspiring concluding reflection as he takes us on *A Walk with Jesus* that will not be forgotten. He brings us full circle back to our original destination and goal— to help those who have committed their lives to bring healing and hope to children in crisis. In the words of Dr. White:

> Welcoming a child in Jesus' name is welcoming Jesus Himself...Over time, I began to learn what it was really like to welcome children in the name of Jesus: to be open to them with my whole being. And I have come to recognize those parents, teachers and caregivers who have opened their hearts to children; who love and respect the children they are alongside. This is the calling of our Lord and Master: full acceptance, appreciation, valuing, respect for children in His name . . .
>
> *. . . the name of Jesus.*

Acknowledgments

We continually remember before our God and Father your work produced by faith,
your labor prompted by love, and your endurance inspired
by hope in our Lord Jesus Christ.
1 Thessalonians 1:3, NIV

This project was birthed out of the desperate cry for help from children-in-crisis workers and caregivers as they expressed their need for resources and training in counseling children and youth in crisis. I cannot count the number of times I have heard these words, "Please send tools that will teach us how to help the children, how to talk with and counsel them. We do not have access to professional help here and we need direction."

I turned to prayer, knowing it would take a team of people with just the right expertise and experience to develop a resource that would be of help. The Lord abundantly and graciously answered by sending a group of highly qualified contributing authors. They are all practitioners in their field of service with many other professional responsibilities; however, they have tirelessly and generously donated their time and talent to bring healing and hope to the children of God's heart. For this I will be forever grateful.

An additional blessing came in the form of editorial assistance provided by an amazing group of workers who did a superb job toward ensuring the clarity, accuracy, and continuity of the project. A special note of thanks and appreciation goes to CLC managing editor, Tracey Lewis-Giggetts, whose contributions have been a tremendous help during this process.

Finally, my heartfelt gratitude extends to those who have been the catalyst for this undertaking—the countless numbers of caregivers and workers who have committed their lives in service to children with hurting hearts. Our sincere prayer is that this handbook would be an effective resource and thereby, in some small way, we can join hands with caregivers in their efforts to help build a hope-filled tomorrow for children and youth whose lives are at-risk and in crisis.

Phyllis Kilbourn

PART I

LAYING A NEEDS-BASED FOUNDATION

ONE

GOD'S PATTERN and PLAN for CHILDREN

Valued, Accepted, Loved

Marjorie McDermid

When I contemplate the value God places on children, my mind immediately goes to my own childhood. I was born in the dust bowl of Saskatchewan, Canada in what we came to term as the "dirty thirties." Talk about dirt poor! That was my family and many of our neighbors as we eked out a living on small grain farms in those dry years.

In spite of being poor, my siblings and I were well-off. We were loved dearly by our parents, who protected and cared for us at the risk of their own health and lives. Beyond that, they brought us to Jesus and taught us the principles of God's Word. I am eternally grateful to God for them.

Susannah has a different story. Susannah lives in South Africa. At the age of eleven, her stepfather raped her. The exploitation at home spurred her to run away. On the streets in Cape Town, a gang run by an organized-crime syndicate recruited her. Initiation into the gang included being raped and prostituted by the young male members. She was introduced to drugs and raped repeatedly. By the time Susannah turned twelve, she had been betrayed by her family, raped at home, living on the street and addicted to drugs.

At one time in a drug-treatment program, Susannah was introduced to Satanism. She went through rituals that included being tattooed while renouncing the Person of Jesus. One design on her body depicted an upside-down cross.

Following six years of exploitation by both men and women, Susannah was rescued by a Christian couple, and found safety and hope. A year after being rescued, Susannah surprisingly and boldly stated, "I am a person!"

What a magnificent moment—celebrating the recognition of her dignity and personhood!

Susannah had met her Maker. She finally knew who she was—*a person*. She had begun to understand who God is and how much He loved her. Her rescuers had not only taken her to a safe place, provided her with food and clothing, and given her protection; they had also given her hope for a future. They taught her about her heavenly Father, and how much He values and loves her. She was no longer a *thing* but a *person*, dearly loved by her Creator. Her spiritual DNA, or hereditary makeup, is now her identity with Christ and her relationship to her heavenly Father.

Valued, Accepted, Loved by God

How much value and worth does God place upon children—*all* children? The answer to that question will affect deeply our commitment to the care and counsel of children who are often viewed to be of little value.

The best place to go for answers to our question is the Word of God, which actually has quite a bit to say about the subject. The Bible speaks to our subject directly, by inference and by example.

Does God Value All Children?

Children are a heritage from the Lord, offspring a reward from him. Like arrows in the hands of a warrior are children born in one's youth.
(Psalm 127:3–4 NIV).

Doubtless, every one who reads this book will expect to see the above verses repeated and won't be disappointed. Don't skip over them; these verses are key.

As I write this chapter, pictures have reached me of newborn Shane, my great-great-great-nephew, and his father. A tear running down the young father's face says it all: this child is a precious gift and part of the heritage of our whole family. Sadly, not all births are greeted with so much pleasure and potential for future well-being as Shane holds. But that fact does not change how God the Father feels about each child who is born.

Valued as His Own Creation

The Lord told Ezekiel to tell the people, "you took your sons and daughters whom you bore to me and sacrificed the . . ." (Ezek. 16:20, NIV). God values, as His own, each child whom He creates through the birth process. We cannot begin to fathom how much God values a child, the gift that He gives to Himself.

Along with all of creation, God refers to children as the work of His hands (see Isa. 29:23; 45:11). As humans, we naturally glory in the work of our hands, those things we can make or create or do. In a small way, then, we begin to understand how God feels about His creation and each child that He creates in His own image.

The book of Job shows us another dimension of this truth when it notes God "shows no partiality to princes and does not favor the rich over the poor, for they are all the work of his hands" (Job 34:19, NIV). God values the children of the poor as much as those of royalty and wealth.

Valued Possessions Are Preserved

Accounts of how God protected children when they were in danger give concrete evidence of how He values them. Remember the young Prince Joash, who was under sentence of death by his grandmother, the queen? She tried to wipe out the entire royal family. God used the boy's aunt, Jehosheba—who just happened to be also the high priest's wife—to hide the child for six years. Seven years later Joash, God's choice for king, was crowned (see 2 Kings 11).

Earlier in history, God blessed the Hebrew midwives who took their lives in their hands when they allowed Hebrew boys to live at birth. Then, He also rescued the baby Moses, who became one of the world's greatest leaders of all time (see Exod. 2).

Still ancient history, but coming into New Testament times, when all boys Jesus' age were threatened with death by King Herod's decree, God intervened. Acting on the advice of an angel, Joseph hurried the toddler and his mother away to safety in Egypt. When the danger passed, he returned the family to fulfill all that God had ordained for Jesus: our salvation and that of the whole world.

Not incidentally, the term *little child/children* is used symbolically in speaking about the kingdom of heaven (see Matt. 18:2-6; Mark 10:15; Luke 18:17). God's plan for the redemption of human souls began with the birth of a child: His only son, Jesus. We need to remember that Jesus was truly human as we look at how the Father related to the Son. He called Jesus His "beloved son" and commended Him (the human son) as being "well pleasing" to Him (the heavenly Father.)

God also uses the metaphor of the birth of a child to describe the birth of our individual, personal relationship to Him (see John 3). The use of that term throughout the New Testament as it is used in reference to Jesus' followers, casts a lot of light on how God views children, what He wants for them and how He cares for them.

Does God Accept All Children?

God's acceptance of children did not stop with those He intended to use for His kingdom.

Alien's Child Preserved

Ishmael's mother, Hagar, was a single, exploited young mother, and her son was *not* the child of God's promise to his father, Abram. God also intervened for this child and his mother, saving them from certain death in the desert (see Gen. 16, 21). Even though God knew the nations that would come from Ishmael would be at enmity with God's purposes and plans, He loved, valued and provided for Ishmael, and preserved his life. We have yet to witness the final act in this theater of the nations. What we do know is that God loves all peoples and is quite equal to the task of being the righteous judge of all nations.

Aliens' Children Get Rights

God further indicates His acceptance of all children when He makes provision for the third generation of children born to aliens living among the Israelites to enter the assembly of the Lord (see Deut. 23:7–8). Later, He instructed Joshua to "assemble the people—men, women and children, and the foreigners residing in your towns—so they can listen and learn to fear the Lord your God and follow carefully all the words of this law. Their children, who do not know this law, must hear it and learn to fear the Lord your God as long as you live in the land you are crossing the Jordan to possess" (Deut. 31:12–13 NIV).

Particularly to us as counselors, what does this example say about the children we serve? Does it not say that God sees every child, regardless of who he or she is or will become, as acceptable and worthy of protection, provision, and possession? God, Himself, in the finality of all things, will judge righteously for each child and will reward us for being the keepers of His created and highly valued human beings.

Children Worthy to Be Cited with Adults

One feature stands out conspicuously while researching children in the Bible. In listings of people, children and grandchildren are seen as worthy to be cited along with adults. They were included in the following:

- prayer and confession

    While Ezra was praying and confessing, weeping and throwing himself down before the house of God, a large crowd of Israelites—men, women and children—gathered around him. They too wept bitterly (Ezra 10:1 NIV).

- praise and worship

  The secret things belong to the LORD our God, but the things revealed belong to us and to our children forever, that we may follow all the words of this law (Deut. 29:29 NIV).

  God said children were ordained to praise Him for a special reason.

  Through the praise of children and infants you have established a stronghold against your enemies, to silence the foe and the avenger (Ps. 8:2 NIV).

- offering sacrifices for sin

  But you and your sons and your daughters may eat the breast that was waved and the thigh that was presented... This will be the perpetual share for you and your children, as the Lord has commanded. (Lev. 10:14-15 NIV).

- celebrations of rejoicing

  And on that day they offered great sacrifices, rejoicing because God had given them great joy. The women and children also rejoiced. The sound of rejoicing in Jerusalem could be heard far away (Neh. 12:43 NIV).

- commands and promises

  So that you, your children and their children after them may fear the LORD your God as long as you live by keeping all his decrees and commands that I give you, and so that you may enjoy long life (Deut. 6:2, see also 5:29 NIV).

Does God Love All Children Unconditionally?

Children are vulnerable and, for the most part, defenseless. Many of the world's children are powerless victims of human neglect, deprivation, abandonment, cruelty and exploitation. God expresses His love for children in His show of outrage against all who abuse or misuse children.

Loves the Belittled and Abused

The Gospels of Matthew (18), Mark (9) and Luke (9) all tell the familiar story of Jesus answering His arguing disciples' question about who would be the greatest in God's kingdom. Using a human object lesson, He called

a little boy to Himself and lovingly held him up as an example of the humble "greatest." What a sails-collapsing, breath-robber for the disciples who
probably thought He would cite one of them! Would it be Peter, the chief
speaker for the group? Or Judas, the treasurer?

Then Jesus added a warning of retribution for anyone who mistreated
this child. He pictured a millstone—so large it took a donkey to turn it
for grinding—being placed around the perpetrator's neck. The idea of the
offender then being dumped into the sea left no doubt as to the fate that
awaited. Jesus indicated that sin so heinous should have appropriate punishment. So much is God's love and regard for children!

Loves the "Throw-aways"

*May he defend the afflicted among the people and save the children of the
needy; may he crush the oppressor* (Ps. 72:4 NIV).

Using a deserted newborn child allegorically to describe God's love for
Israel, the prophet Ezekiel graphically conveys how God feels about this
abandoned child and how He treated her (see Ezek. 16:1–14). He gave her
life (6), made her grow into a beautiful young woman (7), cared for her and
preserved her dignity, then formed a covenant with her that made her His
own (8). He dressed her splendidly and adorned her with jewels (10–13).
These gems may be seen as representative of the gifts and talents He gives
to all children, regardless of their status in life. Can you think of a more de-
lightful picture of how God values and loves the abandoned child?

Loves the Helpless

God had harsh words for those who worshiped another god, thereby
profaning His name. He equaled to idolatry the offering of children in sacrifice to the god Molek.

*The LORD said to Moses, "Say to the Israelites: 'Any Israelite or any foreigner
residing in Israel who sacrifices any of his children to Molek is to be put to
death. The members of the community are to stone him. I myself will set my
face against him and will cut him off from his people; for by sacrificing his
children to Molek, he has defiled my sanctuary and profaned my holy name'"*
(Lev. 20:1–3 NIV).

We can safely assume that today God has the same attitude toward those
who give their children in sacrifice to become temple prostitutes. Perhaps in
the same category are those sold to be trafficked into objects of pornography
and sexual slavery.

Loves the Youth

God's love extends also to the older children or youth. He exhorts them to be aware of their Creator in their youth, before they get old and cynical (see Eccles. 12:1 NIV). The proverbs of King Solomon were given, among other things, "for giving . . . knowledge and discretion to the young" (Prov. 1:4 NIV). Very often Solomon addresses "my son" or "my child."

God values the potential of young people and uses them as His instruments. A captive Jewish servant girl courageously offered advice that brought healing to Army Captain Naaman (see 2 Kings 5). In spite of the disdain of his brothers, youthful David took care of the Philistine giant and won the king's approval as well as his battle (see 1 Sam. 17). Although we have no scriptural proof, it is commonly believed that Mary was a young teenager when she became the mother of our Lord Jesus.

Jesus' Love for the Children

The Gospels of Matthew (19), Mark (10) and Luke (18) all record how Jesus demanded of His disciples that children who were brought to Him for blessing be allowed to come near Him. Mark 10:14 says Jesus was angered by the disciples' actions. When the children came to Him, He took them in His arms and blessed them. What a precious picture and telling example of His value and acceptance of children!

A lovely memory remains from my childhood of a picture drawn to represent Jesus blessing the children. I saw myself as the pretty, little girl in the blue dress. That I had very dark instead of blonde hair didn't lessen my sense of Jesus' love for and acceptance of me.

We don't know to what sort of families these children belonged. Were they poor or, in some way, rejected by people? The actions of the disciples might indicate these parents were not politically or socially "important." Whoever they were, Jesus did not hesitate to touch their children and show His love and esteem for them.

Let's push the speculation a little farther. What if these had been street children? Or orphans? Or children of prostitutes or of parents with addictions? I think it's not hard for us to imagine what Jesus would have done and how He feels about such children today.

Do you ever think as you work with the children—sometimes so humanly unlovable, dirty, deceitful, ungrateful—that Jesus would have died if only for this one child? We cherish that thought for ourselves. Oh, be reminded, if ever we are tempted to think of these children as less than precious, that Jesus died for them too. That's how much He loved them.

Jesus loved the children and regarded them as worthy of His touch and time. He blessed them and made them an example to His disciples—an example of innocence, humility, honesty, trust and those to whom the kingdom of heaven belong (see Matt. 19:14; Mark 10:14). And He says to us, His 21st Century disciples, "Whoever welcomes one such child in my name welcomes me" (Matt. 18:5 NIV).

Jesus Heals Children

Many times, Jesus touched children with His loving, healing hand. How blessed and excited those children must have been! That precious boy in Mark 9, when seized by an evil spirit, gnashed his teeth and threw himself into the fire uncontrollably. We like to turn away from such a scene, but Jesus stepped up and commanded the evil spirit to leave the boy. That act would have been enough to deliver the boy and satisfy the father, but, no, Jesus didn't stop there. He took the boy by the hand and lifted him up to his feet, healed. Try to imagine how that child felt. How did he later tell the story? How loved and respected did he feel?

In another incident Jairus, a ruler in the synagogue, pleaded with Jesus to come to his house and put His hand on his dying daughter (see Mark 5). Now, you would have thought that busy Jesus, in demand by adults and "important" people, might have said some word and healed the child at a distance, as He did on another occasion. But, no, He trudged with the father to the home and entered the room where the twelve-year-old girl lay, apparently now dead. And see what He does? He takes her by the hand and speaks to her. As she stood to her feet and walked around, Jesus, knowing that children are almost always hungry, told the parents, "Give her something to eat (5:43 NIV)." Wonderful Jesus loved this girl-child and considered her worthy of His presence, resurrection power and personal attention.

Jesus Loves to Hear the Children Worship

Sometime later, following Jesus' triumphant entry into Jerusalem, the leading priests and teachers of religious law, having seen the wonderful miracles of healing Jesus had performed, were indignant when they heard even the children in the temple shouting,

". . . Hosanna to the Son of David."

"Do you hear what these children are saying?' they asked him. "Yes," replied Jesus, "have you never read, 'From the lips of children and infants you, Lord, have called forth your praise?'" (Matthew 21:15–16 NIV).

In this case, Jesus' actions toward the children are notable for what He did not do. He did not rebuke the children or ask them to stop their noisy adulation in the temple. Instead, He commended them to the irate leaders for fulfilling the prophetic word of God. He apparently valued the praise of the children above the approval of the influential, religious hierarchy.

God's Pattern and Plan

In His Word, God displays the value He places on children in patterns and plans He has layed out for them and their place in the world.

Multiply and Populate the Earth

As we look at how God, the heavenly Father, values children, let's not miss the obvious: populating the earth and sustaining that population by the birth of human children. God blessed the first parents, Adam and Eve, and commanded them to "be fruitful and increase in number; fill the earth and subdue it" (Gen. 1:28 NIV).

God is still blessing parents by giving them children. Beginning with the birth of one boy named Cain (see Gen. 4:1), children (persons under the age of eighteen) now number into the billions. God's plan outlined throughout the Bible is for a husband and wife to have children and raise them to be godly.

Didn't the Lord make you one with your wife? In body and spirit you are his. And what does he want? Godly children from your union. So guard your heart; remain loyal to the wife of your youth (Mal. 2:15, NLT).

God told His people exiled to Babylon to settle down, marry and have children (see Jer. 29:4–6), promising He had a plan to prosper them as families and not to harm them (see 29:11).

Children in Families

God instituted the family for the care and nurture of the children He would give. As evidence of His love for the children, He designed the family to discipline, protect and educate them, preparing them in every way to take on the responsibility of adulthood. We believe childhood is planned by God as a time of happiness and fun, with children laughing and playing as beautifully described by Job:

They send forth their children as a flock;
  their little ones dance about.
They sing to the music of timbrel and lyre;
  they make merry to the sound of the pipe. (Job 21:11–12 NIV).

God in His wisdom and care knows that, especially when children are young and immature, they need protection both physically and spiritually (see Eph 4:14). God admonishes fathers to "manage [your] children and household well" (1 Tim. 3:12; see also 3:14). As the heavenly Father loves His children and disciplines them, no matter their age (se Heb. 12:6), He instructs earthly parents to do the same (see Prov. 19:18; 22:6; 23:13-14; 29:17). He also warns them against aggravating their children and thus discouraging them (se Col 3:21).

He told the children of Israel to "be careful to obey all these regulations I am giving you, so that it may always go well with you and your children after you" (Deut. 12:28).

God Promises Blessing to Children

The Psalmist saw the "righteous" man as "always generous" and promised that his "children will be blessed" (Ps 37:25–26 NIV).

I will pour out my Spirit on your offspring, and my blessing on your descendants (Isaiah 44:3 NIV).

Educate the Children

Scripture, especially in the Old Testament, speaks a lot about educating children. That which God told us to transmit to our children is not only the knowledge of languages, arts and sciences. He also desires that children be aware of His love for them, the rules of life that will give them a happy, fulfilled life and His strength, as recorded in the wonderful works He has done (se Josh. 4:6; see also Deut. 11:4-6).

Moses recognized the value of teaching the youngsters. He knew the children were the ones who would inherit the land God had promised to him and his forefathers before him. He said to the parents, "Your children who do not yet know good from bad—they will enter the land. I will give it to them and they will take possession of it" (Deuteronomy 1:39, 4:8–10).

The psalmist Asaph and the prophet Joel took up the same idea as recorded in Psalm 78:1–6 and Joel 1:1–3.

Because He loves and values them, God wants children taught the principles and meaning of His Word, and how it applies to them, so they will:

- know that He is the Lord God (se Exod. 10:2)

- learn to fear the Lord (see Deut. 31:11–13)

- know His law to obey it (see Deut. 32:46)

- not conform to a bad example of their fathers (see Ps. 78:6–8, 1 Pet. 1:18).

Conclusion

Let's revisit Susannah's story and notice that it took a year of care and counseling for her to make her bold statement of personhood and hope. Think about what obstacles likely confronted the couple who undertook her rehabilitation. Distrust and fear are obvious guesses, possibly accompanied by anger and a rebellious attitude. Do you think she understood when they told her, "God loves you?" Probably not.

Children who suffer physical or mental disabilities or are enduring/recovering from traumatizing life experiences, will present barriers and perhaps open opposition to your offer of help. How is it possible to relate to them that God values, accepts and unconditionally loves them?

Going to the Heart of the Matter

Only a change of the child's heart will set the child totally free and able to reach his or her potential. Counseling to reach the heart requires a clear understanding of who the child is: a human dearly and deeply valued, accepted and loved by God the heavenly Father. The Christian counselor must be convinced of that truth for herself and for the child. Then, she can minister what the child needs most: love and hope that will bring repentance, reconciliation and a changed heart.

Appeal to the heart. Tell the child, "God loves you." He may not believe it for the first or umpteenth time you say it, but he needs to hear it. You may be to him the greatest or only visible representation of God, His love and the hope He can give. Relationships are key: yours to the child and the child's to God.

Use God's Word

The Bible speaks to everything that has shaped the life and character of this child you have before you. Share God's Word liberally, appropriately and fearlessly.

Get Holy Spirit Help

Jesus promised the Holy Spirit, who would be our Counselor (see John 16:7). He will help both the counselor and counselee, working in the heart. The Holy Spirit pours God's love "into our hearts" (Rom. 5:5), causes hearts to "overflow with hope" (15:13) and ministers the gospel with "power" and "conviction" (1 Thess. 1:5). Prayer facilitates the Holy Spirit's intervention. He will pull down barriers that seem insurmountable.

So then, ours is the joy to teach the world's children the wonderful, transforming Word of God. Ours is the privilege to take on the burden of the broken, hurting children, counseling them and praying for them. We must never forget: God perceives them as precious and sees His glory in their potential. We have the honor of extending our love to them as the extension of His love.

Two

TRAUMA and LOSS

Phyllis Kilbourn

Today, on a global scale, an overwhelming number of children daily are being exposed to traumatic life events. A traumatic life event can be defined as any event that threatens injury, death or the physical integrity (wholeness) of self or others. Such events cause horror, terror or helplessness at the time it occurs. Traumatic life events include: sexual abuse, physical abuse, domestic violence, community and school violence, medical traumas, motor vehicle accidents, acts of terrorism, war experiences, natural and human-made disasters, suicides and any other event that leads to traumatic losses for a child.

There are also traumatic life events that do not stem from violence or natural disasters. Instead, the following events may be considered *normal childhood losses,* although they still are traumatic, childhood losses: death of loved ones and pets, divorce in their or a friend's family, having a family member be deployed by the military, changing schools or grades from year to year, moving to a new house and neighborhood (thereby losing their former house and that which made up their community), losing friends, and abandoning the comforts of childhood to enter the turbulence of adolescence. How children handle their grief over these losses will help determine how children respond to the sudden, unexpected losses for which there has been no preparation.

It is important to note that traumatic life events always result in tremendous loss for children and impact all aspects of their lives: emotional, spiritual, physical, social and mental. Trauma destroys the structures that, in normal times, provide the framework for a child's healthy development.

Carlos, a Peruvian ten-year-old boy, is an example of a child who suffered numerous losses through traumatic life events. As you read his story, you will want to make a mental or written list enumerating his losses.

Four years ago, family violence and sexual abuse by his father forced Carlos
to leave home. He could find no place to live except on the danger-filled
streets of Lima. Carlos often thought of what he missed about home as he
lay on cardboard boxes at night. He certainly did not miss the beatings or
abuse he had endured, but still he loves his mother and father. Too, Carlos
had just started school and a friend had given him Doodles, a fuzzy brown-
and-white puppy. Doodles had become Carlos' most-prized possession.
Carlos knew Doodles understood when he felt sad or lonely. They "talked"
together often and Doodles even tried to protect him during his beatings.
Carlos was quickly swept into many frightening situations to survive, so he
joined a gang for protection. His troubled life consisted of carrying drugs
for the Mafia, prostitution and even being hired for murder. Carlos was
further traumatized by his many arrests resulting in stays in the big city
jail, notorious for its treatment of prisoners. Fear, hard work and lack of
good nutrition all took a toll on Carlos' life. Sick, hungry, afraid and with
no family or friends who cared for him drained Carlos of any thoughts of
hope. How could my life ever become better, he wondered. No one loves
me or cares what happens to me.

Carlos' losses are typical for many of today's children in traumatic circumstances. Like Carlos, any child may experience the loss of: home, family,
parents, pets, friends, education, safety, trust, protection, sense of self-worth,
feeling valued, being accepted and, finally, hope.

The importance of identifying Carlos' losses and the impact they have
had on his life is vital knowledge in effectively helping unravel the tangled
ball of emotions resulting from Carlos' difficult and traumatic childhood.
Once Carlos understands the source and cause of his emotions, he will be
able to work through his losses and eventually bring his trauma to closure.
The same process will be true with each child who receives counseling.

Trauma robs children of precious childhood treasures; treasures that
were meant to lay the spiritual foundation for their lives. Scripture shows
that the robbing is intentional:

> The thief comes only to steal and kill and destroy; I have come that they
> may have life, and have it to the full (John 10:10 NIV)

As counselors, we, too, must be just as intentional in planning interventions, not only to rescue the children, but to help them identify and process
the losses they have experienced. Only then will it be possible for them to
receive the fullness of all that Christ longs to bring to them.

Defining the Losses

A major task for counselors is to help children who have experienced trauma to identify their losses and to understand how those losses affect their lives. Counselors serve as an emotional bridge for children during this process. Through communication techniques, including various forms of play activity or verbal interactions (which will be covered later in the chapter), along with keen observation, counselors can help children identify, name and understand their losses. It is possible for children to work through their emotional difficulties and to begin exploring creative ways to restore their losses and well-being.

Immediate and Long-term Losses

Generally speaking, there are two types of losses: immediate and long-term. Immediate, or first, losses such as shelter, family, food and protection leave children vulnerable, powerless and voiceless, thus exposing them to exploitation. Once children have fallen into exploitation, they experience long-term losses in the areas of trust, acceptance, unconditional love and a sense of value or worth. These long-term losses cause deep emotional wounding and erode a child's spiritual foundation because they represent qualities that are needed for building (or rebuilding) a strong spiritual foundation.

It is important to understand that children who are experiencing loss must find ways to survive while, at the same time, perpetrators are looking for defenseless children to exploit. Vulnerable and powerless, these children become easy prey for perpetrators of evil. The following categories of loss provide an outline for the *immediate* and *long-term losses* that make children vulnerable and open to exploitation.

Identity

Children who have suffered the loss of cherished personal possessions, such as status in their family or community or personal history, experience a loss of identity and a sense of loss of control over their lives. Personal losses can also cause severe psychological trauma when adolescents start asking, "Who am I?" or "Where did I come from?" The identity of children comes from their place in the family, and when the family changes, the child has to search for a new identity. For example, losing siblings forces children to move into a new place in the family system. Or, if a parent remarries, that is yet another adjustment children must make.

Protection and Safety

Children are powerless to protect themselves. They assume that adults in their world—family, school, church and community—will keep them safe. Therefore, the loss of home and family, formerly their safe refuge, is the main cause for losing a sense of safety. This often results in exploitation. In traumatic situations where children have lost needed safety and protection, they experience a loss of belief in parents' or other significant adults' personal power to protect them and keep them safe.

Home and Family

God has put a nurturing home and family at the center of a child's world. Here, children ideally get their first glimpse of the love of God through family members modeling and/or teaching God's foundational spiritual principles: unconditional love, security, trust, acceptance and belonging. Because children depend on others for care, guidance and support, they can be deeply affected by the loss of home and family, whether the loss comes through death or abandonment. This is especially true when children's family losses include provision for their basic necessities, such as food, shelter and protection.

Personal Losses

Losing one's prized personal possessions whether a favorite doll, a pet or a school book, are painful losses. Perhaps even more painful is the loss of a friend, a teacher or a close family member. Children caught up in exploitation usually suffer the loss of their identity papers, including their birth certificate. They now have no way to connect with their place of origin.

Physical Losses

Loss of safety and protection can lead to physical loss and disabilities, especially for children who have been exploited. For example, in war children are put at risk of injury and physical loss by situations such as being forced to clear mine fields or to engage in military activity. Children forced into sexual exploitation are at risk of contracting HIV/AIDS or other sexually transmitted diseases. For children forced into child labor, industrial accidents and poor working conditions can destroy their health, or leave them crippled or wounded. Car accidents and natural disasters can also result in physical losses.

Emotional Losses

The impact of traumatic life events extends far beyond physical damage. The emotional toll can result in a wide range of intense, confusing and sometimes frightening emotions for children. Emotional losses include unconditional love, trust, sense of belonging, ability to love or receive love, innocence, sense of self and one's inner qualities (feelings of inferiority) and hope.

Just as it takes time to repair physical damage, it also takes time to repair emotional damage. Rebuilding lives takes time, especially since the losses are fundamental to a child's spiritual growth and development.

Less Recognized or Ambiguous Losses

Children grieve other, less recognized or ambiguous, losses as well. Children who experience ambiguous losses—such as those resulting from deportation, incarceration or placement in foster care—may feel prolonged insecurity about whether they will see the lost person or homeland again. They may experience repeatedly dashed hopes and renewed grief whenever expected reunions do not occur. In many cases, particularly when a loss is stigmatizing — the result of parental incarceration, for example — children may not feel entitled to their grief.

Children may cloak such losses in secrecy, usually because of stigma or uncertainty. Unlike a clear loss resulting from death, these losses may go unrecognized by others and trigger little, if any, support.

Impact of Trauma and Loss on Children

Trauma-produced losses can change the way children view their world. Assumptions about safety and security are now challenged. The world is no longer a place where people around them keep them safe. Children's reactions to loss will depend upon several factors, including: the severity of the trauma causing the loss, the child's personality and age, and the child's nearness to the traumatic event.

Children's understanding of loss changes as they grow. For example, infants and toddlers have no understanding of object permanency. They enjoy the game of "peek-a-boo" because it helps them begin to accept separation and return. They do not understand that some people do not return, so they cannot conceive of the permanence of death or the loss of a parent due to divorce. If a child of this age loses a nurturing parent, bonding may be broken. Children must now bond with another caring adult, which requires learning to trust again. These children need much emotional support and often could benefit from counseling.

Counselors need to be alert to learn other factors that may bring understanding to the impact of a child's loss, such as the nature of the relationship of the child to the person(s) causing the loss, the history of the loss, the vulnerability of the child and the support system that is currently available.

Behavioral Issues

Loss causes feelings of great sadness. Children feel they must control these feelings. Therefore, behavioral issues can often arise as a direct result of trying to avoid feelings. The dangers children confront without adequate coping skills leave them fearful and alienated by an adult world that all too often has failed to protect them. When they can no longer cope, they scream out for help, but are seldom heard. From a happy, relatively carefree life, loss now results in emotional reactions that may include: fear, depression, anxiety, withdrawal and/or anger. If children are not encouraged to express their emotions, they may never work through their grief and their behavioral issues will continue to manifest.

Regression

Loss often causes children to revert back to behavior at a younger age level. For example, older children and young adolescents also feel sad over the losses they have experienced, but they feel more comfortable expressing their anger than their younger counterparts. They long to retreat to their childhood just when more responsibility is being expected of them. Despite their feelings of anger and guilt, adolescents will try to find meaning in their loss. It is common for children to regress both behaviorally and academically following a trauma.

Acting Out or Outbursts

Children often express their grief over losses through acting out. There may be temper outbursts, aggression, defiance, rebelliousness, "do not care" attitudes or running away. Acting out must be understood in light of the reasons behind it. When children feel powerless, misbehaving, fighting and causing fear in others can give them a sense of control. They may feel abandoned and unloved, and may act out in order to prove that their feelings about themselves are correct. They may be rejecting others in order to avoid intimacy and thus the feeling of rejection that they are certain will come in the future.

Acting out or outbursts may be the only way children know to express negative feelings. Inappropriate behavior must be handled with understanding and in a manner that makes children feel cherished in spite of their negative behaviors. They need to be reminded that they are still loved although their actions cannot be tolerated. While limits must be set for the child, the feelings behind the behaviors also need to be identified and accepted.

Compounded Loss Resulting from Acting Out

Compounded loss is common among children and adolescents with poor conduct. This is, in part, because their behaviors get them into trouble. Anger, fighting, irritability and poor concentration are all natural psychological responses to childhood grief. Adults may have difficulty recognizing these reactions as responses to loss because they are different from typical adult expressions of grief, such as acting sad or crying. Children may act sad or cry, of course, but their grief, like other areas of children's functioning, is influenced by their age and developmental stage. Thus, they also are prone to angry outbursts, tantrums (among the very young), oppositional behavior toward adults (refusing to obey rules, for example) and aggression.

Kevin's story below demonstrates the relationship between trauma, loss and behavior. Kevin was in prison when he described the course of his life and, by his account, the long-lasting negative consequences of a traumatic life event he experienced as a child:

> I have been in the system since I was a young youth. When I was five years old, my father got murdered, and that is when I started getting in trouble. In elementary school, I became a problem child: fighting the teachers, not wanting to listen. Did not care what happened. Because I lost something very, you know, special to me, and that was my father. My mother could not deal with me. I did not want to listen to her. And that led me into boys' homes. Now the courts took over. . . ."[1]

By the age of forty, Kevin had spent almost a quarter of his life behind bars. Over the years, his behavior had attracted attention from professionals—at his school, at youth homes and in prison—who tried to intervene. Yet, it is unlikely he ever received help coping with the early traumatic life event that impacted him throughout his life.

Today, many young children who are grieving similar losses find themselves the focus of school disciplinary systems and juvenile justice systems, much as Kevin did nearly three decades ago. But because the consequences of childhood loss are still too little recognized or understood, adults responsible for addressing youthful infractions often miss opportunities to help such children improve their behavior and, perhaps, their futures.

Loss and Emotions

All losses hurt. However, research has shown that the most problematic losses of all are those that occur under unexpected or shocking circumstances. Losses that are sudden, unanticipated, violent, preventable (the result of not getting timely medical care, for example) and random all have the potential to be traumatic and emotion-laden. It is also important to note that sometimes children respond not to their own emotions, but to the emotions of those around them.[2]

Fear

For most children, loss and fear go hand-in-hand. They do not know what will happen to them. Fear intensifies and complicates the other emotions associated with the loss. For example, a fearful child cannot concentrate in school, will misinterpret comments and sometimes regress to immature or self-destructive behavior (experimenting with drugs, alcoholic drinks or inhalants such as glue sniffing).

The children's losses, fears, alienation and loneliness produce deep psychological scars. Denying their fear and hurt, painful feelings and memories are pushed deep inside them while they struggle to cope with the task of simply surviving. Denial can be a helpful coping mechanism for a while, but eventually frozen emotions have to thaw, enabling the children to get back in touch with their feelings.

Because many children do not identify their loss, they fail to grieve over their experiences. They also suffer because they have not had time to process their losses, nor do they have mature coping mechanisms to handle them. The way children learn to handle losses in childhood impacts their lives as adults. The losses of adult life may actually be compounded by some of the unresolved losses of childhood. Powerless, without a voice to come to their defense and protect them from exploitation or unjust treatment, they continue to live in fear.

Anger and Bullying

Significant losses can result in anger and bullying. In some cases, young people will lose their natural youthful optimism (hopefulness) and their misbehavior can escalate to dangerous levels. Children who experience a traumatic loss because of violence are more likely to have ongoing anger-based responses to their problems.

Guilt and Shame

Children who have experienced traumatic life events may also experience trauma-related guilt and shame. Such guilt and shame refers to the unpleasant feeling of regret that the child feels. This stems from the false belief that she or he could, or should, have done something different at the time the event occurred. Children often feel responsible for their losses.

Guilt is not learning from the past, but getting stuck in the past. To a certain extent, the past can be explored, with the help of a skilled counselor, as a tool to motivate improved behavior. This is because learning from the past often serves a useful purpose in developing character, understanding God's loving presence and more.

The Relationship between Loss and Grief

When children experience a loss in their lives, they also experience grief. According to Therese Rando, grief can be defined as "the process of psychological, social and somatic or bodily reactions to the perception of a loss."[3] She explains that these reactions are natural and expected reactions for children when they have had an attachment to someone or something broken because of loss.

Perceptions of a loss are important, too. What one person may see as a loss may not be perceived as such by another. This difference in perception applies to children, as well. Everyone experiences grief and loss differently and therefore expresses it differently. Not all children will react the same way or see an experience similarly to their peers. Culture may also play a part in how children see loss and the grief response that follows.

However, when children do identify loss, there are similarities in the way children express grief, especially when looking at different developmental stages. This is covered in more detail in the next chapter. Overall, counselors should be mindful of any changes in a child's behavior after experiencing a loss and help that child express feelings of grief.

Responding to Children's Losses

How many adults assume that it is better to avoid talking to children about loss, as bringing up memories long forgotten will only cause them more emotional pain? The fact is: Children do not forget! The assumption should never be made that a child understands what has happened to them. Children often need skilled counselors and caring adults to help them find meaning and seek explanations for traumatic life events.

It is also important to understand that children live in a world of fantasy and magical thinking. They believe that everything revolves around them. If no one explains what really happened to cause their losses, they make up their own explanations. They are filled with anxiety, wondering what has happened to their world and what they did to cause it. Even older children who know logically that it was not their fault still feel in their hearts that they are responsible for what has happened.

Communication (Listening to Feelings)

As counselors, we want children to feel loved and valued. Our communication with children concerning their losses is like a mirror in which children see themselves. Learning to listen carefully for a child's feelings is one of the most important communication skills we can use.

Young children often do not have words to express their feelings (happy, scared, angry, uncomfortable, etc.). Counselors may need to help children label their feelings. One way to do this is through reflective listening, giving a child's feelings a word: "It sounds like you felt afraid." If the observation is wrong, the child can correct it, which causes the child to think about his or her feelings in order to respond. Reflective listening requires sensitive listening to the children's verbal and nonverbal messages, and reflecting back the total message caringly and thoughtfully, without judgment. This kind of communication can be helpful to a child who is having behavior problems because negative feelings always exist before negative acts.

A Counselor's Task

Counselors who have been trained about the role and importance of loss in a child's life will be able to understand and help grieving children. They need to learn the difference between youth and adult grief responses, and the special nature of traumatic loss; how to screen for loss in a sensitive way; how to respond constructively when they learn of loss; and how to help grieving children who start to misbehave.

Counselors need to be aware of children's needs when they have experienced loss. Only then can they bring comfort and understanding into the counseling sessions. Key needs to be addressed include:

- Children of all ages who are grieving their losses may feel sad, lonely, guilty and very angry.

- Children are often in constant motion and many have difficulty concentrating in school. They need an opportunity to express these strong feelings in an appropriate way.

- To resolve the effects of their loss, children need to be bonded to adults they trust.

- Children need to receive accurate information about the cause of their losses.

- Children need to be given a sense of security and a comforting adult to rely on.

- Children must be reminded often that the loss was not their fault.

- Children need to know they are not alone.

Being aware of these needs, a counselor's task is focused on helping children, using age-appropriate strategies, to identify and process their trauma-produced losses so that they can be grieved and resolved. Only then will children be given back their childhoods and be enabled to restart healthy childhood development, including rebuilding essential spiritual foundations.

THREE

CHILDREN and GRIEF

Kim Hoover

Blessed are those who mourn, for they shall be comforted. Matthew 5:4 NASB

Grief is a normal reaction to a significant loss. It is a process, and it is different for each individual. Grief is universal. There is no person who will not experience significant losses in his or her lifetime, and they will likely include the loss of another person. Humans are social beings who are created to form attachments and relationships with other humans. When significant attachments are broken, loss is experienced and the response is grief.

Stages of Grief

Although the grief process is different for each person, it is possible to understand grief in a way that allows one to recognize what another person is experiencing and to help with the process. Elisabeth Kubler-Ross, in her now-classic work "On Death and Dying" (1969) set out stages of grief to help identify the varied emotional responses. Although "stages of grief" seems to imply an orderly progression from one to the next, the stages actually describe mind-sets, or cognitive-emotional frameworks, which are quite fluid. They should be thought of as collectively providing descriptions of the internal state of a grieving person at any moment in time. Over time, one would expect that the internal state is more consistently one of "acceptance." The specific stages of grief are as follows:

Denial

Denial refers to an emotional numbing that serves as some psychological protection from the overwhelming sense of loss. It does not mean the person does not know there has been a significant loss. Rather, it is a state where the full emotional realization of the loss is being kept from flooding a person's conscious awareness.

Anger

Anger is one of the first and strongest emotions to be recognized. Anger is directed *toward* something or someone. It thus serves the purpose of beginning to organize one's emotions and thoughts rather than leaving them in that diffuse, overwhelming and chaotic state.

Bargaining

Bargaining reflects a wish for things to be like they were and for the loss to be restored. It often includes some unrealistic thinking that there is something a person can do to make things go back to how they were, and it includes feelings of guilt and regret as the permanence of the loss is increasingly realized. It allows one to begin to remember and think about whom or what was lost.

Depression

As the reality of the loss becomes fully realized, feelings of emptiness and more intense sadness occur.

Acceptance

Acceptance does not mean that a person feels fine about the loss, forgets the loss or is somehow "over it." Rather, it means the person has accepted a new reality without what was lost and can continue in life.

Factors Influencing Grief

The specific form that grief takes for an individual is shaped by three areas, including personal attributes of the grieving person, support system and the nature of the loss itself. Personal attributes include the individual's age and developmental stage, personality factors, and previous experiences with significant loss. The support system can include faith and spiritual beliefs, presence of family, the family's ways of coping with loss, presence of extended support network, stability of the environment following the loss, and opportunities available for the individual to express feelings. Identifying the specific nature of the loss highlights the many different types of losses that will result in grief. A loss may be loss of a person through death, physical separation, or mental or emotional impairment. It could be the loss of significant things that have great meaning for one's sense of self, such as loss of a home or homeland, destruction of all personal belongings, loss of a lifelong pet, loss of meaningful employment, or loss of part of self due to physical illness, disability, or mental or emotional impairment.

Using "stage of development" as a framework, one can consider how these three areas shape the process of grief in children. Since development from infancy to adulthood proceeds along a certain ordered course, one can think of specific stages of development that roughly correlate with certain ranges of chronological age. Through each stage, new brain connections are being made that allow for development of new motor, language and cognitive skills. Children think differently at different stages in their development and they express their emotions in different ways. Since grief reflects one's state of thinking and feeling related to a loss, then it follows that children at different developmental stages manifest grief differently.

Grief and Stages of Development

Infants (0-2years)

Infants do not have a cognitive awareness of loss, but they do respond with distress if basic needs are not consistently met. Therefore, the loss of a person who can provide consistent caregiving has serious consequences. The quality of interactions with the caregiver is also important, so contact through touch, voice and facial recognition is critical to the infant's well-being. If an infant's caregiver is lost or is replaced by a caregiver who does not provide appropriate interaction and stimulation for the infant, then the damage to the child can be long-term, even lifelong. In addition to physical delays in development, the development of trust will be impaired and can interfere permanently with the ability to establish healthy relationships. Personality factors may also play a role in the infant's response to loss even at this early stage. Some infants are temperamentally more adaptable than others. With a loss, some change in routine is inevitable, and a less adaptable infant will show more distress.

Toddlers (2-3 years)

For toddlers, the primary developmental task is forming secure attachment to a primary caregiver. If the child loses the caregiver during this time through death, separation, abandonment, or physical or emotional disability, then the loss will be shown with symptoms of disordered attachment, as well as general symptoms of distress. These symptoms may include hostile or aggressive behavior, avoidance and withdrawal, sleep and eating disturbances, or regression (reverting back to a behavior more typical for a younger age, such as wanting to feed from a bottle after it had been given up). Again, it is the support system, through consistent caregiving and maintenance of some routine, that most helps a child of this stage with loss.

Preschool (3-5 years)

Children at this stage have a sense of themselves and caregivers as separate, different people. Therefore, loss of a caregiver or someone close to the child will be recognized as a loss, as someone gone. They do not, however, have a clear sense of death being permanent, and so they may persist in looking for or asking about the person's return. These children often exhibit "magical thinking," making a cause-effect connection between two events that occur near each other in time or space but are not logically connected. For example, if a child follows instructions to put on a raincoat in case of rain and then rain actually occurs, then the child might think that putting on a raincoat caused it to rain. Likewise, if a child had misbehaved in some way before the death of a parent or other significant loss, then the child may think his or her misbehavior caused that event. This type of thinking should be expected from a very young child and gently, lovingly corrected, although the full awareness of cause-effect relationships will not come until later. A child's previous experience with death or loss (such as a pet) could also influence the grief process at this stage of development. As with earlier childhood, the child's temperament and personality features, and the presence of consistent supportive caregiving also contribute to the particulars of the grief response. Children may show symptoms including oppositional, defiant behaviors (arguing with or refusing to comply with directions from caregivers), aggression, tantrums, withdrawal, sleep and eating disturbances, regressive behaviors, and increased anxiety and fearfulness.

School age (6-12 years)

Young school-age children have a greater understanding of cause and effect, so they will be better able to process a sequence of events that occurred and resulted in loss. They tend to be concrete thinkers, meaning they often take things literally and do not yet have the ability to grasp abstract concepts. They also tend to be rule-oriented. They may ask many "why" questions with the belief that there has to be a logical explanation for everything. They are likely to ask questions about death that reflect their concrete thinking, such as wondering what a deceased person will eat. Children at this stage often have concerns about body integrity (more attention to any physical damage to their bodies) and physical well-being. When they hear things about death like a person's heart stopping or their body wearing out from old age, they are likely to worry that the same thing could happen to them or to others close to them. Their anxiety may then be manifested by many physical complaints, clinginess or need for frequent reassurance. Unwillingness to attend school, a decline in school performance or changes in behavior at school may appear since anxiety over separation from family is heightened.

In addition to the factors previously mentioned (personality, previous experience with loss, presence of family support, consistent caregiving and routine) being important, supports outside the family also become more important. Since children at this age are in school and often involved in sports or social activities separate from the immediate family, these areas can all contribute to helping the child cope with a loss. These activities can nurture a healthy grief process, both by allowing for the continuation of a comfortable routine, and by allowing for support from other significant adults and peers. In addition to more physical complaints and worry about the well-being of others, grief at this stage can be demonstrated through emotional and behavioral changes (withdrawn and sad, explosive and aggressive), sleep disturbance, development of new fears and regression to earlier stages.

Adolescence (12-18 years)

A major psychological task of adolescence is the development of a sense of identity. Identity develops through the accumulation of experiences, relationships and increasing self-awareness. The ability to think about abstract concepts also develops during this stage and helps establish a sense of identity as the individual can think from different perspectives, can think about the future, and can clarify values and beliefs.

Since the development of identity depends largely on an individual's relationships, then loss of a significant relationship through death, separation, abandonment or illness can have a profound impact on the young person. While earlier stages of development have led to a child's awareness of being a separate physical being who can function when not in direct physical contact with the parent (or caregiver), adolescence fosters the sense of psychological separation. Adolescence is like a dance around a relatively stationary central figure (the parent or caregiver). Sometimes the young person moves in close, demonstrating characteristics and values very much like the adult. Other times he or she moves far away, perhaps temporarily taking on exaggerated, opposite characteristics. Sometimes the movement is fast, sometimes slow, sometimes with a regular pattern, sometimes random. Eventually, the movement becomes more calm and steady, and the parent-child relationship includes an adult-adult connection. If that central figure is lost, or if external circumstances become overwhelming, then the young person may also feel "lost." Without a central organizing figure, the dancer may spiral out of control or drift aimlessly.

All the different factors that can shape one's grief come into play at this stage. The adolescent's personality, whether more introverted or extroverted, whether directing feelings inward or outward, can shape the appearance of grief as more emotional or behavioral. Previous experience with loss can provide some framework to help the adolescent organize thoughts and feelings. Depending on those experiences, that framework can be healthy and supportive ("I know I'll be alright.") or unhealthy and destructive ("I must be a terrible person because terrible things keep happening to me."). The support system might now include more established friends, additional trusted adults and even a more intimate relationship. The relationship of the adolescent to the person lost and the nature of the loss are important in the grief process. How far along that process of psychological separation the adolescent has come and how central to identity the lost person or object is will influence how lost the adolescent feels.

The more lost the adolescent feels, the more likely the grief will be expressed more strongly through changes in mood, behavior, difficulty concentrating and performing in school and in other areas (such as sports or social activities). With intense emotional pain, the youth might turn to drugs or alcohol for escape or emotional numbing. The anger may feel overwhelming and may be expressed outwardly through aggression, hostility or rejection toward people once close. The anger may be directed inward with guilt or self-blame, and it may appear as self-harmful behavior or sabotaging one's own success. If the adolescent has moved further along the process of establishing a clear sense of identity or has other people who can become that central organizing figure(s), then the loss will be challenging and painful, but is less likely to be devastating.

Interventions and Support for the Grieving Child

At this point, the opening words to this chapter bear repeating: Grief is a *normal reaction* to a significant loss. Grief is not a pathological process, a disorder for which we seek a cure. In working with grieving children, our goal is not to cure them of their grief or to stop their grief. It is instead to facilitate the normal, healthy process of grief. We want to encourage the process, not stifle it.

The grief process is different for each individual. We do not facilitate the process by imposing our own idea of what grief "should" look like or how long the process "should take." We *do* facilitate the process by helping the child identify the losses, express feelings and strengthen supports.

Identify the Losses

Sometimes, the loss that has triggered the grief response is obvious, as in the death of a parent. Other times, the loss may be less obvious, as in a child with a chronic illness who has some restriction on activities, or who periodically requires hospitalization or surgeries. Sometimes, as in cases of severe catastrophic trauma, there will be multiple losses. Since grief is a response to loss and since the nature of the loss helps shape the grief, then identifying the loss or losses is an important first step. Identifying the losses can best be accomplished by obtaining information both from the child and from other sources. People who knew the child before the loss occurred can help one understand personality features, interests and talents, and the child's routine, which can all shed light on what has been lost beyond what is most obvious. The child is also an important source of information. This statement may seem absurdly obvious, but it is important to remember that the grief is the child's grief and needs to be understood from the child's perspective. For example, if a family loses its home and all its belongings in a fire, the adults may be experiencing loss of a permanent home, loss of financial security and loss of meaningful things that represent a family history. However, the four-year-old child who still has security in the presence of his parents, who does not have the collection of memories and hopes for the future, does not experience these same losses. He may be most affected by loss of a beloved teddy bear he hugged to sleep every night, and be inconsolable at bedtime until this loss is identified and restored or replaced.

Express Feelings

"Jesus wept." (John 11:35)

Although grief is a normal, healthy process, children need adults to help them through the process. They need opportunities to express their feelings, whatever they may be. They need the means to safely express these feelings, and they need to feel that they will have help containing these feelings if they become overwhelming. It is adults who meet these needs. Providing opportunities for a child to express grief means not ignoring the child even when there seems to be people or circumstances demanding attention. It means making time for one-to-one contact with the child, free from distractions, when total focus and attention can be on the child. It means actively "listening" to what the child is saying with his or her words, questions, fears, emotions and behavior. Active listening requires the listener to participate, not just by passively hearing or observing the child, but by clarifying, restating, encouraging and validating what is being heard. Finding out what the child is trying to express is much more important than telling the child what he is expressing. Sometimes just taking the time to be with the child, to be a consistent caring presence when the world seems to be turned upside down, is enough to facilitate the natural grief process.

Providing the means for a child to express his or her feelings requires some willingness and ability to enter into a child's world. All adults were once children and therefore have some ability to connect with children. Children do not always have the words to describe their feelings; nor do they always experience an adult asking many questions as someone who is trying to understand. The children may be afraid their feelings are so big that letting them out will annihilate anyone in their path.

A child's world is one of fantasy, imagination, play, colors, sounds and activity. Tapping into these features will allow a child to express his or her feelings in a very natural and comfortable way. Playing with figures in a dollhouse or sandbox, imaginative play-acting, drawing, finger painting, manipulating Play-doh or clay, making or moving to music, and physical activity all become the means whereby a child will "tell" you what he or she is feeling and thinking. These means of expression allow the child as much distance as they need from direct associations with the loss, which may be overwhelming, but allow the feelings associated with the loss to come out. When this occurs in the presence of a consistent, caring adult, then the feelings become less overwhelming, more organized and more directly accessible.

While it is the presence of the adult providing the means of expression of feelings that is most important, some examples of specific interventions may be helpful. These examples are provided, not as a formula to follow, but rather to stimulate the creativity and imagination of those working with children.

- Draw a picture of self or family before and after the loss
- Paint (or draw) feelings
- Make an outline of the child's body and ask him to draw in feelings
- Identify animals associated with different feelings and have the child act them out
- Create puppets and act out scenes involving loss, feelings, safety

- Make a "scream box" to scream into when feelings get very big
- Make and string "worry beads" to hold and manipulate when anxious
- Play "fruit ball" (like baseball, using fruit and vegetables for the ball)
- Identify different ways to make music and try them out with different feelings
- Listen to different types of music and create movement for each one
- Create a journal, scrapbook or poster pertaining to losses
- Create a memorial ceremony and perform it (releasing balloons, lighting candles, planting a flower or a tree)

Some children will find it easier to express their feelings in a group with same-age peers who are also dealing with grief. In a group setting, feelings of isolation and "different-ness" can be overcome by the awareness of others in similar circumstances. Hearing others' experiences can facilitate a hesitant child to verbalize his own, and children will experience support of peers in a different way than from adults.

Strengthen Supports

Since humans are by nature social beings, no individual lives in total isolation. However, if a child has lost a very meaningful person so that the development of trust, attachment or identity is disrupted, then feelings of isolation or abandonment are likely to occur. Reaching out in support can be a lifeline, and strengthening existing supports the child has can be critical. If a child has experienced loss, then other family members have as well. Helping the adults close to the child manage their own grief will be important so that they can continue to be available to the child. Friends, neighbors or the church community providing meals, transportation or help with daily tasks can provide support to a grieving family and give them room to deal with their emotions. Some extra attention from a friend's parent, a teacher, coach or minister can help a child continue to feel connected to others. Mobilizing the child's faith community in prayer and acts of kindness will help a child feel embraced at a time of greatest need.

The Road Ahead

There is a time for everything,
    and a season for every activity under the heavens:

a time to be born and a time to die,
a time to plant and a time to uproot,
a time to kill and a time to heal,
a time to tear down and a time to build,
a time to weep and a time to laugh,
a time to mourn and a time to dance - (Eccl. 3:1-4 NIV)

Children continue to grow and develop physically, emotionally, cognitively and spiritually. Although a child may seem to move through grief and come to a sense of acceptance and peace, this state is always subject to change. As particular milestones in life are met or events occur that bring attention to a previous loss, then all the feelings associated with grief can reemerge. As a child's thinking develops, the previous loss will need to be revisited to be processed in new ways. For example, a young child may be comforted by thinking of a deceased parent in heaven, but becomes an adolescent with the ability to think abstractly and critically, and is full of anger over how a loving God could allow suffering. The reappearance of grief and the need to again express feelings—have these feelings validated—and experience support is not a setback. It is rather a testimony to the miracle of life and the gift of grief that allows us to heal from the hurts of loss.

Part II

Counseling: Principles and Strategies

FOUR

BASIC COUNSELING SKILLS

Mary Beth Young

This chapter is an overview of the process of counseling and the skills needed when working with young people in crisis. It serves as a guide for those who want to serve the Lord by meeting the emotional and psychological needs of children and adolescents. To help adapt the concepts and principles in this chapter to another culture, read carefully the chapter on cross-cultural counseling.

Counseling can be complex and requires many specific skills. To learn more about counseling, enroll in one or more courses, attend training workshops and continue reading books on the topic. Most importantly, ask God for guidance and wisdom as you begin to counsel young people. God has given us the Holy Spirit who is *our* Counselor and who guides us when we are obedient, open to Him and listen to Him. God has also given us the Bible to learn how Jesus interacted with others. Ask a mature, godly Christian who has experience counseling young people if you can regularly meet with him or her. God created us to need others to help us grow and learn, and an experienced counselor to consult with provides you with protection and guidance as you learn about counseling.

What Is Counseling?

Counseling is the process of providing emotional support to people to help them figure out how to deal with what is concerning them. This chapter's focus is on an overall view of counseling that will help you to minister to children (ages five to twelve) and adolescents (ages thirteen to nineteen) who are in crisis. An important difference between counseling a child under the age of twelve and an adolescent is that focused play is generally the approach used with younger children. The counseling skills discussed in this chapter are appropriate for all age groups, but if you work with children under twelve, apply these skills in the context of focused play.

Counseling as a Journey

Before we discuss the skills of counseling, it is helpful to think about counseling as a three-phased journey. For example, in the beginning of any journey, it is important to know where you are going and how you plan to get there. In counseling, the person who requests counseling defines where he or she wants to go. You, as the counselor, are a guide who assists the person in identifying and reaching the target destination.

During an actual journey, you may encounter unexpected obstacles, delays, and detours along the way, and you may need assistance. In the same way when it comes to counseling, unexpected issues may surface, the process may require additional time or the target destination may change.

At the end of the journey, you arrive at your chosen destination. In counseling, when a person arrives where he wants to be, then he no longer needs a guide. Hopefully, as this person matures, he may be able to guide others to where they want to go, too. We could label the beginning, middle and end phases of the counseling journey as assessment, intervention and closure.

The assessment phase is the beginning of the journey when you help a person identify where he or she wants to go in counseling. (For children under age twelve, adults in the child's life usually identify the child's counseling goals.) During this phase, obtain background information (family history, educational history, history of abuse, medical history, vocational history, strengths, talents, gifts and so on) to get an understanding of the person and the events that shaped the person into who he or she is today. The assessment phase begins the counseling process, but continues throughout the process.

The intervention phase is what happens during the journey. You assist in determining how the person wants to handle his or her current situation. This is often the longest phase of the process and provides an opportunity to impart skills (problem-solving, decision-making, coping and so on). Encourage the young person to practice new skills in counseling (or in play) and to apply them to current life situations. Avoid telling the person what decision to make, but work alongside him or her in thinking through the pros and cons, as well as the potential consequences of the available options. (For children between ages five and twelve, this is addressed in the context of play.) Discuss what is working and what is not, and collaborate with the person to identify alternate ways of approaching the current situation. A variety of counseling skills to use during the intervention phase are discussed later in this chapter.

Closure is the end phase of the journey. When the person has resolved the issue (reached his destination) for which he originally sought counseling, he no longer needs a guide. This can be a sensitive phase of the journey, as the person may have shared intimate details of his life with you and may find it difficult to think about separating from you. While closure is the end of the journey, you must consider closure from the beginning of the journey. The counseling goal is not only to assist the person in reaching his destination, but also to empower him or her to become increasingly stronger so that, eventually, counseling is no longer needed.

It would be great if learning how to counsel were as easy as following the steps in a recipe, but counseling is much more complex than that. The three phases of counseling do not always occur in order and the phases often overlap. For example, closure of the counseling relationship may be premature (occurs before the person has reached his destination) or unanticipated (circumstances prevent the person from continuing in counseling.) Let's look briefly at the skills you will practice most often during the counseling journey.

Introducing Eight Key Counseling Skills

Before we look at each skill in detail, let's consider how the three counseling phases integrate with them. Together, the phases and the skills represent a framework for counseling. Counseling skills include the following:

1. Developing a relationship
2. Observing
3. Interviewing
4. Developing a knowledge base

5. Using an array of communication tools
6. Obtaining referrals
7. Initiating closure
8. Managing documentation

As stated previously, the three phases may not occur in order, often overlap or may occur simultaneously. The same is true of each of the skills. Table 1 maps the phases of the counseling journey to the specific counseling skills most often associated with each phase.

Journey Phase	Counseling Phase	Counseling Skills Used
Where am I going? What is my goal? Sometimes the answer to 'Where am I going' changes as counseling progresses.	I. Assessment Assessment is ongoing and occurs throughout the counseling process.	1. Developing a relationship 2. Observing 3. Interviewing 4. Developing a knowledge base
How will I get there?	II. Intervention The counselor assists in determining how the person wants to handle his or her current situation. Usually this is the most lengthy phase of the counseling process.	5. Using an array of communication tools 6. Obtaining referrals
I have arrived at my destination.	III. Closure The person has achieved his or her counseling goal(s).	7. Initiating closure 8. Managing documentation

Table 1: Each journey phase is connected to the appropriate counseling skill(s).

Your role as a counselor is to coach or guide, but the person does the work of making decisions and/or changes in his or her life. The person has to figure out what changes to make and whether he or she wants to make them. As a counselor, you listen, assess, ask questions, give feedback and suggestions, and so on; but it is up to the person to decide what he or she will and will not do. Jesus instructed people, "If any man will come after me, let him..." (Luke 9:23 KJV). Rather than using force, a counselor extends the same freedom of choice that God has given us. In counseling, the relationships you build with people can have lifelong effects.

Skill 1: Developing a Relationship

The counseling relationship may begin because you are a caregiver at a drop-in center, orphanage or group home; do outreach work on the streets; or teach Sunday school. Maybe you regularly visit an institution that cares for children, or you minister to young people by teaching Bible stories, sharing information about healthy hygiene practices or providing structured playtime in a group setting. You may notice a person who often looks sad, angry or scared; acts more aggressively than the others; is withdrawn from the group; is ostracized from the group; is acting differently than usual. Any of these signs might lead you to the conclusion that this person may need counseling. Furthermore, caregivers at the institution may share concerns with you about an individual child. No matter how the counseling relationship begins, developing a relationship is the cornerstone of everything else you do in counseling. Children need three things to develop a healthy counseling relationship: quality time, opportunities to develop trust and someone who genuinely listens.

Spend Time Together

Spending quality time with the children you counsel allows them to get to know you—and you to get to know them. As adults, we are often used to being in charge and telling young people what to do, but they need that same sense of being in charge. Allow and encourage them to choose the activities or to direct the conversation during a session. Play the games that they want to play, talk about what they want to talk about, tell jokes when they want to tell jokes, or be silly when it is an OK time for silliness and fun. Giving children choices lets them know that you value and respect them, and gives them more control over how their time is spent.

Spending quality time together helps you get to know the children; but, more importantly, time is an important factor in deciding whether they want to trust you.

Build Trust

Trust develops over time as children learn through the repetition of an adult's actions whether the adult is reliable and consistent. Do you show up when you say you are going to show up? Do you follow through on doing what you say you are going to do? Do you treat those you counsel with respect and communicate (verbally or through your actions) that you value them? Do you keep your word? If the answer is yes to these questions, then, over time, a person learns that you are reliable and will most likely begin to trust you.

In infants, trust develops primarily through the attachment cycle between the mother and her infant:

1. The baby has a need, which could be hunger, discomfort or pain.

2. The baby expresses his need through a rage reaction, which could be crying or screaming. The infant's rage reaction elicits a response from the caregiver in which the infant's need is acknowledged and resolved.

3. The mother or caregiver satisfies the infant's need through touch, eye contact, facial expressions, motion (rocking, walking) or food.

4. Consistent gratification of the infant's need leads to the infant trusting his mother.

The repetition of the attachment or trust cycle thousands of times in the first two years of a child's life results in a strong trust bond—or attachment—between the child and the mother or caregiver (see Figure 1).

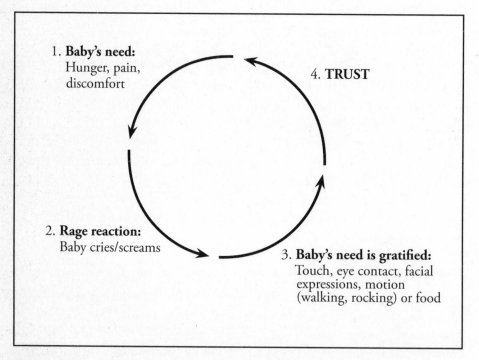

Figure 1: How Trust and Attachment Develop

Trust or attachment plays a crucial role in the development of a child. This primary relationship between the mother and her infant strongly influences how the baby/child interprets feelings, perceptions and behaviors in future relationships. Because the mother or caregiver is a mirror for the child, if the mother sees the infant as valued and consistently meets the infant's needs, the infant views himself or herself as a person of value and has the healthy expectation that he or she can trust adults to meet his or her needs. The same process applies when you begin a counseling relationship. Like the mother, you are a mirror for the child. When you view the person as valued and consistently meet his or her need for a stable, healthy relationship, the person acknowledges his or her own intrinsic value and develops the healthy expectation that he or she can trust you.

A mother's response to her baby's distress not only builds trust, but also teaches the child how to manage his or her own emotions. When she responds in a healthy manner by rocking, cuddling and holding the distressed baby, the mother sets the foundation for the baby to learn how to eventually soothe or calm his or her own emotions. As you develop a counseling relationship and you comfort someone who is in distress, you are modeling self-soothing skills. Children and adolescents do not master the developmental skill of self-soothing until they progress in their maturity.

As we minister to children and adolescents, they learn to trust us through the repetition of our behaviors in response to their needs. For children who have not had a healthy or trusting attachment with their mothers, this may be the first healthy relationship they have experienced with an adult, where they know they are valued and their best interests are the counselor's primary concern. The counseling relationship may be a child's first experience of being able to trust an adult and receive the comfort that adult offers when the child is in distress. The counseling relationship can provide an important corrective experience for the child who did not have a healthy, trusting relationship with his or her mother, or caregivers. You must be reliable, consistent and make the child's needs your first priority to ensure that trust develops.

Genuinely Listen

Listening "is an active process by which we express a genuine desire to connect with a person"[4] and "is at the core of building a [trusting] relationship with a child. When children know that someone is [taking the time] to genuinely listen to them, they become more trusting and accepting of themselves."[5] Young people need to talk about what is important to them, and listening also gives you an opportunity to assess their needs and determine the best way to meet them. Effective active listening requires the following skills:

- Acknowledging what a person is communicating and validating or confirming that what the person is communicating is important.

- Providing feedback (you are a mirror).
- Asking relevant questions.
- Expressing understanding.[6]

Active listening increases your understanding of not only what the child has experienced, but also the child's understanding of what has happened. Listening to the details of what young people have experienced is not enough; you must also understand what these situations mean to them. What are the messages learned from these events? Children come to believe these messages about themselves and the world. Often, the messages communicated to or perceived by the person are not accurate or true. The counselor then needs to help the person to correct these distortions or lies. Genuinely listening to a child meets the child's need to be heard and noticed.

A common effect of trauma is the person who experiences it is silenced.[7] As a result, secrets related to the trauma develop, and a child begins believing the lies he or she may have been told. Because silence is a result of trauma, the child now needs to have a voice.[8] Counseling is an opportunity to give children their voices back. Provide opportunities for young people to express themselves in healthy ways—first in the counseling relationship and then in other relationships. Diane Mandt Langberg, Ph.D., provides an excellent explanation of how God's image is reflected in each person and why one of the characteristics of personhood is having a voice.

> Our essence is expressed in our voice. To be in the image of God is to have a voice and to speak that voice out into the world. Anything that distorts the voice of God results in the destruction of the person.[8]

Allowing children to have a voice and to speak out about their experiences is one way for them to regain their sense of value.

Create a Safe Environment

Ask open-ended questions to encourage young people to share. Listening means that you remain quiet and allow for silence. If culturally appropriate, establish eye contact with the child. To provide a sense of equality, sit in close proximity to the child where you are both at the same level. If the person sits on the floor, you sit on the floor too. Create a space that is private, comfortable and in which the young person feels safe. Avoid potential interruptions so that you can fully focus on the person.

Skill 2: Observing

A counselor learns about a person through observation. Assessing your observations also gives you valuable information about a person. When observing, repeatedly ask yourself, *What might this* [whatever I've observed] *tell me about this person?* Several broad areas of observation can guide you in knowing how to interact with someone:

- Physical appearance

  What is your first impression? What is he wearing? Is he clean and well-groomed? What is his facial expression? Does he appear happy, sad, scared or mad? Does he have any visible scars or bruises? If he is carrying anything, what is he carrying and why is he carrying it? Does he seem small or large for his age? Is there anything unusual or striking about his appearance? What is the tone of his voice? What is his attitude?

- Body language

  Does he maintain eye contact with you, if this is culturally appropriate? Do his eyes dart around as though he is watching out for someone or something? Does his body seem relaxed or tense? Is his body posture stiff or rigid? Is he tapping his fingers or shaking his leg? Does he keep his hands in his pockets (what might be in his pocket?) or can you see his hands?

- Environmental factors

  Where did you meet this person? Was he alone or with an adult? Did he seem to be part of a group of other young people? Did you meet him in a typical place for people his age? How did the conversation begin? Did he initiate the conversation or did you? If you initiated the conversation, was he receptive to you or did he seem to want to avoid you? Do you generally see him at this location, primarily during the day or night or at a certain time of day?

- Responsiveness

  Does he seem interested in talking? Does he want something specific from you? Is he hurried or relaxed? Does he appear focused on the conversation or easily distracted? Does what he says match the way he acts or what you may know about the way he acts? Does he seem alert or is he sleepy or groggy? Does what he says make sense and does it sound reasonable? Does he appear to be getting annoyed (impatient, angry, excited, scared, nervous) about something you say or something that is happening in the background? Does he tend to seek attention for himself, or does he tend to be reserved or cautious?

- Your own thoughts and feelings

  Be aware of your own responses to the person because they may provide insight into how others may feel about him. Are you at ease talking with him or are you becoming distracted with something else? What is your body language, tone of voice, attention span and so on communicating to him? Are you beginning to feel annoyed (impatient, angry, excited, scared, nervous) about something he says or something that is happening in the background? Does what you say make sense? Do you feel safe with this child, or do you feel that you are in danger or uncomfortable?

After you have observed the child and observed yourself in response to him or her, what do all of these observations tell you about the child? In every interaction you have with the child, assessment is something that you are constantly doing. Counseling involves thinking through (evaluating) and assessing your observations. By assessing what you have observed, you can tell whether a child is or has been physically well cared for (healthy, sick, good or poor hygiene, proper nutrition, clothing, etc.); whether a child is angry, scared or lonely; whether you need to be concerned about your own safety with a child; whether a child has concerns about his or her own safety; whether a child seems to be at the appropriate developmental level as other kids the same age (or more mature, delayed, etc.); whether a child is responsive to you and so on.

Skill 3: Interviewing

Asking questions is critical to the counseling process and helps you to understand how others view their current situation, themselves and their abilities to solve the current problem. Asking questions gives you information that helps determine how to proceed with the counseling, which resources are available to solve the current problem, and whether the person wants to resolve a particular issue or problem. If the person tells you about an event and it does not make sense to you, ask questions to clarify the details and the person's feelings about the event. Interviewing provides you with insight in three key areas:

- A person's personality, preferences and background.
- The events and experiences that have shaped a person's current outlook and values.

- The type of assistance a person wants from the counseling relationship.

Asking the Right Questions

Open-ended questions are helpful because they allow people to provide information about themselves or their situation, rather than yes or no answers. Examples of open-ended questions include:

- What happened?

  (What was going through your mind when this happened? What did you do when this happened? What did others do when this happened? What message did you learn from this event? What happened next? What concerns you most about that?)

- How did this unfold?

  (How did this affect you? How did this hurt or help you?)

- When did this happen?

  (What was the context in which this event occurred? Was it when you were a child, a teenager? When you think about what happened, how do you make sense of what happened?)

- Who was involved?

  (Who helped you through this situation? Who did you tell about this at the time?)

- Why was this important?

  (Why do you think your mother made this decision? Why do you think you chose to tell your aunt what happened? Why do you think you're ready to talk about this now?)

One question that must be answered in the counseling relationship is what assistance does this person want from the counseling relationship? Sometimes people have a particular issue or problem that they want to solve or get guidance about. Other times, an adult may have suggested a particular issue that a person may need help with. Ask the person to confirm whether the issue another adult suggested is an area where he or she needs assistance. If you believe the direct question is too intrusive, allow the person to talk about what is important to him or her, and then see if you can bring up this topic (that the adult suggested) within the conversation.

A person may enjoy talking with you, but may not know what he wants or where he wants to go in counseling. Over time, he may open up more about himself, which demonstrates that he is beginning to trust you. Through conversation, you may observe particular area(s) of his life or issues, and assess that he needs support or guidance. In this case (once trust develops between you), give the person feedback about what you see in his life. Ask questions such as, "Have you noticed this?" and "Is this something you want to address in depth?"

When a person does not know exactly what he wants or needs from counseling, your task is to help him become aware of what he may need. Asking questions helps a person discover what patterns of behavior he is demonstrating.

Inexperienced counselors often assume that they know why a person is seeking counseling and what he or she needs from counseling. If you insist that someone pursues the counseling goals you think are most important, you risk conveying the message that you do not have confidence in him or her to think independently and figure out what is important to him or her. The person being counseled is the one who does the work involved in self-growth; therefore, only after you have a clear idea about what the person wants from the counseling process can you move forward.

At the beginning of this chapter, counseling was defined as a process that provides emotional support to help a person figure out how to deal with what is concerning him. Counseling is not about figuring out how to deal with what is of concern to the counselor! When a person trusts you, then part of the counseling process is to give feedback about the issues you see in his or her life and ask whether they might be something he or she wants to address in counseling. To motivate people in counseling, encourage and assist them in defining their own counseling goals—not the goals you think they need to work toward in counseling.

Additionally, a child under age twelve typically cannot verbalize his or her specific counseling needs. Gather information from the child's caregivers to identify the needs. These adults often identify issues, behaviors, emotions or patterns of behavior they feel the child needs to address in counseling. Again, with the younger child, use play, rather than direct conversation.

Interviewing Guidelines

General principles for interviewing include the following:

- Ask only questions for which you need answers.

   Know your reason for asking a particular question. Young people can sense when you are asking questions because you want to assist them and when you have an unnecessary curiosity about their experiences.

- Begin with general questions and then move to questions that are more personal.

   The counseling relationship begins the first time you meet a person. Starting with general, more superficial questions helps the person feel comfortable and encourages trust to develop. Be sensitive to the timing of personal questions. Some questions can be asked only after you have established trust. Asking personal questions prematurely not only can hinder the relationship, but the person may also feel that you are intrusive and may no longer want to discuss any personal matters with you.

Effective interview questions are most likely the same questions we ask when talking to a friend who is making a decision. The difference is that counseling is a structured way of using many of the communication skills that we use in everyday life

Skill 4: Developing a Knowledge Base

Healthy human development, abnormal psychology and theories of human interaction are standard areas of study in the counseling field. To be an effective counselor, you must have a general understanding of how people develop physically, socially, emotionally, cognitively and spiritually. As the counseling relationship develops, you must be able to assess whether the person's issues are typical of most young people, whether the person may be delayed in some area or developmentally affected by circumstances and experiences. A more experienced counselor can assist you in assessing what is going on in the person, as well as suggest specific ways to move forward in counseling this person.

To increase your knowledge, take courses, read books or visit reputable Web sites about counseling. If you do not have access to courses or books in your native language, observe human nature and consult with someone who has wisdom about young people. If you have children of your own, you have a general idea of when developmental milestones are expected to be achieved. If you have worked with young people for a significant amount of time, you may have observed that people demonstrate similar patterns of behavior or thinking during different stages of their lives. Your casual observations of young people are helpful; nevertheless, I strongly recommend that you begin a formal program of study.

As you study and learn more about healthy human development, abnormal psychology and theories of human interaction, you gain insight and direction about how to counsel most effectively.

To become the counselor that God wants you to be, you must also rely on the Holy Spirit for wisdom and guidance. Yet, the inexperienced counselor or young Christian who believes reading the Bible and praying are the only requirements to becoming an effective counselor and that completing an advanced course of study is unnecessary because it is "secular knowledge," makes a grave error in thinking. Suppose you needed surgery. Whom would you choose to perform the operation? Someone who has read the Bible and prayed about doing surgery but has never studied biology, anatomy, surgical procedures and so on? Someone who has studied human anatomy, the body's organs, the body's diseases, and who has studied and learned how to perform surgery under a more experienced and learned medical practitioner? Or, someone who has studied both disciplines?

Skill 5: Using an Array of Communication Tools

Counseling is a structured way of using many of the communication techniques that we use in everyday life. However, a counselor needs to know which technique is most appropriate for a particular situation. Choosing the right technique naturally and skillfully comes with experience. When working with children, use age-appropriate words and language. Remember, when working with children under the age of twelve, use these communication tools in the context of play.

Conveying Hope

Loss of hope is a common experience when life does not go as planned, expected or wanted. Conveying hope reminds people that things can be different. Counselors provide hope when they share counseling experiences they have had with other young people in similar situations who are now living healthy, productive lives. People often ask me whether counseling gets depressing because I hear about so many problems. One reason it is not depressing is that I counsel many people who get better and make healthy changes in their lives. When you introduce the possibility of things changing, people get the idea that things could get better for them and they feel hopeful. Until a person begins to experience change as a result of counseling, he or she often does not believe that change is possible. Peer counseling with others who have experienced change in their lives is also a valuable way to provide realistic hope to people.

Avoid making blanket promises that "things will get better" because a person might feel that you are discounting his or her current situation. To offer realistic hope, you could say, "Let's give this a try and see how things go." This allows for the possibility of change and demonstrates respect for people, letting them evaluate whether things are, in fact, getting better.

Providing Information and Knowledge

Often young people honestly want to do things differently, but do not know how. This is when the counselor needs to provide information or knowledge about the way something works. For example, a person may admit to feeling angry all the time, but does not know why. After interviewing the person (to find out about his or her background and to assess what may contribute to his or her being angry all the time), use information to help the person figure out where these angry feelings are coming from. For example, you could explain where feelings come from or what contributes to a person's feelings. Table 2 lists other examples of how to use information in counseling.

Knowledge Area	Example
Human development	Communicate that it is normal for an adolescent to begin thinking about who he is and who he wants to be as he becomes a teenager.
Abnormal psychology	Inform the person that studies have shown that children who have repeated or prolonged separations from their parents have a higher rate of depression than adults.
Theories of human interaction	Explain that people who have been abused often see themselves as worthless, or explain that people who grow up around someone with an addiction have difficulty trusting others because the person with the addiction made multiple promises that were not kept, and so on.

Table 2: Counseling involves providing people with information and knowledge.

If you intend to be a valuable resource for the people you counsel, increase your knowledge about human development and consult regularly with an experienced counselor.

Providing Guidance

As discussed previously, during the intervention phase, the associated skills do not always occur in a particular order and they often overlap. If providing information/knowledge is the first step in the previous example about the person with anger issues, then guidance is the next step. Guidance is another word for teaching. As a counselor, you teach young people new ways of handling conflict, strong emotions, decision making and so on.

Providing Validation

Validation is the act of confirming and legitimizing a person's ideas, values and emotions.[10] Everyone needs validation. We all want to know that what we think or say is valued. Validation is important for people who grew up in an environment where thoughts, feelings and opinions were put down, made fun of or ignored. When you provide validation in the counseling relationship, people begin to see their ideas, values and emotions as being worthwhile and worth listening to, and they generally feel encouraged to continue to express their thoughts and feelings freely.

When the counselor says "yeah," "exactly" or "uh-huh," the counselor is validating what the person said. Other validating responses include "absolutely!", "I couldn't agree more," "yes," "that's right" and so on. Choose validating responses that you feel comfortable saying, and that fit your personality and style.

Using Reflection and Feedback

As discussed previously, active listening builds trust as you develop a relationship with a young person (see Skill 1). Reflection is a type of active listening in which you repeat back to a person what he or she said to you in order to ensure you heard and understood the person accurately. Reflection allows the person to correct you if you misunderstood what he or she communicated. After you reflect back to the person what was said, confirm your understanding by asking, "Is that right?" or "Is that what you're saying?" Reflection does not need to be a rote repetition of exactly what the person said, but it could be. Paraphrasing is an alternate way to reflect back what was said. In any case, use reflection to maintain clear, open communication.

Whereas reflection is mirroring what a person said, feedback is observing a person and then commenting on what you saw or heard. For example, suppose a group of young people goes outside to play every day, and a counselor notices that the young man she is counseling does not interact with anyone and stays to himself when outside. She may give her feedback to the person by saying, "I've noticed that whenever we all go outside, you sit by yourself." He may or may not be aware he is doing this. Feedback helps increase his awareness. To use this feedback as an opening for further conversation, the counselor may ask, "Is there a particular reason why you sit by yourself every time we go outside?"

When giving feedback, describe what you see or hear, but do not include judgments. In the previous example, if the counselor says, "I've noticed that whenever we all go outside, you *always want* to sit by yourself," the counselor is making a judgment about the behavior. Feedback is information about what the counselor sees or hears, not what the counselor thinks the person may be feeling.

Making Suggestions

A suggestion is an idea that the counselor proposes as possibly being helpful to someone and worth trying out. The person then decides whether the suggestion is something he or she thinks will be helpful. Suggestions are a valuable tool in the counseling relationship, but, as previously discussed, the person must choose whether he wants to make changes in his life—not the counselor. Adults sometimes forget that they cannot "make" anyone do anything. An adult can encourage a person to make certain choices or provide incentives or consequences, but ultimately it is up to the person to decide what he will and will not do. People are more inclined to try suggestions that appeal to them. For example, if you are counseling someone who has anger issues and you know the person enjoys playing soccer, you could say, "How about playing soccer or practicing kicking goals when you're angry? And why not try saying, out loud or under your breath, what you're angry about as you kick the ball?" This suggestion allows the person to make his or her own choices about how to deal with anger. While suggestions are the right counseling tool for some situations, giving instructions can be a more effective tool in other situations.

Providing Instruction

An instruction is a directive that describes what the counselor wants or expects someone to do. To effectively use instructions as a tool, you must have a thorough understanding of the person you are counseling and have an idea of how he or she will respond to a direct instruction. Often a person is willing to follow your instruction(s), but this usually occurs later in the counseling relationship after you have developed trust. Rather than making a suggestion, as in the previous example, you could give an instruction instead. You could say, "I want you to play soccer or practice kicking goals when you're angry. I want you to say, out loud or under your breath, what you are angry about as you kick the ball." The difference between making a suggestion and giving an instruction is subtle. Instructions are useful when you want someone to try something that he or she might not ordinarily be open to trying. Because choice is so important, even when you give an instruction, say something like, "How does that sound?" after giving the instruction. This gives the person an opportunity to tell you whether he or she thinks the instruction is reasonable. If so, then he or she is more likely to follow through. As the counseling relationship grows, you can begin to probe deeper into specific issues.

Planting Seeds

Planting seeds is a counseling technique in which you initiate and take the lead in talking about sensitive subjects, such as trauma or abuse, and you respond to questions a person might have about sensitive subjects. When you observe a person becoming open to talking with you about personal issues, you could plant a seed by saying something like, "I know there have been some extremely hard things that you have had to face in life. If you ever want to talk about these things, I'd be willing to listen." Then move on to the next subject. You are laying the groundwork for dealing with trauma or other difficult experiences that the person may want to talk about at a future time in counseling.

To steer a conversation in a highly personal direction, plant a seed first. For example, preface questions that are more personal by saying something like, "I'm going to ask you some personal questions now. I've worked with many young people who tell me about what they've experienced and how they've had to deal with difficult experiences in their lives." If abuse, neglect and exploitation issues come up during an interview, you can plant even more specific seeds. For example, suppose you interview a young man who has been living on the streets and ask him a question about whether he was abused or exploited. If he says he was not abused or exploited, you could respond by saying, "Wow, that's great. Several young people whom I've talked with who have lived out on the street have told me that they've been forced to do things—sell drugs or have sex—just to survive." This lets him know that you are not shocked by and will not judge him for things that he may have experienced or been forced to do when he was living on his own. If he understands that sensitive or difficult subjects or issues are perfectly OK to bring up in counseling, he is more inclined to share.

Planting seeds gives people the choice and the opportunity to bring up sensitive issues. Be sensitive to a person's readiness to discuss difficult topics. Insisting that a person discuss something that he or she is not ready to work on, or does not yet feel comfortable addressing, can be extremely harmful.

Creating Corrective Emotional Experiences

Corrective emotional experiences are emotional experiences in which losses the person has experienced (such as safety, control, power, trust in adults and hope) are restored either in the counseling relationship or through other relationships. A common thread throughout this chapter is allowing people to make their own choices in counseling. Generally, minors are dependent upon the adults in their lives and have no control over the situations in which they have lived. Whether a situation involves abuse, abandonment, neglect, exploitation or living with addiction, young people most likely feel powerless to stop the trauma, isolated by the situation and hopeless that the situation will ever end. To correct these negative experiences through counseling, give people control over where they want to go, what they are willing to work on and the pace at which they work on issues in counseling. Over time, the counseling relationship may allow a person to experience hope that his or her life will not be forever affected by the trauma. Through counseling, he or she corrects the experiences of feeling hopelessness.

Not all corrective emotional experiences occur in the counseling relationship. More often, corrective emotional experiences occur when caring adults are willing to step into a person's life and work to restore the losses that he or she has experienced.

- A caring woman regularly visits an orphanage to spend time with a young girl who has not had the benefit of a loving mother.

- A loving family welcomes an abandoned young boy as their own son to their family and home.

- A Sunday school teacher gets to know a young person at church who has been exploited or abused all of his life and takes time to listen to him, values him for who he is, asks this young man to join his family during church, invites him home for lunch after the worship service and is available throughout the week.

The only requirement in all of these examples is a caring adult who goes the extra mile to provide corrective emotional experiences.

Life Skills Development

People who have not had the benefit of a caring adult in their lives may need to learn skills that many people take for granted. A person can develop the following life skills in individual and group counseling situations.

- Decision-making

- Problem-solving

- Expressing needs by asking rather than demanding

- Developing friendships

- Relaxation techniques to calm nervousness or anxiety

- Being assertive without being aggressive

- Identifying and expressing a range of feelings

  (a person may be good at identifying anger but less able to identify hurt, disappointment, frustration and other negative emotions)

- Developing recreational interests

  (this is important for young people who have used drugs)

- Making a good impression with new acquaintances

- Managing anger, depression /sadness in healthy ways

- Being a member of a family

The list could go on. Many of these skills are best learned in a group setting in which the participants role play situations or practice different skills. Individual sessions may be more effective for the reserved or shy person. As the person gains confidence, encourage him or her to join the group. Both children and adolescents benefit from group work, but they have different ability and maturity levels, so it is best to keep children and adolescents in separate groups.

Encouraging and Empowering People

Everyone needs encouragement! Encouragement is like a breath of fresh air. Encouragement is positive input about the characteristics or changes you see in a person. Many young people in crisis have not experienced encouragement in their lives. Rather, they have been repeatedly told or shown that no matter what they do, it is not right. Encouragement motivates people when they feel low and sends the message that you have confidence in them and in their abilities. Encouragement builds realistic confidence when it is truthful and factual. An encouraging counselor helps people to change their self-perceptions and see themselves more like God sees them.

Empowerment is knowing and experiencing that you are capable of doing things for yourself. Assisting people in recognizing their strengths and abilities, and encouraging them to use these strengths and abilities to improve their circumstances empowers them. However, fostering dependence on the counselor is never the goal of counseling. Empower people to use their strengths and skills so they can eventually apply what they have learned in the counseling relationship to other areas of their lives.

Asking Questions

Questions are an important tool during the structured interview (see Skill 3) and when you do not fully understand what a person is trying to communicate. Questions also assist people in thinking through issues and encourage them to figure things out independently. Human nature is such that we learn better when we experience something ourselves, rather than someone telling us how to do something.

Observing and Confronting Discrepancies

The counseling relationship must be truthful. The Bible encourages us to "speak the truth in love" (see Eph 4:15). When we hear the truth about something we would rather not face, we can either reject it and change nothing or accept it and see what we can learn. Confrontation is a method that points out contradictions in what a person says or does. When you confront someone, your goal is to make the person aware of this discrepancy and to allow the person to examine it. The counselor's attitude toward the apparent discrepancy is not that of "gotcha," but is nonjudgmental. When you discover a discrepancy in what the person says or does, gently and kindly bring this to the attention of the person. He or she may be unaware of the contradiction or may be hoping that you will not confront him or her. In either case, confrontation is a sign of respect and shows that you care enough to bring this contradiction to his or her attention.

You take a risk when you confront someone, but if you use an approach that communicates that you love and care about the person, this may be one of the few times when he or she is confronted in a loving and kind way, rather than in an accusing or aggressive manner.

Verbalizing the Other Person's Difficult Feelings

If identifying feelings or verbalizing feelings is difficult for someone, make an educated guess about what the person might be feeling and then ask the person if this might be what he is feeling. Encourage the person to tell you whether your guess was accurate, so that, together, you can identify the correct feeling. When you model for someone how to identify and verbalize difficult feelings, the person learns how to identify and then verbalize these feelings independently. Creating an "emotions" poster is an activity that helps children under the age of twelve identify and verbalize feelings. For the poster, use photographs/pictures (from magazines) of individual children demonstrating a variety of emotions (happy, sad, scared, angry, embarrassed, shy, confused and so on). Ask the child to point to the picture that expresses how he or she is feeling.

In some situations, it is appropriate to verbalize for someone what he or she does not know how to say. For example, suppose you are counseling a young girl and you suspect she is having a hard time with the death of a loved one. As you explore the situation together, suppose she says, "I think if I had only done something sooner, he would have lived." You could say, "I'm wondering if you felt it was your fault that he died?" She can then either confirm this or correct your perception. It may be hard for her to come right out and say that she thinks it was her fault that he died. Acknowledging that this might be how she is feeling gets the thought out in the open where it can be worked through.

If a person tells you about either physical or sexual abuse or exploitation, it is not appropriate to verbalize what the child cannot say. Instead, ask open-ended, non-leading questions or make objective statements. For example, you could say, "So tell me what happened when you were with this man." Let the person describe what happened. If you do not understand a particular word that a person uses, then ask for clarification. Ask questions such as, "What happened next?" or "How did you feel when this was happening?" These open-ended questions allow the person to tell you what occurred in his own words. In these situations, take care not to ask leading questions, which suggest what might have happened or how the person might have felt: So did this man hurt you? Did he hit you with a stick? Did he tell you not to tell anyone? Were you scared?

Assigning Homework

Homework assignments encourage people to do the work of counseling outside of the counseling session. The more a person can transfer what he or she is learning (in counseling) to everyday life (outside of counseling), the more successful the person will be in implementing change. Studies have shown that people who complete homework assignments outside of the counseling sessions make the most progress in counseling. Completing homework assignments is not a magic wand, but demonstrates a person's motivation and willingness to integrate what he or she is working on in counseling with everyday life. The more a person practices the skills he or she is learning and can apply them, the more he or she will see change in everyday life.

Decide on homework assignments together. During the earlier stages of counseling, you may take the lead in assigning homework and ask whether it sounds reasonable. As the counseling relationship deepens, you may ask the person for ideas about what he or she wants to work on for homework. Homework assignments do not have to be given at every counseling session. Decide together if a homework assignment will be given and what it will be. Homework assignments could include:

- keeping track of what triggers drug use
- keeping track of what triggers fights
- practicing going to several places of employment and asking about job openings
- practicing how to ask for something without being demanding
- practicing healthy ways of dealing with anger or frustrations, and so on.

Skill 6: Obtaining Referrals

At any time during the counseling relationship, a person may share that he needs medical care, clothes, food, shelter and so on. While a counselor's role may be to focus primarily on emotional needs, a counselor is well aware that a person is made up of body, mind, emotions and spirit. Experienced counselors know that people cannot focus on their emotional needs if they are constantly hungry or cold or in danger, and their priority is survival.

They need to get warm, to get fed and to be safe. Be aware of community resources that may be available to minister to these other physical needs.

Depending on the country in which you minister, there may be public resources available to young people. If so, refer the person to the appropriate resource so that he or she can get connected to someone who may be able to help. Oftentimes, however, no such public resources are available to young people. In these situations, network with other agencies serving young people. Ask these agencies if they are aware of any other informal community resources, such as a church that provides a hot meal once a week or medical personnel who treat young people in counseling. Ask about the interest level or funds available for the development of specific resources that are currently unavailable to young people.

As you get to know a person, you may realize that his or her problems are beyond your counseling ability or skills. This is an extremely important assessment to make. Explain that while you would like to assist him or her, you know that you do not have the knowledge, training or skills to help. Ask him or her for written permission for you to contact another counselor. Referring a person to someone new can be difficult for the person to understand and, generally, no one wants to change counselors after developing a relationship. Before the other counselor meets the person, schedule a few more counseling sessions to ease the transition. These additional sessions help the person adjust to the idea of seeing a new counselor and process his or her feelings about leaving the original counselor. You can also review with the person what he or she has already accomplished in counseling and say good-bye to each another.

Skill 7: Initiating Closure

A counselor is aware that the counseling relationship will, at some point, end, and strives to empower people to eventually leave the counseling relationship and live their own lives in a healthy and satisfying way. A counseling relationship may be brief, such as when the counselor meets with someone one time. Or the counselor and the young person may meet on a regular basis for a few months. Or, possibly, the counseling relationship lasts for one or more years. Still, the counseling relationship will end at some point. Closing a counseling session and determining whether you will meet again can be difficult.

Ending the Counseling Session

A counseling session may begin as a casual conversation with someone or it may be a scheduled appointment. In either case, be aware of your time limits. If a conversation begins over playing cards or a board game and is moving toward more personal issues, and you know you have to be somewhere in ten minutes, it would be best to say, "I'm interested in what we're talking about. I'm sorry that I have to be in a meeting in ten minutes because I'd like to continue this conversation. Since I'll have to go in the next few minutes, would you be open to scheduling a time later today [or another day] when we can get together to finish this conversation?" Then schedule a time for later that day or another day, and be sure to initiate and follow through with this meeting time.

If you schedule appointments, let the person know at the beginning of the meeting how long the session will last. Usually for children under age twelve, a thirty minute session is appropriate, although some children this age may do well with a forty-five minute session. For adolescents, determine whether they can stay focused and engaged for sixty minutes or if a shorter time frame is warranted.

Having a specific time limit for the counseling session provides boundaries. For young people who are hesitant about counseling, having a specific time limit to talk or play provides security because they know that the session has a definite beginning and end time. Ten minutes before the session ends, you could say, "In a few minutes, we'll need to start wrapping up." If the current discussion could take more than ten minutes, say, "We won't have time to finish this activity because we need to start wrapping up in a few minutes." This cues the person that the counseling time is nearing its end for that day.

At the close of the individual session, say, "So when can we meet again?" This initiates the expectation that meeting again would be important. You might also query the person: "I enjoyed talking with you today about this. I'm wondering if it would be helpful for us to meet again so we can see how you're doing with what we talked about today." This allows the young person to express whether he or she thinks meeting again would be helpful.

Ending the Counseling Relationship

Throughout the counseling relationship, as you observe progress, provide feedback to the person about the changes he is making and how you see that he is moving closer toward his goal.

Over time, a natural progression of meeting less frequently occurs as the person becomes better able to manage what is going on in his or her life. Initially, you may meet with a person weekly, but as he or she makes changes and appears better able to manage concerns, you may suggest meeting every two weeks. As the person continues to move forward, initiate and discuss the idea of meeting once a month. At this stage, you may want to begin talking about ending the counseling relationship.

Skill 8: Managing Documentation

Documentation may sound like an unusual skill for counseling. In the discussion about interviewing (see Skill 3), we looked at an example of a structured interview. When you ask multiple questions, write down the responses to keep track of and remember the information. Written documentation is important because you may need to share this information with others who minister to the person. Documentation should be shared only:

- if appropriate,
- if the person knows what specific documentation is being shared and with whom it is being shared, and
- if the person has given permission for this documentation to be shared with specific individuals.

Not all documentation needs to be shared with everyone who ministers to the young person. Exercise discretion and sound judgment when assessing who needs to know when it comes to sharing documentation. Keep documentation in a secure location that is accessible only to those who need to know and to whom the person has given permission.

Documentation does not have to be lengthy, but it does need to be meaningful. Take notes about what was discussed in each counseling session to keep track of:

- each session's focus,
- the level of progress being made toward one or more goals and
- other observations.

This chapter has provided you with a broad framework for counseling to guide you in ministering to young people. God gives us a blessed opportunity each time we get to know and counsel young people. They are amazing and precious gifts, and we never know how what we say or do may influence them in their growth in the Lord. Counseling is a sacred trust and requires each of us to be fully dependent on Christ for our wisdom and discernment. I pray you will draw closer to Him as you seek to provide comfort, wisdom and guidance to those the Lord has entrusted to your care.

Suggested Readings

You may want to read Chapter 11 in *Healing the Children of War*, Phyllis Kilbourn, editor.[11] In this chapter, Mickie Heard, M.A., gives a thorough explanation of what organized play is and how to use it when counseling children. Phyllis Kilbourn has developed curriculum related to organized play in the training manual *Offering Healing and Hope for Children in Crisis: Module 1: Trauma and Crisis Care.*[12]

FIVE

HEALING through FOCUSED PLAY

Mary Beth Young

It is amazing to watch children! They can play for hours and hours on end. Their play may be loud, or active, or quiet, or funny, or destructive, or entertaining. God has created children so that they play in order to learn about their world. If we, as adults, want to understand children and learn what is going on inside of them, one of the best ways to do this is to pay close attention to their play.

When I was first learning about how to interact with young children through play, I found this to be an intimidating concept. I felt inadequate to competently communicate with a young child, much less get to know him and work with him to resolve any emotional issues through his play. I was very comfortable talking with teenagers and getting to know them, but children—this was a whole new experience for me. Now that I've been working with young children for years, it has become quite natural to sit down with a young child and provide an environment where he is encouraged to play spontaneously. Through his play, I can learn how he thinks, how he perceives the world, and hopefully, help him make sense of difficult things that he may have experienced in his life. All of this is accomplished through *play* with him. I may not ever talk with him in the here and now about 'him' or 'his life' or 'what he is experiencing.' I do not have to ask him directly, "What are your worries?" or "What are your concerns?" Everything I need to learn and communicate with him can be done through interacting with him while he *plays*. This kind of play has been referred to as organized play or focused play and will be referred to as focused play in this chapter.

The purpose of this chapter is to help caregivers learn how to engage in focused play with a child in order to: (1) discover what psychological-emotional-social-spiritual issues he may need to address, (2) help him heal from (and hopefully resolve) these psychological issues and (3) guide him to be able to move forward in his life. This chapter will describe the basics of the process of focused play along with the skills needed and used by a caregiver during focused play. There are so many children in our world who have experienced what no child should ever have to experience. Yet, sadly, too many children witness violence toward others or experience this violence being inflicted upon themselves. Too many children have suffered the brutal effects of abuse, exploitation, discrimination, violence and the loss of any safe haven to which they can flee. Our desire is to point these children to the Lord, who is our Refuge. There are a growing number of Christian believers throughout the world who are committed to assisting these children. This chapter is written to assist these believers who are ministering to children in crisis.

In addition to focused play, a caregiver will want to interview the adults who live with the child, as well as other adults who know the child well (family members, etc.) to get a complete picture of the child—if such adults are available. These interviews will provide valuable information that the caregiver may not be able to obtain from engaging the child in focused play. So, while focused play is one way to get to know a child, it is important to interview the adults who know the child well in order to obtain the most accurate and complete picture of the child, his strengths and his emotional needs.

There are several resources that utilize the different forms of focused play activities, such as role play and drama, art, music, puppets, playroom, sand tray, etc.[13] While this chapter will not go into detail about each of these forms of focused play, the skills presented in this chapter can be used in each type of these play activities in order to uncover a child's emotional concerns and assist a child in resolving these issues.

First Things First

As we begin to learn about focused play, some important reminders are in order. Our first approach when ministering to children in crisis is to get on our knees and go to our heavenly Father. God knew each child before he was born, and He can guide and lead us to minister to a child in ways that uniquely fit the child and that would provide a tender touch from the Lord. God has created and gifted each child, and no two children are the same. Even when two children grow up together in the same home and experience the same event, each child may understand and make sense of this experience differently. The Holy Spirit gives us wisdom and discernment as we minister to children who have encountered tremendously difficult situations. God has also given us other, more mature believers with whom to consult about difficult situations that children in crisis may have encountered. None of us know all the answers. Proverbs encourages us to heed the instruction of wise counselors (see Prov. 19:20). While you may not know a more experienced caregiver or live in close proximity to one, if you have access to the Internet, this is a way to learn and consult with other skilled caregivers. There are experienced, Christian caregivers throughout the world who would be more than happy to answer your questions and walk you through how to work with children in crisis. We all need guidance and others to consult with about difficult issues when we minister to children in crisis. Consulting with a more experienced caregiver provides support to you, and either confirms how you are ministering to children in crisis or lets you know areas in which you may need additional instruction or guidance.

What Do Children Accomplish through Play?

There are a number of reasons why a child plays. A child accomplishes so much through play and often adults are unaware of all that is accomplished by a child when he plays. Here are some ideas about what occurs through his play. He may:

- learn new skills necessary for his development
- practice and build skills for life (independence, how to get along with others, how to play by the rules or not)
- test out these new skills in a variety of situations
- figure out what he is capable of
- create a world in fantasy that he can master
- have control
- figure out if he has any power in the world
- solve his problems
- learn to make sense of his world
- project himself into his play
- learn to negotiate new situations
- demonstrate what he knows
- learn how to entertain himself
- figure out his own rhythms of energy and rest

- release emotions
- release energy
- form trusting attachments with parents/caregivers or peers
- develop his personality
- work on what he may need to learn (such as learning how to share, how to take turns, how to demonstrate anger in a healthy way, etc.)
- demonstrate how he solves problems

What Is Focused Play?

Focused play is an opportunity for a child to express—*through play*—what is on his mind. Focused play involves a caregiver or counselor introducing the child to a variety of play items or activities so that the child decides what to play with and how to play. The adult provides an emotionally safe, private, neutral place—where there will not be any interruptions—so that the child feels emotionally safe enough to express what is on his mind through play. This time of focused play is structured. In other words, the caregiver structures the amount of time spent with the child, as well as the play items and activities the child has access to. As you know, young children will not sit down and have an extensive conversation with an adult about their worries or about what is troubling them. Children do not have the verbal capabilities to explain what they are thinking. In focused play, children often learn how to better verbalize what the play characters are thinking and experiencing, which then allows the child to better verbalize what he has experienced. Since play is the language of a child, a child can "tell" a caregiver what is on his mind if a caregiver is willing to take the time and "listen" to the child's play. There are a number of skills a caregiver uses to learn what is going on in the child's mind and what the child is experiencing emotionally.

What Is the Purpose of Focused Play?

The primary purpose of focused play is to provide a safe emotional environment where a caregiver can assist a child to heal from emotional wounds through play. Focused play allows the child to process difficult or painful emotional issues. Because there are so many different situations that a child may bring to focused play, there can be an equal number of purposes to focused play for a child.

If a child has experienced trauma, the child may work toward understanding the trauma and making sense of the trauma through his focused play—with the assistance of a caregiver. If a child has difficulty verbalizing his feelings, a caregiver can assist him to learn a variety of feelings and begin using words to express when he experiences these feelings. A caregiver may introduce focused play to a child in order to assist the child in processing a difficult situation the child has experienced. Therefore, the purpose of focused play will depend entirely on the needs of the child.

What Are the Benefits of Focused Play?

As everyone knows, children are immensely different from adults in many ways. A child's thinking process is one such difference. Children between the ages of seven to eleven think and communicate in a concrete and literal way. This is because his brain is not yet capable of abstract thinking or reasoning. When a child is in this stage, he understands words and concepts in this concrete and simplistic way. Therefore, adults need to communicate with him on this same level. Play is one such way an adult can communicate with a child in a way that a child can understand. Since play is the language of a child, if we want to communicate effectively with a child, then we need to use his language. Through play, the adult can communicate with the child in a nonthreatening way.

We also know that children are great imitators. That is how a child learns so much in life: by watching and learning to copy what others around him do. Focused play is often an imitation of what the child has experienced in his life. Focused play is nonthreatening to a young child because when a child is playing, he is involved in his world of fantasy. The child does not have the capacity yet to understand that what he is demonstrating in play is a reflection of what he has experienced or what he wishes could happen. Therefore, when a young child plays spontaneously, he does not feel he is communicating anything in particular through his play. By remaining in his fantasy during his play, the child senses that the play is about "someone else" and this provides the child with a sense of safety. While an adult who observes a child's play may see reflections between the child's play and the child's life, the child is only able to see the fantasy of the play. This allows the child to remain open and spontaneous about what he is sharing in his play. If the caregiver were to leave the child's fantasy of play and begin asking the child direct questions about his life, most likely the caregiver would not get as much information from the child in this type of direct conversation. Play is the medium that allows the child to demonstrate symbolically and safely what is going on within him.

Why Is Healing Important?

The answer may seem obvious, but let us look at this a little more closely. When a child has emotional or psychological issues, these issues may prevent him from developing in a normative manner. In other words, his emotional-social-psychological-spiritual growth may be impacted. Depending on the degree of a child's emotional issues, a child will use his emotional energy to protect himself. This kind of emotional protection takes a lot of psychological energy and prevents the child from using his energy toward normative developmental tasks such as reading, writing, making friends, praying, getting to know God, learning how to solve problems, etc. Emotional issues can lead to problems related to anger, isolation, withdrawal, bitterness, vengeance, aggression, depression, confusion, etc. Through healing of these emotional issues, a child is freer to focus on the developmental tasks of growing up.

When Can Focused Play Begin?

A child is able to engage in meaningful, focused play when he is living in an emotionally and physically safe environment. God has created us so that when we are in difficult situations, we have psychological defenses that we use to protect ourselves. These psychological defenses are used to protect the child until the child is ready to deal with these difficult or traumatic situations. When a child is living in a physically or emotionally dangerous situation, the child will use most of his emotional energy to bolster and maintain his defenses so he can survive the danger emotionally.

Psychological defenses are automatic. In order to understand psychological defenses, let us begin by looking at an example of an automatic *physical* response to danger. When you believe a person is going to hit you, your automatic defense is to put your hands up to block the attack. You do not consciously think, "Now I'm going to put my hands up so I can defend myself against this other person who is trying to hit me." Your hands automatically respond to the threat by trying to block the attacker's strikes. The same occurs with psychological or emotional defenses. A child does not consciously choose to use a psychological defense. A child automatically uses whatever psychological defenses he can to prevent the dangerous situation from overwhelming him. Using these psychological defenses takes a lot of emotional energy from the child because he is trying to protect himself from an onslaught of emotional harm. Once the child is in a physically and emotionally safe environment, and knows that the danger has passed, the child no longer needs to exert a substantial amount of his psychological energy to protect himself through defenses. Now that the child is in a safe environment—where there is no threat of harm—the child can begin to relax; this is usually when a child begins to express and process his concerns—through play—with a caregiver. It is unrealistic to think that when a child is in the midst of danger he will be able to process his concerns. This is because most or all of his energy is being used to protect himself emotionally from this danger and to survive the danger. Once the danger is removed and is replaced by a safe, caring environment, the child can now use his psychological energy to deal with the danger that he previously experienced.

The following is another example to help bring understanding to this concept. If a child comes to your ministry and he has not eaten in a few days, what would you do? Of course, you would give him some food, make sure he had enough to eat and assess what other physical needs he may have. You would not start reading the Bible to him or begin introducing focused play to him while he is hungry. He would not be able to focus on what he is listening to or engage in meaningful, focused play when he is hungry. His primary need at that point is to be fed. This is similar to a child who is still living in a dangerous situation. When a child continues to live in a dangerous situation, his primary need is to be in a situation where he is physically and emotionally safe. Focused play will only be engaged in by a child when he is far away enough from the difficulty or danger, and when he does not have to use his energy to guard against the difficulty or danger. When he is in the dangerous situation, he will use most of his psychological energy to survive the danger, not to process it.

Timing is critical when introducing focused play to a child. While a child may reveal or disclose trauma while he is experiencing the trauma, it is *harmful* to a child for a caregiver to encourage him to begin dealing with or processing his trauma.

What Is Emotional Safety and How Is It Provided?

Emotional safety is provided when the child has formed a safe, caring relationship with the caregiver where only the child's best interests are the priority. This is when the child experiences from the adult unconditional acceptance and the adult does not make judgments about what the child shares through his play. This nonjudgmental attitude by the caregiver is critical for the child's healing. If a child is going to share intimate details—through play—of what he has experienced, he has to know the caregiver is emotionally strong enough to handle what he may reveal. In other words, if a child reveals he has experienced something the caregiver may have strong beliefs about (sexual abuse, same-sex experiences, human trafficking, etc.), the caregiver needs to maintain a nonjudgmental attitude toward the child. If a child senses the caregiver is shocked or disgusted by what the child is sharing through his play, the child will immediately shut down and will no longer share information through his play. If a child stops sharing information through his play, a caregiver cannot help a child process what he is sharing. It is this processing that is necessary in order to promote the child's healing. A caregiver needs to provide a neutral, nonjudgmental environment where the child can express his play spontaneously. While it is not the caregiver's role to judge, it is the caregiver's role to teach and to provide information about healthy boundaries between adults and children ("Adults know adults are not to engage in sexual acts with children," or "Adults know they are not supposed to give drugs to children," etc.). A caregiver needs to think through how sensitive subjects will be discussed with a child in his focused play, so children know that the adult is responsible for what the child may have experienced.

Confidentiality is a part of emotional safety because the child needs to know that what he shares in his play with the caregiver will not be shared with others—except in some situations. As the caregiver develops the relationship with the child by providing this emotional safety, the child will progressively share more of himself and his concerns or needs through his play. There may be times when a caregiver may share some of what the child has disclosed in play with others, such as other team members. When this occurs, sensitivity and respect for the child's privacy has to be considered. This chapter cannot address all aspects related to confidentiality, so it would be best to consult with a more experienced caregiver about when it is necessary to share information with other team members and when it is not.

Where Does Focused Play Take Place?

Often ministering to young children is done in a small group such as ministering at an orphanage or an after-school Bible ministry. Focused play needs to take place in an individual situation, not in a small-group setting. A caregiver will want to have the use of a comfortable and child-friendly room where toys are available to the child. The size of the room needs to be big enough for the child and caregiver to be able to spread some toys out on the floor and play freely. It is important that the caregiver use the same room each time she meets with the child. The consistency of the same room lets the child know what to expect (provides security) and therefore allows the child to feel emotionally safe.

While a child-friendly room is the optimal place for focused play to take place, not all caregivers will have access to such an environment. If this is not available, a private place where the caregiver and child will not be interrupted will do nicely. When working with children, a caregiver has to be flexible. So it may be that the only available place for a caregiver and a child to play together one-on-one is off in a corner of a room away from the rest of the children. If this is the situation a caregiver finds herself in, then she should be flexible and do the best she can in this environment.

How Does a Caregiver Initiate Focused Play?

A caregiver may begin by letting the child know that she has some "special" or "fun" toys and activities that the child may enjoy playing with. Most children are curious and will want to see what toys and activities are available. A caregiver may say something like, "I am really enjoying getting to know you and want to keep playing with you. I have some toys and activities that you might enjoy playing with. Would you like to come and see these toys and keep playing together?" You will want to put this in your own words and what is comfortable for you.

When the caregiver and the child are in the playroom, the caregiver will want to briefly show the child the toys and activities that are available. A caregiver may want to say, "Here are some toys you are welcome to play with," and then show the child the toys. The caregiver will want to let the child know about some of the rules of being in the playroom with her.

Why Rules in Focused Play?

Yes, simple rules are needed as rules provide both structure and security to a child. A child feels more secure when he knows what to expect, when he knows what his limits and boundaries are, and when he knows an adult is going to adhere to these limits. Rules demonstrate that the caregiver is going to make sure the environment is safe for the child.

Rules That Guide Focused Play

You will want to keep the rules to a minimum. The rules need to be kept simple, framed in a positive manner and in a way that a child understands. Most rules will be about safety and confidentiality. Some basic rules may include:

1. "When you come into the playroom to play, the first rule is that you keep yourself safe and play with the toys in a safe way."

2. "The next rule is that if you would like to come back and play in the

playroom next week, you have to clean up the toys that you got out today and put them back where you found them before you leave the playroom."

A good rule of thumb is for the child to clean up one play activity before he starts on another play activity.

3. "And the last rule is that what you and I talk about and what we play will be kept private between you and me. The only time I can't keep private what goes on in the playroom is if I think that someone is hurting you or if you are hurting someone else."

The caregiver here is referring to abuse, suicidal thinking or homicidal thinking—but generally, the caregiver does not need to use these specific terms (i.e., abuse, suicide, homicide) until the caregiver knows the child a little better.

It is helpful to let the child know how long he or she can play in the playroom. This is another way to provide structure and security for the child. A child feels more secure when he knows what to expect and when he knows how much time he can play (even when the child is too young to fully understand the concept of time).

What Are Some of the Suggested Play Items and Activities to Have Available?

First and foremost, the play items that are available in the playroom need to be items that most children in your culture would normally play with. A caregiver will use creativity in the selection of play items, since she may not have many resources or play items available. There are two lists provided of play items and activities that may be helpful. The first list is when a caregiver may only have limited access to toys or play activities. These items can be easily used to draw pictures, tell stories about these pictures and make up skits (puppets and dress-up clothes) to allow the child to create his own stories in his play. While a caregiver may not have all of these items or even most of these items, a caregiver who can be flexible and creative, using whatever he has available, can be highly effective. Even if a caregiver does not have any of these items, pictures can be drawn by a child in the dirt or sand, and stories can be solicited from the child about the pictures. The caregiver should not be discouraged if she does not have any of these items available. She should simply use whatever natural items are available to her (stones, twigs, acorns, etc.) for play items. It is a child's imagination that is the necessary component for focused play and often caregivers must be creative when resources are lacking.

Some basic items for a playroom may include:

- crayons, colored pencils, paint and paint brushes, magic markers
- paper (white and construction paper)
- clay or playdough
- glue
- scissors
- chalk
- pipe cleaners and/or craft sticks
- puppets (can be made of: socks with buttons for eyes and nose, yarn for hair; can be cardboard cut outs or hand-drawn pictures glued onto a craft stick)
- sunglasses (children often feel invisible when they are wearing these)
- baby dolls which reflect the ethnic diversity of the children you are ministering to
- toy baby bottles, baby blanket, baby clothes for doll, etc.
- play telephones
- a mirror
- old clothes/hats/shoes for dress-up (be sure to include clothes that boys can dress up in as well)
- board games

The next list contains additional play items that often spark a child's interest and fantasy. If you have access to the following items, these can provide rich play experiences for children to express what is on their mind:

- a dollhouse with separate rooms for a kitchen, living room, bathroom, bedroom, backyard area
- people figures (such as adult figures that may be used as a mommy, daddy, aunt; community figures: teacher, police officer, doctor, fireman, etc.; and child figures that may be used as a sister, brother, other children)
- household furniture items for the dollhouse (couch, chairs, table, beds, bathtub, toilet, dishes, etc.)
- animal figures (zoo animals, farm animals, dinosaurs or stuffed animals)

- nature figures (trees, bushes, lakes, rivers)
- a play medical kit (with a play stethoscope, thermometer, bandages, etc.)
- angel figures
- castles, knights, dragons
- sheriff badge
- bridges, fences
- farm buildings or houses
- creepy-crawly creatures
- pirates, skull, skeleton, tombstones, or a cross
- bride and groom
- a medium-size plastic container filled halfway with sand (a child may use this as a sand tray where he re-enacts play with toy figures in the sand)

THE PROCESS OF FOCUSED PLAY

What does the caregiver do while the child is playing? In other words, what skills does the caregiver use to guide the child to heal (resolve) his emotional wounds or issues? While there are a number of skills that could be used during a child's play, the following are the primary skills that a caregiver practices during focused play. These are:

- observation
- patience
- active listening
- open-ended questions
- assessment
- the five corrective experiences approach

As with all skills used by a caregiver, practice, practice and more practice is what enables the caregiver to feel more comfortable and competent using these skills. Utilizing each of these skills does not always fit nicely into a progression of using skill #1, then skill #2 and so on. A caregiver may use these skills simultaneously. For purposes of clarity, these skills will be presented as separate skills. A caregiver needs to remember that the use of these skills will often overlap during focused play. Again, this is another reason why every caregiver needs a more experienced caregiver with whom to consult on a regular basis about the child's play and how the caregiver is interacting with the child through focused play.

The first skill is **observation.** The adult gives *undivided attention* to the child's play. An effective way to communicate to the child that the caregiver is giving him undivided attention is through the caregiver's body language. If the child is playing on the floor, then the caregiver should be on the floor with the child. The caregiver wants to be close enough to the child so she can carefully observe the child's play. Observation is one of the most valuable skills a caregiver demonstrates, particularly when a child is engaged in focused play.

Observation by the caregiver is *active.* Observation may appear to be a passive skill, but as the caregiver observes the child's play, the caregiver is actively observing and making mental notes about:

- the sequence of the child's play (what happened first, next and last)
- what is/are the theme(s) of the child's play (this will assist the caregiver later to assess the child's emotional issues)
- what is the emotional expression on the child's face while he is playing
- does the child's facial expression match the content of his play or not?
- is the child playing quietly or talking out loud as he plays?
- is the play appropriate to the situation or is the play more aggressive or violent or passive than what would be expected from a child this age?
- does the child play alone or engage the caregiver in his play?
- does the child's speech match what is going on in the play?
- is the child hesitant or confident in his play?
- is the child looking for approval from the caregiver?
- does the drawing of the child match what the caregiver would expect for a child this age?
- is there anything unusual or out of the ordinary about the child's play? (either the subject matter or the child's perspective about the play?)
- is there anything inappropriate about the child's play or that raises questions in the caregiver's mind?

When a caregiver makes these mental notes based on her observations of the child during play, it allows her to begin to get a picture of the whole child.

The second skill that is necessary for a caregiver to develop when engaging in focused play with a child is **patience.** Caregivers often need to develop the skill of 'being with the child,' and just focus on allowing and encouraging the child to play. Children will reveal exactly what needs to be addressed in counseling *if* the caregiver is patient enough to observe and listen to the child's play. While a child is engaged in focused play, he is open and spontaneous in his play. His play will reveal whatever emotional issues are going on inside of him. A caregiver needs to take the time to allow the child to play spontaneously and let the child's play "speak" for the child. A caregiver may be tempted to rush ahead and begin working toward healing or resolution of the child's emotional issues before the child has fully expressed these issues. The caregiver needs to be patient with a child in focused play to allow the child's play to reveal different pieces of the puzzle to the child.

Another skill that is critical when a child is playing is to provide **active or reflective listening** to the child. Active listening is when the adult summarizes or paraphrases what the child is doing in their play. Active listening allows the adult to communicate back to the child what the caregiver is seeing in his play and allows the child to let the caregiver know if what she is perceiving is accurate or not. Active listening is "where you make a conscious effort to hear not only the words that another person is saying but, more importantly, try to understand the complete message being sent."[14] A child often does not have the words to express what the characters in his play may be demonstrating. This is why active listening is so important. The caregiver reflects back to the child what the caregiver *observes* in the play. An example of reflective listening is: If the child is playing with people figures in a dollhouse and the play figure whom the child has referred to as "daddy" is acting in an angry or harsh manner, the caregiver may say, "It looks like the daddy is angry." This allows the child to confirm that the daddy figure is angry or for the child to say, "No, daddy's not angry, he always acts like this. When daddy's angry, he yells."

Always keep your feedback related to the child's *play*; do not address your feedback to the specific child. Do not say, "I'm guessing your father was angry, that is why you're making the daddy figure angry." This feedback is too direct and too threatening to the child. Remember, play allows the child to express things he cannot express verbally or is too uncomfortable with expressing verbally. If the caregiver *interprets* the child's play directly to the child, this does not allow the child to feel safe. The caregiver must always keep her reflective listening and observations directed toward the child's *play*—not at the child's current or past life situation. Another way to explain this is *the caregiver needs to stay in the metaphor* of the child's play. The child's play is a metaphor of what is going on inside of the child. So, in order for the caregiver to effectively communicate with the child, the caregiver must make active listening statements that are reflective about the child's play—not reflective about the child himself. The reason active listening is so important is because by reflecting back to the child what the caregiver sees in the child's play, the caregiver is being a mirror for the child. By the caregiver being a mirror to the child, this reflective feedback allows the child to become more aware of what his play characters are doing and helps the child learn how to verbalize what the play characters are doing. Being able to verbalize what the play characters are doing in the play allows the child to use this skill in his own life to learn how to verbalize what is going on in his life.

Another benefit of active listening is that it encourages a child to continue to freely express his thoughts and feelings through play. A cardinal feature of focused play is for the child to be able to play spontaneously. A caregiver does not want to say or do anything that will 'lead' the child to say something or to play in a particular way. A caregiver wants to provide a neutral, safe environment where the child is able to express his thoughts and feelings through play. A caregiver must be sensitive to his own body language and what he says to assure these are not 'shaping' or influencing the child's play. A young child has a strong desire to please the adults in his life. If when a child is playing, a caregiver makes statements about the child's play such as "that is cool" or "I like that," these statements can subtly shape and influence the child's play. That is why it is best for a caregiver to primarily use active listening to reflect back to the child what his play is demonstrating.

The fourth skill a caregiver uses when a child is playing is to **ask open-ended questions.** Open-ended questions are used to clarify or to obtain more information about a child's play. If a child is drawing a picture, the caregiver may ask an open-ended question such as, "What is going on in this picture?" or "What is the little boy feeling [or thinking] in this picture?" If a child is using puppets, the caregiver may ask, "What is this puppet doing?" or "How did the little girl puppet feel when the adult puppets were calling her names?" Or, if the child is playing with family figures and the daddy figure hits the mommy figure, the caregiver may ask, "I'm wondering what the little boy figure thinks about why the daddy hit the mommy?" These open-ended questions will give the caregiver additional information about the child's perspective on the situation that cannot be obtained through the other skills used by the caregiver.

Open-ended questions also provide the child an opportunity to think through some considerations he may not have thought of previously. If a child's play is focused on two child figures arguing and disagreeing, the caregiver might ask, "How can these children figure out a solution to their disagreement?" This gives the child the chance to think about a solution to the conflict rather than the caregiver introducing the solution to the conflict. This type of open-ended question allows the caregiver to encourage the child to think and problem solve for himself, along with some subtle guidance from the caregiver. If the child comes up with a solution that is far-fetched, the caregiver can ask another open-ended question to redirect the child to think about the consequences of this far-fetched solution or to assist the child to think toward another more reasonable solution.

These first four skills: observation, patience, active listening and open-ended questions are used to allow the caregiver to obtain information about the child from his play. When a caregiver has spent time playing with a child and has obtained enough information from the child's play, the caregiver will then put together all the various pieces of what she has learned about the child and make an **assessment** of the child's emotional needs. Assessing the child's emotional needs takes time. *One of the most common mistakes of inexperienced caregivers is to make an assessment prematurely before the caregiver has gathered the necessary information to make a sound assessment.* As stated earlier in this chapter, interviewing the adults closest to the child is a vital part of a caregiver's assessment in order to obtain the most complete and accurate picture of the child.

One of the contributing factors for a caregiver to make an accurate assessment of the child's emotional issues is for the caregiver to assess the theme(s) of the child's play. An example of this is when a caregiver asks the child to draw a picture of whatever he wants to draw. Once he has drawn the picture, the caregiver asks him to tell the caregiver a story about the picture. Often children will say, "I do not know a story." The caregiver will need to gently encourage the child to make up a story about what is happening in the picture he drew. A caregiver may need to point to an object in the picture and begin asking the child open-ended questions, such as "Tell me about the truck. Who's driving it? Where is it going? What happens when he gets there?" The caregiver then needs to allow the child to tell his own story about this picture. It is through the child telling the story that the caregiver can assess the general *theme* of the child's story. If a child has drawn several pictures and told a story about each picture, a caregiver will often observe a pattern of the theme(s) represented. The themes that are represented in a child's story can be endless. Some themes may be related to: safety, danger,

anger, happiness, being fearful about something, fun experiences, not having enough, abandonment, security, honesty, dishonesty, lack of trust in others, naiveté about others (i.e., trusting others too much), guilt, protection or lack thereof, being disappointed by others, others making promises they do not keep, secrets and more. Assessing the theme(s) of the child's stories allows a caregiver to more easily understand what psychological-emotional-social-spiritual issue(s) the child needs to address in focused play.

Providing **corrective experiences** through play is a critical component of helping the child heal. It will take some time to develop this skill, but with the guidance of a more experienced caregiver or counselor, a person can become more competent in the use and the eventual proficiency of this skill. A more experienced caregiver can guide a less experienced caregiver in the timing of the use of this skill. It is helpful for the caregiver to have a variety of corrective experience approaches to choose from, since one approach will not fit all situations. These corrective experience approaches include:

(1) providing opportunities for the child to think through different solutions to the situations he has presented in his focused play

(2) asking the child questions to gently redirect his play

(3) teaching the child new skills through his play

(4) assisting the child to *understand* (make sense of) his emotional-psychological-social-spiritual issues

(5) allowing the child to *demonstrate* the new skills he has learned or *how* he has put into perspective the emotional dilemma that was illustrated in his play scenario

Here's an example and a brief description of the use of each of the five corrective experience approaches to help you understand how to use these corrective experience skills. If a child enacts a scenario in his focused play where the daddy figure is stomping around the house in anger, yelling at the mommy figure and hits her in front of the children figures, the caregiver may ask open-ended questions to find out additional information. The caregiver may ask, "What prompted the daddy figure to get so angry?", "How did the child figure feel about what is happening to the mommy figure?", "What did the child figure do when the mommy figure got hit?" and "What did each of the other family members do when the mommy got hit?" The caregiver will encourage the child to *continue to play* and observe how the child allows his focused play to unfold so the caregiver can observe how this play scenario ends. If the play scenario ends with the mommy going to her room, the daddy stomping out and leaving the house, and the children going in to watch television, the caregiver may use any of the following corrective experience approaches to assist the child to figure out, *through the play,* how to best handle this situation.

Scenarios Using the Five Corrective Experience Approaches

In the use of each of the five corrective experience approaches, it is expected that *before* the caregiver begins using a specific corrective experience approach, the caregiver has first used her observation, patience, active listening, open-ended questions and assessment skills. A caregiver does not rush into using corrective experience approaches without first using the skills that allow and encourage the child to play spontaneously. The child is then able to express and begin to become more aware of the emotional issues demonstrated in his play and how to process these emotional issues.

Corrective Experience Approach #1

Provide opportunities for the child to think through different solutions to the situation(s) he has presented in his focused play.

After the caregiver has used observation, patience, reflective listening and open-ended questions to allow the child to complete his play scenario, the caregiver may say: "I'm wondering what would happen if the mommy had a plan of what to do when the daddy began stomping around the house when he first got angry?" This introduces the child to the idea that possibly there is a different solution to this scenario. A different observation is that the mommy begins to realize that when daddy is stomping around the house, this may mean that he is getting ready to become physically aggressive toward mommy (or the children). The solution may include the mommy *having a plan* of what to do when daddy starts stomping around the house—such as the mommy and the children leaving the house and going to a safe place. The caregiver then has the child reenact this play scenario where the daddy figure starts getting angry and the mommy figure quietly gets herself and the children out of the house. In this example, after the focused play with the child, it would be important for the caregiver to talk with the child's mother. The caregiver would <u>not</u> tell the mother that the child acted out the scenario of the daddy character hitting the mommy character in his play. The caregiver would ask the mother open-ended questions about conflict in the home, how people express their anger in the home, etc., in an effort to encourage the mother to share about the difficulties that are going on in the home. The caregiver would then discuss with the mother ways—or a plan—of how she can keep herself and her children safe when these diffi-culties occur.

Corrective Experience Approach #2

Ask the child questions to gently re-direct the child's play.

After the caregiver has used observation, reflective listening, patience and open-ended questions to allow the child to finish his play scenario, the caregiver might say: "I have an idea. Let us go back and try this. When the daddy was getting angry and stomping around the house, I want you to show me what would happen if the child figure slipped out of the house and told his grandmother, who lived next door, that he was scared because daddy was getting ready to hit mommy." The caregiver then allows the child to play this scenario out, demonstrating what he believes the grandmother's response would be. This use of redirecting the child's play by introducing a possible solution or an event into the play situation helps the child see there may be some things that can help the situation—and that would provide a different ending to the play. This also provides the caregiver with informa-tion about whether or not the grandmother may or may not be a viable resource for this family during times of high family stress.

Corrective Experience Approach #3

Teach the child new skills through focused play.

Teaching a child new skills opens up so many possibilities in focused play. A caregiver, *through play,* can teach a child how to keep himself safe, how to make friends, how to cope with his feelings, how to grieve and how to tell adults when "bad" things are happening to him. Any emotional-so-cial-psychological-spiritual issue a child experiences can most likely be ad-dressed through the use of teaching new skills through focused play. In the example above, the caregiver may teach the child the new skill of telling a trusted adult—who can help the mommy problem solve to keep herself and the children safe—when mommy is getting hit at home. In the play scenar-io, the caregiver may encourage the child to finish his play scenario through the caregiver's use of observation, patience, reflective listening, open-ended questions and assessment skills. The caregiver may then say, "Can I play for a little bit?" If the child agrees to the caregiver's request, the caregiver then begins moving and controlling the family figures in the play scenario. The caregiver may set up a play scenario where the family is at an aunt's house or the child is attending an after-school Bible ministry. The caregiver enacts in her play how the child tells the aunt or tells the Bible ministry teacher that mommy is getting hit at home and how when mommy gets hit, this makes the child character feel very scared. The caregiver then enacts the aunt or the after-school Bible teacher sitting down privately with the mommy and talking about what she can do to help the mommy. In addition to teaching the child to tell a trusted adult when he is scared about things going on at home, this also teaches the child that adults are the ones who have to figure out how to make things safe for children.

Teaching—in focused play—is especially important when a child has experienced some type of abuse. Children have a very strong sense of justice and a child is generally going to look at 'whose fault' it is when something happens. Because a child is dependent on caregivers for all of his needs, a child will do 'mental gymnastics' in order to protect the caregiver in his life who has abused him. When a child is abused, the child will come up with an explanation of why the abuse happened. This explanation is generally going to protect the abusing caregiver. It allows the child to believe the caregiver loves him, thus allowing the child to maintain his attachment to the adult. One such explanation, when a child has been abused, is that a child believes, "It was my fault. I deserved it." It is necessary—during play—to teach the child that no child "deserves" to be abused. Because caregivers often justify their abuse of a child by telling him, "I would not hit you if you listened to me" or something similar, it is particularly important for the caregiver to take the time to teach the child and help him understand that adults are responsible for keeping children safe from harm. When an adult sexually abuses a child, he may tell the child, "You wanted" the sexual abuse or "You enjoyed" it. Again, this is where teaching is critical for the child to understand that adults are responsible for keeping children safe from harm and there is nothing the child did to invite this sexual aggression.

Corrective Experience Approach #4

Assist the child to understand (make sense of) his emotional-psychological-social-spiritual issues.

This is the approach that allows the child—through play—to put his real world experiences into an understandable and healthy context in his life. A way to do this in the play scenario of the daddy figure hitting the mommy figure is the following: The child may have been coming to see the caregiver weekly for a few months. During this time, the child has learned, through focused play, how to express his thoughts and feelings, how to cope with these feelings in a healthy way, and how to tell adults about when mommy is getting hit at home so trustworthy adults can listen to him and assist the mommy character to figure out how to deal with this situation at home.

In order for the child to move on in his life and use his emotional energy for the normal developmental tasks of life (reading, writing, playing, making friends, getting to know God, developing interests, etc.), the child needs to have some type of understanding of, "*What was the purpose of this emotional issue in my life?*" Put another way, "*Why did this happen to me and can anything good come from this?*" A child is not going to say in his play, "The experience of the child figure living in a home where his daddy hit his mommy happened because..." We know children do not think, talk or play this way. Yet, within his own developmental understanding, a child does need to make sense of what he has experienced in his life.

In focused play, the caregiver may ask open-ended questions to get the child to think about this. A caregiver might ask, "What has this little boy learned about himself from growing up in a family where there have been some very difficult times?" Or, "What has this little boy in the play learned about solving problems by living in a family that has some troubles?" This allows the child to begin thinking about and realizing the positive aspects that have come from difficult situations he has experienced. The positives may be that the little boy in the play scenario learned there were trustworthy adults in his life to whom he could go for help; he may have learned he could tell others what he thinks and feels in order to feel better; he may have learned there are solutions to his problems; he may have learned his family really loved each other, but that daddy needed to learn some new ways to handle his anger and so on.

The caregiver will want to assist the child to look at his play scenarios and see what positives the play figures learned from any difficult experiences demonstrated in the play scenarios. Patience on the caregiver's part is important here, as is gentle redirection. Only the child can reach this point in his play as he progresses to this internally. While a caregiver can ask these types of questions to guide the child toward thinking about this, only the child can do the internal work of getting to this point.

It may be helpful to the caregiver to think about how adults do this in order to understand this concept with children in focused play. When an adult experiences a traumatic situation, in order for the adult to fully heal, he needs to reach a point where he accepts what he has experienced (the grieving process) and puts this experience into a healthy framework in understanding his life. God created us so we have a desire to understand and put into perspective difficult situations that we have experienced. The

Bible speaks to this and guides us in doing this. Genesis 50:20 says, "But as for you, you meant evil against me; but God meant it for good" (NKJV) and Romans 8:28 states, "And we know that all things work together for good to those who love God, to those who are the called according to His purpose" (NKJV). You may have heard stories of individuals who have been through horrific experiences (survivors of abuse, rape, domestic violence, torture, prisoners of war, human trafficking, etc.) While these individuals would never have chosen to go through these experiences, they are able to acknowledge that these experiences have contributed to who they are now as people, as well as having grown in ways they would never have known they were capable of growing. You may have heard them say they have experienced God's presence and sustaining grace in ways they had previously not known. Even if it is not a traumatic situation, adults try to put into perspective any difficult situation they have experienced. And this is what children who have experienced difficult situations need to do in focused play in order to fully heal.

Corrective Experience Approach #5

Allow the child to demonstrate the new skills he has learned or how he has put into perspective the emotional dilemma that was illustrated in his play scenario.

There will come a time when the child will naturally demonstrate in his play the healing (resolution) of his emotional issue. This is the culmination of the use of the caregiver's skills as described in this chapter, as well as the child's internal 'work' that he has accomplished, which is reflected in his play. It is the use of the previous corrective experience approaches that lead the child to this point of healing. Once the caregiver observes this healing in the child's play, the caregiver will provide reflective listening related to the resolution of his emotional issue. This gives positive feedback that the child has learned what he needed to learn and has accomplished what he needed to accomplish in his play. When the caregiver observes this healing in the child's play, the caregiver will be very specific in verbalizing what the play character has learned or resolved in his play. The caregiver should make a big deal about what the play character has accomplished in the play scenario. Children need a lot of positive encouragement in order to learn. The caregiver may say something like, "Wow! Your little boy character has really learned how to tell adults whom he can trust when he feels scared. He has also learned how to tell adults what frightens him. Now that he is able to let someone know when he needs help, he has been able to get the help he needs instead of just being scared all by himself." This verbalizes and reinforces to the child what he has accomplished in his focused play.

Who Is the Ultimate "Healer"?

Thankfully, Jesus is the Great Physician and He has a variety of ways to heal children who have emotional scars. One way of healing He uses is focused play. It is a creative approach to helping children heal from emotional wounds and move forward in their lives. Jesus tells us, "The thief does not come except to steal, and to kill, and to destroy. I have come that they may have life, and that they may have it more abundantly" (John 10:10 NKJV). God's desire for children is that they come to know Him and live an abundant life in Him. The Lord has given each of His followers a tremendous opportunity since He has invited us to be His hands and feet on earth. My prayer is that this chapter will better equip caregivers to minister to the beautiful and precious children whom the Lord has brought into our lives. May the Lord give you wisdom and discernment. May He lead you to wise and godly caregivers who can guide you as you seek to serve Him through ministering to children in crisis.

Six

COUNSELING SEXUALLY EXPLOITED CHILDREN

Esther Buff

Scripture records the tragic story of Tamar's rape by Amnon, David's son. We can learn much from this story about how children who have been raped or forced into sexual exploitation feel and think about their experiences. Counselors can also gain insight into how to counsel the "Tamars" who come to them for counseling.

> In the course of time, Amnon son of David fell in love with Tamar, the beautiful sister of Absalom son of David. Amnon became frustrated to the point of illness on account of his sister Tamar, for she was a virgin, and it seemed impossible for him to do anything to her. Now Amnon had a friend named Jonadab son of Shimeah, David's brother. Jonadab was a very shrewd man. He asked Amnon, "Why do you, the king's son, look so haggard morning after morning? Won't you tell me?" Amnon said to him, "I'm in love with Tamar, my brother Absalom's sister." "Go to bed and pretend to be ill," Jonadab said. "When your father comes to see you, say to him, 'I would like my sister Tamar to come and give me something to eat. Let her prepare the food in my sight so I may watch her and then eat it from her hand.'" So Amnon lay down and pretended to be ill. When the king came to see him, Amnon said to him, "I would like my sister Tamar to come and make some special bread in my sight, so I may eat from her hand." David sent word to Tamar at the palace: "Go to the house of your brother Amnon and prepare some food for him." So Tamar went to the house of her brother Amnon, who was lying down. She took some dough, kneaded it, made the bread in his sight and baked it. Then she took the pan and served him the bread, but he refused to eat. "Send everyone out of here," Amnon said. So everyone left him. Then Amnon said to Tamar, "Bring the food here into my bedroom so I may eat from your hand." And Tamar took the bread she had prepared and brought it to her brother Amnon in his bedroom. But when she took it to him to eat, he grabbed her and said, "Come to bed with me, my sister." "Don't, my brother!" she

said to him. "Don't force me. Such a thing should not be done in Israel! Don't do this wicked thing. What about me? Where could I get rid of my disgrace? And what about you? You would be like one of the wicked fools in Israel. Please speak to the king; he will not keep me from being married to you." But he refused to listen to her, and since he was stronger than she, he raped her. Then Amnon hated her with intense hatred. In fact, he hated her more than he had loved her. Amnon said to her, "Get up and get out!" "No!" she said to him. "Sending me away would be a greater wrong than what you have already done to me." But he refused to listen to her. He called his personal servant and said, "Get this woman out of here and bolt the door after her." So his servant put her out and bolted the door after her. She was wearing a richly ornamented robe, for this was the kind of garment the virgin daughters of the king wore. Tamar put ashes on her head and tore the ornamented robe she was wearing. She put her hand on her head and went away, weeping aloud as she went. Her brother Absalom said to her, "Has that Amnon, your brother, been with you? Be quiet now, my sister; he is your brother. Don't take this thing to heart." And Tamar lived in her brother Absalom's house, a desolate woman." (2 Sam. 13:1-20 NIV)

A beautiful young lady gets raped. What a sad story. We still have millions of 'Tamars' today. Innocent, good-hearted boys and girls full of dreams, who, in one terrible day, have their whole lives changed. They are still told, "Do not tell anybody" or "Do not take these things to heart." So, they suffer for the rest of their lives as desolate women or men. The Tamars of today do not tear their clothes and put ashes on their heads, but their hearts are still torn and their lives are burnt to ashes. In South Africa, one out of every three girls is raped. And, as in Tamar's situation, they mostly get raped by family members: stepbrothers, stepfathers, uncles and cousins. And, they are strongly warned, "Do not tell anybody."

Causes of Sexual Abuse

If we are counseling children who have been raped or forced into sexual exploitation, we first must ask ourselves, "How did this happen?" "Why were these children sexually attacked?" Working with girls in South Africa, I discovered shocking answers to these questions. These are questions counselors need to seek answers to in whatever context they are working.

Living in Poverty

One factor of sexual assault is poverty. Children who live in a one-room house are at higher risk when both boys and girls must share one bedroom. More often than we sometimes realize, boys molest other boys or girls. The children have no privacy and, therefore, they are vulnerable. From changing clothes to bathing, they are always in public view. I once asked a girl to draw a hut and then, inside the hut, draw how she felt. She drew only one bed in the big hut; her deepest desire was "to be alone, to have my own bed, my own privacy, my own four corners."

A Societal View that Encourages Male Promiscuity

Another risk factor for sexual abuse is the beliefs and attitudes toward sex that are formed during a child's early years—from birth to six years. Many shocking sex-related proverbs are prevalent in Africa. While they are shocking, we need to know and understand them if we are to gain a deeper understanding of the forces behind and the impact of sexual abuse. For example, one proverb says, "A bird in one valley can never get fed." To understand the meaning behind the proverb, it is important to be aware that proper names for the male or female sex organs are not commonly used in Africa. The vagina is referred to as a *biscuit* and the penis a *bird*. Imagine a huge bird with a huge beak flying from biscuit to biscuit, tasting each one: "I get a taste here, I get a taste there." A bird is never satisfied with only one biscuit.

Similar proverbs exist in other cultures. In one language, a man is a goat. Does a goat stay behind its fence? No, a goat eats everything it finds and preferably wants to go outside the fence. In another language, the penis is referred to as a bull. When I asked my students, "Does a bull have only one cow?" They answered, "No, he has a whole herd." The idea that a man must have many girls or wives is deeply engrained in the thinking of children. As part of their core belief system, this attitude does not quickly leave people when they convert; it takes education and much prayer to change a person's established worldview.

Lack of Appropriate Sex Education

Another reason for rape or sexual exploitation is that teaching creation, and how babies are formed in the mother's womb, is not known. So, most children think we are just a sex product, we are just here to extend the family, or to keep the name or to keep the plot in the family in order to inherit more land. They are not seen as individual miracles formed by God. I am reminded of a time when my daughter was working in a preschool and the staff was always talking about boyfriends. They did not believe my daughter had not slept with a boyfriend at her age. She told them, "If you want to mess up your life, your future and your character it is up to you, but I am too special to be spoiled." Sadly, we do not have many girls who understand they are precious and too special to be spoiled. Many grow up already feeling like they are trash or a mistake; therefore, they do not know how to protect themselves.

Social Vulnerability of Girls

In one language, the vagina is called "mashed tomatoes." How can a mashed tomato fight for her rights? There is no way. A woman does not have a purpose and a vision for life; she is expected to extend the family. Therefore, it is difficult for girls to know how to take care of themselves. They are vulnerable to men who think they are "goats or birds." Many children are fatherless, so they are not looking for a boyfriend, but are in great need of a father.

Unmet Emotional Needs

While visiting my neighbor, I saw a grown-up daughter sitting on her father's lap. The mother was confused and felt badly about it. I told the mother, "You know what? That is the nicest thing I have ever seen. That is why your daughter is the only girl on our whole road that does not have a baby at her age and is not married." The mother looked at me with big eyes. I told her, "Daughters must be hugged and loved by their daddies, and boys by their mothers." But sadly, we have a fatherless nation. Many girls do not even know who their father is. Without a father, they are trying to fill their emotional well with a boyfriend.

A teenager on our farm attended a Christian youth group where the leader asked, "According to your opinion, is it necessary to have a boyfriend?" They all replied, "Yes." He asked, "At which age do you think you need one?" The average answer was at age fifteen. He said, "OK, that is interesting, but why do you think you need a boyfriend?" Their answers were: "We need someone to talk to; we need someone to have time for us; we need someone that understands; we need someone who can just love us and have fun with us." The leader's next question was, "What do you do when you get together with your boyfriend?" Their answers were: "We talk; we hug; we kiss; we have sex; we have a baby and then we separate." And so the cycle continues for many children who are growing up without daddies.

Most boys and girls do not know why they were born a girl or a boy. Nobody tells them the truth that they are created in God's image to glorify Him, and that He has a plan and a purpose for their lives beyond having a baby at age fifteen. It is a challenge for us in ministry to tell the children the truth about who they are, why they are here and God's purpose for their lives.

How Do We Find Today's "Tamars"?

How do counselors find the "Tamars"; those who, like Tamar, have suffered sexual abuse and are in need of counsel and guidance? Remember, children are normally told, "Do not tell anybody or I will kill you." Sometimes those who would rape them have a gun and seriously threaten them. If a child is bold enough to tell his or her mother, many times the mother does not believe them. If they are willing to report it to the police, they are usually told, "Oh no, it was your boyfriend. You wanted to have sex with him. You cannot call this rape." Scripture clearly shows that we are called to find and minister to the Tamars.

> Speak up for those who cannot speak for themselves, for the rights of all who are destitute. Speak up and judge fairly; defend the rights of the poor and needy. (Prov. 31:8-9 NIV)

> The Spirit of the Sovereign LORD is on me, because the Lord has anointed me to preach good news to the poor. He has sent me to bind up the brokenhearted [like Tamar], to proclaim freedom for the captives and release from darkness for the prisoners, to proclaim the year of the LORD's favor and the day of vengeance of our God, to comfort all who mourn [like the millions of Tamars], and provide for those who grieve in Zion—to bestow on them a crown of beauty instead of ashes, the oil of gladness instead of mourning, and a garment of praise instead of a spirit of despair. (Isa. 61:1-3 NIV)

God wants to use you and me to help the Tamars experience life again. How can we find them?

Educate Yourself

I believe first of all you should educate yourself and know what a healthy child looks like. How does a child develop? At what age do they talk and walk? How does a child play? How is a child curious? What can a child discover and at what age? I always say we do not have ignorant children; we have a lot of highly traumatized children. When something bad happens to a child, the mental and emotional development gets stuck. So, he or she looks like an underdeveloped child or like a slow-learning child, but many times it is just a child that has been abused at home. So, observe the healthy children and then you can quickly see whether this girl or this boy is developing well or not.

Be an Observer

Observe the children on the playground and at school; study their faces and their eyes. You might have a game with them and observe a little girl who just stands outside the circle not wanting to join you. The little girl has no smile on her face, looks tired and does not want to jump up and down with you. But you say, "Come on! Jesus loves you! Jump!" This is more abuse because when the heart is broken, there is no energy for any fun. God created the children in His image so they are creative, they are clever, and they are curious to know more and more. But when a child has lost those things, there is a reason.

- **Observe school performance.**

   Because the child's mind is so preoccupied with the pain, "How am I going to survive tonight without my daddy raping me?" she cannot think and concentrate at school. This results in her getting bad marks and bad reports, and we tend to think she is a naughty child who does not want to listen. That is not the case.

- **Observe eating patterns.**

   Do they eat healthy food? Do they ever feel like eating? Do they eat far too much?

- **Observe sleeping patterns.**

   Do they sleep properly? Do they have nightmares that keep them from sleeping well? Do they want to sleep all day?

- **Observe washing/bathing patterns.**

   Do they shower once a day, as is normal, or do they wash all the time?

- **Observe talking and social patterns.**

Are they introverted, quiet, moody or do they have normal friends and mix with them? Any behavior that you think is not the way God originally created the child can be a sign something bad happened in his or her life.

Best Practices for Assessing a Child

There are different ways to assess the abuse and resulting needs of a child. You need not be a psychologist; you just need to be willing to let God use you. You first need to remember that you are just the facilitator of the miracle God wants to do for an abused child. He is the Healer and the Restorer of life. Many people are afraid to meet Tamars because they always think, "What am I going to say? What am I going to do?" If you have a heart full of compassion for the lost, the traumatized and the forgotten people-group of Tamars, God can use you. Pray, "Here I am Lord, use me." He will answer your prayer and will use you in helping those who have been deeply wounded through sexual abuse. God does the healing, but there are some basic principles to follow as you communicate His love to these broken ones.

Lead Drawing and Discussion Activities

One best practice is learning to teach children Bible lessons that are concentrated on their feelings and how that looks in their hearts. This can be accomplished by giving the children an opportunity after the Bible story to draw something that depicts their feelings. You can call this section "Arts and Crafts," but you also are using it as an assessment tool to discover what is going on in the child's heart. This can be followed by helpful discussions based on what you have learned about their feelings:

- When teaching creation (Genesis 1), you can ask them to draw a picture showing what their heart is telling them about how special they are. Sexually abused children usually have negative feelings about themselves, thinking they are damaged or spoiled goods.

- When telling stories about families, such as David, Joseph or Jacob, ask the children to draw how they feel about being in their family or to draw their family showing where they fit in.

- When you tell the story about the disciples crossing the Sea of Galilee in a boat, let them draw a boat and then ask, "How does it feel to be in that boat? Where did you come from? Where do you want to go?" Just ask some imaginary questions until they reveal inside how they feel in their lives.

- There is a lady in the Bible who lost her coins. When you finish teaching that Bible lesson, let them draw what they lost in their lives. Give them an opportunity to draw or express it.

- Many stories in the Bible, like that of Tamar, involve sexual abuse. We like to jump over stories that include sexual abuse because we are not comfortable talking about them. That is why the devil has a chance to spread all his lies. Make opportunities to teach about sex in your normal Bible lessons. After telling the story of how Tamar got raped, for example, say to the children, "If anybody touched your private parts or has done something wrong, come and see me. I am here to help you." Give invitations that make the children feel free to come and see you, not just to talk about their sin, but also how Jesus wants to restore their hearts and set them free from their pain, shame and anger.

Be Supportive

When the children tell you about their picture or their stories, it is important that you always believe fully what they say. Never laugh, make a critical comment or say, "What's this?" That is hurtful and you have closed the door to their sharing what is in their hearts. Never force them to tell you, but always give them the choice to choose. For example, questions like these help children choose what they want to do: "Would you like to show me your picture?" "Would you like to tell me more about it?" "Would you like to see me alone after the lesson?" "Would you like me to help you?"

Be Trustworthy

Children are sensitive and they quickly find out if they can trust you or not. Once you earn their trust, they will come to you on their own and even ask, "Can I talk to you?" Be aware when children do not want to leave after the club or wherever you are meeting them; they may just hang around and not be bold enough to say something. Do not tell them, "Time is up! You have to go home." They might be in need of personal attention. If a child opens up her heart to you, it is important that you promise it is all confidential. That you are not going to tell anybody anything about it without the child's permission. At this initial stage, there is no way one can say, "We are going to report it to your mother or the police" because the child is so afraid. The abuser probably told the child not to tell anyone, so you have to promise you are not going to tell anyone without the permission of the child. When trust has been built between the child and the counselor, the need of sharing a child's story can be discussed in more detail.

Create a Safe Place

When you see the child alone, it is important you make or create a safe place. No one else must be able to hear what is going on. In Africa this is difficult because most houses are crowded and there is no quiet room to be alone, so it is good to ask for a room in the church. Other possibilities are an office in someone's house or sitting under a tree in a park where no one else hears what is going on.

Give a Child Time to Heal

It is important not to be in a hurry when counseling a child. It is the work of the Holy Spirit to help the child open up and to do the healing; if you look at the time every few minutes because you have to rush somewhere else, a child will not feel free to open up to you. Plan adequate time for an effective counseling session.

Communicate with Parents

It's important you let the parents of the child know when and where you are meeting the child. The child may tell her parents she is visiting a friend or going to the market because she does not want them to know she will be with someone with whom she can share her problems. If the parents find out the truth on their own, trust will be broken.

Assemble a Supplies Kit

When you find a Tamar that is willing to open up to you, you must have a first-aid kit. Like a doctor needs some tools to do an operation, so also do counselors need some tools to help a child's heart heal. You may be a heart specialist, but the healing is God's work. It is helpful if you have a bag or a box to take into the counseling session with you. Items to put in the box include:

- tissues for the times when the tears are flowing
- a Bible
- plain paper, colored pencils, paint
- play dough or clay
- a mirror
- a heart-shaped container
- a rope
- an ugly figure to represent the wicked man or woman who rapes

Also, have some reassuring Bible verses or pictures in your kit. The Bible is full of descriptions of who we are and why God created us. Ask the Holy Spirit to show you the right Bible verses that will be encouraging. Print them nicely on a card so you always have something to give to the child to put up where she can see them or place them in her Bible to remind her of how special and valuable she is.

Help Children Express Their Loss

Give the children paper and pencils, and ask them to write what they have lost through the bad things that have happened to them. If a child has confided in you what that bad experience was, you can mention it by name. Their losses could include *trust, confidence, virginity, worth, hope, future dreams, education, good performance at school, childhood, motivation, security, courage, identity, healthy understanding on sex, healthy socializing with the opposite sex, friends, joy, peace, healthy sleep and rest, pride of who I am and the dream of getting married.* As you read this list, you can see that what the Tamars have lost are their lives. But there was never a funeral to memorialize their lives. What do they get back for the things they have lost? *Fear, guilt, shame, low self-esteem, curses, a confused mind, a broken heart, poor school reports, open doors for prostitution or any boyfriend, self-hate, anger, misunderstandings and loneliness.*

Next have them draw the shape of a heart and ask, "How do you feel in your heart?" They can draw or write their feelings. Their feelings will be descriptive and will help you understand the pain they are feeling over their losses. The following have been common responses: *I am trash. I am worth nothing. God doesn't love me, in fact, nobody loves me. Nobody cares. Death is better than life. I'll never get married. I am a mistake. I will never trust again, it only hurts. I can't make a decision, it will always go wrong. I have always been overlooked. There is no one to protect me. I can't trust anyone—no one will believe me, anyway. It is my fault; I deserved it. I am cheap. I am too small to take care of myself. I'm dirty; I'll always remain filthy. I am nothing. Nobody needs me. I am a burden. I was never supposed to be born. God can never accept me the way I am. I am not wanted. Something is wrong with me. I don't know what is going on with my life.*

As Christians, we know all these responses are lies given to them by the devil, the Father of Lies. The devil has been so clever to exchange the good things God has given the children with his destructive lies. As counselors, we must depend on the Holy Spirit's guidance in responding to these lies. Only God, our Creator, can restore the value and the belief system of the Tamars who enter our care. It is not our job to say, "Oh no, it's not true that you are rubbish." Or, "You are so wonderful." That will only give "Tamar" the impression that you do not know or understand how he or she feels. And that could close the door to a much needed counseling opportunity. It is important that you try to put yourself into Tamar's experience, imagining how you would feel if it happened to you. What would you want to hear a counselor say to you? Probably something like:

- I believe you.
- It's okay to feel like that.
- I am sorry that it hurts so much.
- I am here for you.
- I am proud that you can talk to me about this.
- You did a good thing to tell me.

- I understand why you feel that way.
- I care about you.
- I see the pain.
- It is normal to feel like that.

The Four Phases of Healing

What are the four steps the Tamars must go through?

1. Tell their story. Create the opportunity for children to talk and be listened to.

2. Recognize Satan's lies. Are the child's feelings a result of truth or lies?

3. Move beyond the lies. It is the child's decision whether she or he wants to exchange the lies for the truth.

4. Commit to the journey back to health and peace. A child needs time to rebuild the foundations; it can take years.

Step 1: Tell Their Story

Children need an opportunity and the time to talk about the things that trouble them. They also need someone to take time to genuinely listen to their stories. Listening is one of the most vital aspects of a counselor's job. All that has been stored up in a broken heart must come out. It can be anger, lies, tears, fears or hatred. I always pray in my heart, "Oh, Lord, let it flow. Empty the trash in that heart even though I become the trash container. It's OK, as long it comes out." Your giving time to a child who is hurting is like opening a bottle that is about to burst. It may explode, but the contents— here, the children's pain—must come out.

An essential part of the healing process is for a person to have the opportunity to talk while someone listens. The listener must also pay attention to the nonverbal communication. How does the child sit or feel? What kind of facial expressions is she showing? Once the heart is emptied, and the tears have stopped flowing, you see how Tamar released her burden of pain.

Do not try to stop a child from crying. Assure her it is good and helpful to cry. She will know when she has cried enough. Of course, you must help the child to not let her emotions get out of control. A release of tears can help a child understand the issues surrounding his or her trauma much clearer. Counselors must be careful not to express their own sorrow over a child's pain. This can be difficult because a child's pain touches the heart.

Step 2: Recognize Satan's Lies

Remind the children of the negative feelings they expressed during their written assignments. For example, "I am nobody," "I am worthless," "I will never make it." Guide the children in thinking if those are true or false statements. Ask questions such as: "Do these words describe what God has created you for?" "Do they tell what God planned for your life?" It is the child who must make the decision whether he or she wants to exchange the lies for the truth. However, that child must understand God's plan for his or her life and the implications of choosing or not choosing to continue to believe Satan's lies.

Step 3: Move Beyond the Lies

A child must go through steps 1 and 2 before she will be ready for step 3. Plan a concrete exercise that gives the child an opportunity to move on from Satan's lies into God's truth. For example, have the children cut in strips the list of lies written in the earlier exercise and place them into a heart-shaped tin or paper box. Then, have the children take a strip of paper from the box, one at a time, and tell what they want to do with it or how they want to change that lie to the truth. Make sure they understand the significance of the box—it represents removing Satan's lies from their hearts. Be sure that every child who wants to participate is included.

Some answers have been: *"I want to get my life back, I don't want the lie 'I'd rather die.' I want to break the curse of sexual immorality; I don't want to remain in that vicious cycle. I want to leave revenge to God; I don't want to pay back the rapist. I want to forgive; I don't want to remain tied to this man who ruined my life. I want to fill my head with Scriptures that tell me the truth about me; I want to get rid of the lies. I want to report the case to a social worker or a police officer; I don't want to keep quiet anymore."*

Conclude this exercise with prayer, asking the Holy Spirit to give the children strength to stand against the lies of Satan. Also, give the children an opportunity to pray, asking for God's help.

Step 4: Commit to the Journey Back to Health and Peace

The last step, and the goal, is to be totally healthy (physically, emotionally, spiritually, intellectually and socially) and living in peace with themselves, God and others around them. Each child needs his or her own time to reach that goal. You may be needed to walk with the child for a long time.

A healthy heart is one that is free from fear, shame, guilt and sin. It can be a long walk, but with your help, and the help of the Holy Spirit, it will be possible to help the Tamars to come back to a normal, healthy life.

Planning a Counseling Session

What does a counseling session look like? In reality, there is no set plan to follow. The Holy Spirit will give insights into each child's counseling needs. Every child is unique with his or her own set of needs. The following is an example of the process of planning a counseling session.

Start with Prayer

Anyone who has worked with sexually exploited children is aware of the spiritual warfare issues involved in seeking their deliverance. Satan does not want the children set free from their bondages and will use all sorts of tactics to prevent that from happening. However, it is now God's time for healing and restoration, and we must stand against Satan's attempt to hinder God's plan and purpose for these sessions.

Be Quiet and Listen

Do not think you have to always be talking. You only have to listen and help "Tamar" discover the lies of Satan in her life and replace them with the truth. Let the child express what happened through drawing, telling, playing, or even with using play dough or clay. Show understanding, compassion and acceptance. Do not ask any questions about the details of the artwork, "Why are those hairs black or brown?" It's not about art; it's about the heart and a child's feelings over the traumatic events. It is important you keep a professional distance. Do not touch, hug or stroke the child because physical touch was part of the child's trauma. The child, not knowing your intentions, may be scared to be touched.

After the child has shared what happened and expressed his or her pain over the ensuing trauma-produced losses, we must think about closure—a time for the funeral to mourn his or her losses. As the child talks about her losses, have her think about whom she might need to forgive for those losses. A willingness to forgive those who do wrong to us is needed for inner healing. Children might first need to express their anger toward the perpetrator who has caused them so much pain. Children also need to be reminded that forgiving someone for a wrong committed against them does not mean the person is no longer responsible for what was done. The following passage describes God's view of the wicked man.

Why, O LORD, do you stand far off? Why do you hide yourself in times of trouble? In his arrogance the wicked man hunts down the weak, who are caught in the schemes he devises. He boasts of the cravings of his heart; he blesses the greedy and reviles the Lord. In his pride the wicked does not seek him; in all his thoughts there is no room for God. His ways are always prosperous; he is haughty and your laws are far from him; he sneers at all his enemies. He says to himself, "Nothing will shake me; I'll always be happy and never have trouble." His mouth is full of curses and lies and threats; trouble and evil are under his tongue. He lies in wait near the villages; from ambush he murders the innocent, watching in secret for his victims. He lies in wait like a lion in cover; he lies in wait to catch the helpless; he catches the helpless and drags them off in his net. His victims are crushed, they collapse; they fall under his strength. He says to himself, "God has forgotten; he covers his face and never sees." Arise, Lord! Lift up your hand, O God. Do not forget the helpless. Why does the wicked man revile God? Why does he say to himself, "He won't call me to account"? But you, O God, do see trouble and grief; you consider it to take it in hand. The victim commits himself to you; you are the helper of the fatherless. Break the arm of the wicked and evil man; call him to account for his wickedness that would not be found out . . . You hear, O Lord, the desire of the afflicted; you encourage them, and you listen to their cry, defending the fatherless and the oppressed, in order that man, who is of the earth, may terrify no more. (Psalm 10:1-18 NIV)

It is touching when a child reads these verses where the wicked man (for a sexually abused child) is the rapist and the victim is the child who got raped. And when the child can hear someone read, "Lord, You break the arm of that wicked man who raped me, and You stand up for me, the victim. I, the victim, commit myself into Your hand. You are my Helper, and You will call this wicked man to account." Many passages in the Bible affirm that God will pay back those who do evil. Revenge belongs to God; He will treat that wicked man in His own righteous way. And that is such a release to know that man will get punished by God, and it's not the child's job to do it.

Uncover the Lies

After all the anger toward the abuser has been released and the tears have been flowing for all the losses, a child can look at the lies of Satan in light of the truth. For example, say to the child, "You say you feel worthless. Where do you get your worth from? Who gives you your worth?" As the child begins to think about this, she will discover she is still special.

- When the child says, "I am filthy," give her the mirror and let her look at herself. She can see that she is still fearfully and wonderfully made. Give her an opportunity to think about what she said.

- When the child says, "Nobody wants me," ask her, "Is there anyone in your life that is still kind to you? Write their names down. Do you know anyone who loves you? Then write their names down too." Usually, a child will write down your name as a counselor, they might write down God, or the name of a teacher or someone that is still caring for the child. Then, the child realizes the statements about her identity are not true. There are those who love and care for her; to think that no one does, is a lie of Satan.

- When the child says, "It was my fault," ask her, "How could an ant fight an elephant?" And then the child laughs when she realizes an ant cannot fight an elephant. There was no chance for her to run away, so assure her that there was nothing she could have done about it.

- When the child says, "I am useless," ask her, "What did you do today?" If she says, "I got dressed" or "I washed the dishes," you should praise her: "Wow! That's wonderful. You know, your hands are so special. You need those hands of yours. You are so worth it. You have done such a good job." You can never encourage and praise children too much.

Help them discover the small, good things they are still doing. This will help them see with their own mind that what they said is actually not the truth. Sometimes they have already changed their mind about the abuser. They start to find out that man or that woman was also a victim, and that is amazing. That is the work only the Holy Spirit can do.

Exchange the Lies for Truth

When you have sorted out every statement that was a lie, let the children write down the statement that is true and put that one back into the heart-shaped box that says, "I am special." Examples of truth statements are: *"I am not guilty. I am wonderful. God still wants me. I am God's creation. I can still do many good things."* They are now ready to embrace the truth, refuting the lies of Satan.

At this stage, the children may be ready to accept Christ as their Savior. If they are ready, encourage them to do so, but do not push them if they are not. Part of their readiness is if they have been able to forgive and release the person hurting them into God's hand. It also is the time to decide whether the child is willing to report his or her abuse to someone.

Be Available for Legal and Medical Matters

An abused child has probably been told, "Don't tell anybody." According to the child's emotional health, she might now be able to tell a social worker or report her abuse to the police. The counselor should offer to go with the child, even though doing such may be dangerous, especially if you are asked to accompany the child in court. Do not be afraid. You are speaking up for the innocent and standing up for those who have no voice.

The Tamars of today also live in constant fear that they may be HIV positive. Because the chances of becoming infected are high, encourage them to be tested. Ask, "Would you like to go for an HIV test?" If he or she consents, say, "Would you like me to come with you?" or "Do you want to go on your own?" or "Is there anyone else who can go with you?" Be available to the children as much as possible through this stage.

Ask God to Break All Curses

The Bible says that through sex you become one flesh, so it is likely that curses have entered into the life of the Tamars through the rape. It is time to break the curses.

A good prayer for the children to say is: "Lord, on behalf of the rapist I ask for Your forgiveness and that You cleanse me from that sin of sexual immorality, and in the name of Jesus, we break the curse of all of the sins that have come to me through this person who raped me. In the name of Jesus." I use a piece of rope to illustrate unforgiveness or being tied to curses. I wrap the rope around Tamar's hand and let Tamar say in his or her own words, "I set myself free, in the name of Jesus, from the curse of sexual immorality, in the name of Jesus. I am free and I release the rapist that trampled my heart for so many years, in the name of Jesus." And the victim can set herself free from the rope symbolically wrapped around her hand, which will allow her to feel the freedom that Christ wants to give. God wants to set her and so many others free, and He does. The rope helps the child to understand what is happening in the unseen world.

It is also important to encourage children to learn to trust again; that to live in the freedom and joy they experience in that moment, will take time. You can look at their facial expressions and you see the burden is gone, the lies are gone and the joy has come. It is just so wonderful to see how that comes alive. It's a witness of the Holy Spirit, but the devil hates it. So tell them, "It takes time. Don't expect from now on just to have a mountaintop experience nonstop. You might still be afraid of men. You might still be afraid to go to the shop or anywhere alone, or sleep in that house." Sometimes specific actions may need to take place, like making arrangements for the child to stay somewhere else because the danger they experienced may still be present in the home. However, all those further decisions must be made with the child's agreement.

End the Session with Prayer

Close each session with prayer, thanking God for the victories won in the hearts of the children. Give the children Bible verses that will encourage them in their walk with the Lord.

- Give them a copy of Psalm 91 to read and encourage them to insert their own name into the passage.

- Give them pictures that depict God's loving care for them. The Good Shepherd holding a lamb in His arms, for example, can assure children they can be safe in the presence of Jesus.

It is a wonderful thing to witness how God restores broken hearts, and it is equally wonderful to know that He wants to use us to bring His message of healing and hope to those who have been deeply wounded through sexual abuse. Do not be afraid to answer His call to work with children in crisis!

SEVEN

PRINCIPLES for
GROUP COUNSELING

Leah Herod

Everyone will encounter stress at some point in his or her life, and nearly 70 percent of people will endure some type of trauma—whether it be natural disaster (fire, hurricane or flood), man-made disaster (war or terrorism) or personal trauma.[15] Many children will be able to cope and survive the trauma, and become stronger because of it. Other children will have enduring difficulty because of the trauma. The problems in coping may interfere with a child's daily living (problems in school or home; difficulty with peers, teachers or family members). The child may have behavioral, cognitive or social difficulties. She may regress, or revert back, in some of her developmental tasks. For example, a child who has been toilet trained may start soiling her clothes. Or, a child may want to suddenly act younger than her age. The impact of a trauma can be addressed through counseling. Individual and group counseling can assist in coping by processing the trauma, addressing the symptoms that are causing problems in a child's life and teaching coping strategies. Both individual and group therapy are acceptable and effective forms of counseling children. There are differences in the two forms of counseling, however, and there are also differences in working with children as opposed to adults. This chapter outlines general considerations in group counseling and provides specific suggestions for working with children in a group setting.

General Considerations

Group Counseling Differs from Individual Counseling

A group is more than the sum of its parts. It is more than a collection of individuals. A group is a type of system that develops rules and norms for relating and interacting. Group counseling, therefore, will have somewhat unique considerations when compared to individual counseling.

Overall, group counseling is an accepted form of counseling—it is effective and offers a number of benefits to participants. In order to have a successful group, planning is necessary. Consideration should be given to the type of group, the structure of the group, qualifications of the leader and characteristics of the group members. In addition, leaders should consider ahead of time how to introduce the group and set rules from the first session. By attending to these matters, it is more likely the group will be successful.

Effectiveness of Group Counseling

Questions have been raised as to whether group counseling is as effective as individual counseling. Research suggests that, overall, it is. In general, researchers have concluded when individual and group treatments are compared, they are similar in both effectiveness (how well the treatment works in a counseling setting) and efficacy (how well the treatment works in a research study).[16] Group therapy has been demonstrated to be as effective as individual therapy for children and adolescents who have suffered some type of abuse (including physical and sexual abuse, neglect or general maltreatment),[17] been exposed to trauma such as war,[18] or been diagnosed with a variety of disorders such as depression,[19] phobia and anxiety.[20] There are a variety of types of groups. It has been established for some time that group treatment is effective with children and adolescents, regardless of whether it was a preventative program, psychotherapy, counseling, guidance or training group.[21] There are general benefits to group therapy and no one type of group (such as interpersonal, psychoeducational, cognitive-behavioral or other approach) has consistently been shown to be better than others.[22]

Benefits of Group Counseling

Practically speaking, there are benefits to group treatment related to cost and personnel when compared with other forms of treatment.[23] This can be especially relevant in the case of large-scale disasters, where there may be many people in distress. Obviously, more people can be treated in a group setting than in an individual setting. Therefore, the mental health professionals may be able to attend to the psychological needs of more survivors of the disaster by using a group format. This can be helpful when the needs of the survivors are greater than the resources available.

On a deeper level, there is a suggestion that there are benefits to the actual process of group counseling, relative to other forms of psychological treatment. Although it is a complex process, Yalom[24] identifies twelve primary ways that group therapy is beneficial. These 'therapeutic factors' with a brief description, are as follows:

Interpersonal input	Learning from group members how their behavior impacts others (such as annoying habits, mannerisms and the impression they give to others)
Catharsis	Expressing positive and negative feelings to others, and gaining relief because of doing so
Cohesiveness	Having a sense of belonging and being accepted by others
Self-understanding	Gaining greater awareness of one's own reactions in the present and how they are sometimes linked to past experiences (rather than present circumstances)
Interpersonal output	Learning how to relate better to others and increasing trust
Existential factors	Learning to take responsibility for life, realizing that life is sometimes unfair and that there is no escape from life's pain or death
Universality	Recognizing that others have had similar experiences, feelings and problems
Instillation of hope	Encouragement by seeing that others have improved and overcome similar problems
Altruism	Helping and giving to others
Family reenactment	Realizing the link between current behavior and the patterns of interacting with family members as a child (i.e., realizing they are interacting with group members today in a way that is similar to how they interacted with their family as a child)
Guidance	Receiving suggestions and advice from group members and/or leaders
Identification	Modeling/imitating the mannerisms or style of someone who is respected

Table 1: Therapeutic Factors

The therapeutic factors were originally derived from interviews with clients following treatment and revised with input from therapists.[25] The factors are listed above in order of importance to group counseling, with the ones at the top of the list being more relevant. Based on the rankings, it appears that the greatest benefit of being a part of a group relates to the learning that occurs in the interaction between group members, the emotional release (referred to as catharsis) in a group setting, and the sense of belonging and acceptance.[26] It should be noted that these factors are not totally independent of one another and do overlap.

Researchers have since investigated which, if any, of these factors were specifically determined to be a part of the benefit of group counseling over individual counseling. Group cohesiveness is increasingly being viewed as the most powerful in the group setting.[27] Cohesion is positively related to client improvement.[28] If cohesion is present, a group with younger members (adolescents) will change more than a group with older members.[29] Therefore, it is important for group leaders to set the tone of acceptance and find ways to enhance a sense of belonging in the group.

Benefits to Trauma Survivors

There are benefits overall to participating in group treatment. There is an indication that group processes are particularly salient for trauma survivors.

> "Traumatic events destroy the sustaining bonds between individual and community. Those who have survived learn that their sense of self, of worth, of humanity, depends on a feeling of connection to others. The solidarity of a group provides the strongest protection against terror and despair, and the strongest antidote to traumatic experience. Trauma isolates; the group re-creates a sense of belonging. Trauma shames and stigmatizes; the group bears witness and affirms. Trauma degrades the victim; the group exalts her. Trauma dehumanizes the victim; the group restores her humanity."[30]

This quote emphasizes the notion of universality and the sense of "I am not alone," combined with the cohesion and intimacy of a group as some of the primary curative factors in the healing of a trauma survivor.

Many research studies have investigated the benefits of group counseling to trauma survivors, with adults as the group participants. Benefits are also evident when the group participants are adolescents. One study conducted with adolescents in Bosnia who had been exposed to war, indicated that participants' positive benefits of being in the group included acquisition of coping skills and attitudes, improved interpersonal relationships, and a willingness to advocate for peers.[31] The 'ability to communicate openly with others' was the most frequently noted skill acquired as a result of treatment. Participants also indicated they had more hope for the future, better problem-solving skills, self-esteem, cognitive restructuring and insight. Adolescents shared the information they learned with others. When asked about problems in regard to group participation, the adolescents said initially they felt stigmatized by others (peers and teachers) by being in the group. This later decreased, as they shared some of the strategies they learned with others and improved in their interpersonal relationships. This study highlights that adolescents, through their self-report, value the therapeutic factors of interpersonal learning and catharsis. Overall, it can be seen that there are a variety of benefits to trauma survivors when they participate in group counseling.

Types of Groups

In general, counseling groups can be separated into three basic types: support groups, psychoeducational groups and process or insight-oriented groups.

Support Groups

A support group consists of people who share a common issue, and who meet for mutual encouragement and sharing of coping strategies. A mental health professional may or may not be present, although the expectation is that the group is not designed to provide professional counseling. There is an emphasis on mutual sharing and developing relationships with others in the group. Group members are expected, typically, to give and receive feedback from others. Participants discuss their feelings and there is a great deal of interaction between members. Support groups may be run continuously, allowing people to come when they want without an expectation that every member will be present each week. The structure in a support group varies, with some having specific teaching components, while others have a general topic or theme for the session.

Psychoeducational Groups

Psychoeducation, simply put, refers to providing education about a psychological difficulty or diagnosis. The information is provided by a counselor or other mental health professional who has factual knowledge about the disorder. Often, this entails information regarding what the diagnostic label means, course and prognosis (i.e., the disease process and typical expectations for how the diagnosis manifests) and includes ways of treating or coping with the difficulty. Participants in a psychoeducational group may include several people who have been given a particular diagnosis and/or their families. Unlike a support group, the aims are clearly defined. In a psychoeducational group, members may learn specific strategies for coping. Sometimes knowledge/skills are expected to build from week to week, although a group can be designed with sessions that are independent of prior knowledge.

Process-Oriented Groups

A process group is generally led by a trained mental health professional. The process-oriented group may also be referred to as a psychodynamic or interpersonal group. The goal of this type of group is for members to gain insight about how their way of relating impacts others, and become more aware of their unconscious ways of relating. In a psychodynamic group, the assumption is that past experiences, especially from childhood, relate to how a person interacts with others in the present. These current ways of relating may not be adaptive or helpful, but the person is operating in ways similar to how he did with his family of origin (parents and siblings). These patterns are unconscious. It isn't a matter of skill deficit, per se. According to the psychodynamic approach, change occurs through learning from others, getting feedback, gaining insight and having a corrective emotional experience. The leader aids through the modeling of 'healthy' communication patterns and interactions.

Researchers also consider a Cognitive Behavioral Therapy (CBT) group as a separate category, but actually CBT groups can be viewed as a combination of psychoeducational groups with therapeutic skill building and process/insight oriented groups. Often they are structured, the leader is a highly trained mental health professional, and the focus is on a particular psychiatric disorder or set of symptoms. CBT approaches have, in recent years, been manualized, making it easier to replicate treatment. The table below summarizes key features of each type of group.

	Support	**Psychoeducational**	**Process**
Counseling knowledge/ training	Low	Medium	High
Leader activity	Low to Medium	High	Medium
Member involvement	High	Varies	High
Structure	Low to Medium	Medium to High	Low
Open versus Closed	Open	Either	Closed

Table 2: Type of Group and Typical Features

A support group can be facilitated by a lay counselor or community member who has experience in the topic of interest or who has training in leading a group. Psychoeducational groups should only be led by those who have specific knowledge of the topic area and who can provide accurate information regarding the disorder. With adequate training, the leader of a psychoeducational group can also teach coping skills. It is recommended that only counselors with adequate training and supervision run a process group.

Application: Planning a Group with Children

What factors make a difference in the actual success of a group? General considerations related to group counseling, as contrasted with individual counseling, have been highlighted. However, there are more specific factors that influence the success of a group. Characteristics of the leader, participants and structure determine whether the group will be successful.[32]

Organizing a group well is essential. The benefits to group counseling are dependent on how well the group is initially set up, introduced and then executed. The leader(s) need to take time to adequately plan a variety of aspects of the group, from the participants to the structure of the group. For individuals who have experienced trauma, this is especially important.

> "In order to be successful, a group must have a clear and focused understanding of its therapeutic task and a structure that protects all participants adequately against the dangers of traumatic reenactment. Though groups may vary widely in composition and structure, these basic conditions must be fulfilled without exception."[33]

Characteristics of the group members and group structure will be outlined after highlighting characteristics of the leader. Specific considerations related to when the group is comprised of children will be woven throughout to aid in planning and execution of the group.

Leader Characteristics

Regardless of specific technique or goals, there is an overriding importance of the counselor/group leader in the counseling activity. In fact, the relationship between the counselor and counselee has been identified as the most important factor in change. Group leaders who demonstrate empathy, acceptance and concern toward the child (or children) are more effective.[34] However, the concern must be genuine. The group leader can choose from a variety of techniques and make a number of different plans, but counseling will not be as effective if there is not a consistent and positive relationship between the counselor and the child. This doesn't mean the group leader is always positive. As a counselor, the group leader needs to challenge and encourage growth in the child/children. The counselor can work with the children to promote changes in an affirming, warm manner. When considering the difference between the counselors who are successful and those who are not, the ones who are more successful focus on strengths in the child. The counselors who aren't successful focus on problems and neglect strengths.[35] Characteristics of the child are also important, but the ability of the counselor to establish a positive relationship is the most influential factor in counseling.

If the group is comprised of children or adolescents, it is important for at least one leader to have experience working with that age group, even if it is on an informal basis. It is optimal, and strongly recommended, to have two adults present when working with children. Group members who have two leaders experience greater benefits than those who only have one leader.[36] Given that working with children is different from adults, there are recommendations that group leaders have the following professional qualifications:

- A thorough understanding of the developmental tasks and stages of the particular age group

- A good understanding of counseling skills, especially as they pertain to group work

- Awareness, knowledge and skills necessary to work effectively with children from culturally diverse populations

- Supervised training in working with children in groups before leading a group alone

- Knowledge of the literature and significant research pertaining to counseling children and adolescents within a group setting[37]

Meeting these criteria is ideal, but not always realistic. At the minimum, for inexperienced group leaders, there should be someone who is available as a resource who has experience in working with groups.

Group leaders who are flexible, creative and energetic will likely have an easier time working with children. The leader may come to the group with a plan, but realize it is not working well at that time with the children. If the children get restless, the leader should have the flexibility to add in a break or some type of physical activity. The physical activity might be a stretching exercise or it could be a song with movements the children imitate. Of course, the leader will need to consider the child's age, as a song that is appropriate for preschoolers will likely not work with adolescents. The leader may need to be creative in the moment, to enhance the learning by the group members. It can be helpful to present the topic in multiple ways for children to grasp the idea. This may be done by designing multiple activities that relate to the topic with a given group session. The topic can be presented through a story, a game, a song or some other activity where the child is active in learning about the topic. It can take a lot of creativity to engage children. A group leader who is energetic and entertaining can have an easier time getting children to attend and participate. Listening to a group leader explain a topic must occur only in short segments, if necessary. The ability to focus attention increases with age, so the developmental level of the children will make a difference in how long they can attend. Group leaders who are overly rigid or who ignore how well the children are attending, are likely to encounter problems in leading a group with children.

Participant Characteristics

The characteristics of group members are largely determined by the purpose and goals of the group. Group leaders should have clarity in who they are attempting to serve, what problem they are attempting to address and what purpose they are attempting to accomplish. In planning a group with children or adolescents, it is necessary to determine characteristics of the group members, also known as selection criteria. The criteria include age range, target problem or diagnosis, sex and exclusionary factors.

Age Range

It is obvious that group counseling with children is different from adults. A primary difference is due to developmental considerations. Children develop in fairly predictable stages, and some of the physical, cognitive, social and emotional changes are rapid. This makes the age a more important factor in selecting participants for a group with children. A wider age range is acceptable when adults participate in a group; however, for children and adolescents, the age range needs to be narrower. Age has a huge impact on attention spans, activity levels and comprehension levels. The younger the child, the narrower the age range of group members should be for optimal understanding and participation in the group.

Developmental considerations become greater in working with children who have suffered a traumatic event or crisis. Children who have endured a trauma or crisis are particularly vulnerable to disruptions in the normal sequence of development. A crisis is often a surprising event that a person views as life threatening, causes a high degree of stress and that overwhelms a person's normal ability to cope. Children may have less awareness of their own distress, although parents and other adults may be able to identify a child's distress. When children have experienced a traumatic event, their development can be disrupted. When explaining the impact of trauma on development, Saltzman et al.[38] stated:

> "Of particular therapeutic concern, traumatization may *delay, interrupt,* or in some cases *prematurely accelerate* the initiation of developmentally inappropriate tasks. This developmental disturbance may manifest in a variety of forms. These include uneven development of the self-concept; distortions or maladaptive changes in beliefs about the self, others, the world, and the future; disruptions in primary relationships; decreased academic performance; and alterations in future ambitions, planning, and preparation" (Saltzman, Layne, Steinberg, and Pynoos 2006, 678).

This highlights a major difference in working with children and adolescents, compared with adults. Developmental considerations must be attended to when working with children.

Commonality

Often a group will be designed to address a particular problem. Reviewing the purpose of the group can help in narrowing selection criteria because it relates to why the group was originally developed and what problem the group was intending to address. There should be some type of commonality that all group members share. The commonality could be a similar behavior, characteristic, psychological diagnosis or a common experience (such as witnessing domestic violence or surviving a hurricane). It is important to pay attention to selection criteria especially with children, because combining children with very different qualities can cause significant problems in carrying out the purpose of the group. For example, having a group of socially inhibited children joined by aggressive peers can make the group difficult to facilitate and make it difficult for the children to have a positive experience.

Culture and Gender

Cultural considerations also need to be taken into account. Cultural factors may help determine the appropriateness of single-sex or mixed-sex groups. In some cultures, it may be inappropriate to have girls and boys together in the same group. The separation may occur at a specific age or developmental period. With increasing age, it is more likely that this would be important. Once again, this will depend on the cultural context (where the group is being held and the norms for that culture). Even if it is OK with the culture, the leader(s) may realize it is easier to facilitate a group of all girls or all boys, especially if they are adolescents.

Exclusionary Criteria

Not all interested people are suitable for participating in a group. The group may not work well if some people are included that would cause disruption and not be able to adequately participate. For example, if the person is frequently suicidal or has hallucinations (i.e., sees and hears things that aren't really there), then attention may be directed toward that person, thus distracting from the group as a whole and the goals/purposes of the group.[39] One study targeted children's social skills and concluded that children with high anxiety (overly fearful) and special needs should be excluded due to causing disruption within the group. The study also noted that children who succeeded in the group had the ability to reflect on their own behavior and how their behavior impacted others.[40] There are some children who would best be served by services other than group counseling, and group leaders need to be attuned to characteristics of a child that could make it difficult to have a successful group experience.

Parental Consent

There are different ages at which a child can legally give consent to receive counseling. In general, it is recommended that parents give permission for their child until the age of eighteen, even if the child can legally seek counseling at an earlier age. It is good practice to have written permission. A 'consent form' might list the general purpose of the group, as well as a brief description of confidentiality and the limits of confidentiality. The parents should be aware that the counselor does not plan on providing details about the group sessions, but will tell them if there is concern about the child's safety.

Purpose and Goals

One of the first tasks in designing a group is to determine the group's purpose and goals. The purpose is essentially the reason for having the group in the first place. The purpose of having a group flows from the problem. For example, the problem may be that there are aggressive children who are fighting and being kicked out of school. The purpose of developing a group might be to decrease the number of children who are kicked out of school for fighting. This could be done by teaching children other ways to cope with a situation, instead of aggression, that will enable them to stay in school. The goals will then be developed from the purpose.

There are general goals that could hold true for any group, and then there are specific goals for the group based on the problem area (symptoms/diagnosis) that is targeted. General goals might include things such as finding better ways to solve problems, offering helpful suggestions to others and becoming more self-aware, to name a few.[41] Specific goals for a group of adolescents who are aggressive might include learning other strategies for dealing with anger (instead of hitting), how to express feelings with words and how to take another person's perspective. It is best for goals to be specific and clear.

Group Structure

After the purpose and goals are developed, then the group structure can be planned.

When designing a group, consideration must be given to the structure. Structure refers to the framework, or basic plan for the group. It answers the practical questions regarding joining the group, number/frequency/timing of group meetings, and values that will link to group rules.

Open Versus Closed Groups

The leaders need to decide whether the group will be open or closed. If it is designed so that participants can join at any time, then it is an open group. This is ideal when each group session is understood without prior knowledge and can stand alone. Open groups are less likely to require approval to join. A closed group typically has a point, maybe within the first two sessions, beyond which no additional group members will be added. This is ideal when it is expected that information will build on the previous lesson or when group bonding is a prominent feature. It is presumed that adding another person after the first couple of sessions could disrupt the bonding or could be a distraction without the previously acquired information. There is a potential for greater connection and intimacy of group members in a closed group. Closed groups may require approval to join.

Frequency and Duration

The leaders should plan how many times the group will meet and how long each session will last. First, the leaders can evaluate how many sessions are necessary to accomplish the goals. Some psychoeducational groups have as few as four sessions. More commonly, however, it may take between eight to twelve sessions to adequately cover a topic and the associated goals. Games and activities can be included that emphasize a common theme for the session. For children, the activities during the group session will make a difference in how long they will be able to maintain attention. It is common for a group session to last between one to two hours. One hour may be enough time to accomplish the weekly goals when working with children.

Group Rules

It is important to have rules for the group so that members know what to expect. Often, even with children, the group members can make contributions to the group rules. This should be done in the first group session. It is beneficial for the leaders to already have determined what rules they value. An example of how this may be done is provided by Herod and Briant online at www.crisiscaretraining.org.

Confidentiality, respecting others and listening when others are speaking are commonly included guidelines/rules in a group setting. Of course, simple words should be used with children so they understand. It can be helpful to have the rules posted as a reminder for children. Using pictures to represent the rules is one way to simply convey them. If possible, state the rules in a positive way. For example, "Don't interrupt" can be positively stated as, "Listen when others are talking." Some group leaders ask that group members let them know if they are going to miss a session. Many times there is a value of timeliness, although the cultural context will need to be taken into consideration with this rule. What is common for the culture in regard to timeliness? In one culture, someone is considered to be on time if they arrive within five minutes of the start time, while in other cultures, they are considered on time even if they arrive twenty minutes after the stated start time. Regardless, clarity should be established at the outset regarding timeliness, as well as the other rules.

Purpose	What is the purpose?
	Is the group designed to address a certain problem (anxiety, depression) or common experience (witnessing a traumatic event, surviving a natural disaster)?
	What are the general goals of the group?
	What are the specific goals of the group?
Structure	Will the group be open or closed?
	How many sessions are needed?
	How often will the group meet?
	How long will each group session last?
Leader(s)	How much counseling training does the leader have?
	How much experience does the leader have with groups?
	How much experience does the leader have with children?
	How much experience does the leader have with the topic?
Participants	Who is allowed to participate?
	What will be the selection criteria for participants (behavioral symptoms, diagnosis, referral by parent or teacher, etc.)?
	What is the age range?
	Will it be a single-sex or mixed group?
	Are there cultural factors that influence selection?
	What is the minimum and maximum number of participants?
	What are the exclusionary criteria?
	How will parent consent be obtained?
Rules	What are the values that leaders want to convey in the rules?
Recruitment	How will the group members be recruited?
	How will the group be advertised?
Feedback	Will there be a way to determine if the group is effective (obtain feedback)?
	Who will provide feedback (group member, parent, teacher, doctor)?

Table 3: Planning for a Group

Tasks Before, During and After a Group

Before a group is established, participants will need to be recruited and consent obtained. Participants should be prepared for the group, before it begins and during the initial session. After the group has ended, it is beneficial to obtain feedback and determine how well the group was executed.

Recruitment

After the group has been designed and planned, a brief description of the group and logistical information can be distributed or posted. Since the target group will have already been identified, leaders can evaluate how to get the information to the parents or children who share the problem or diagnosis. Leaders may contact teachers, church workers, doctors or other people to identify children who could benefit from the group. Information about the group could be posted at a school, community center or other location where it would be visible. If there is access to the web, information could be posted electronically or e-mailed to people who might be interested. As previously discussed, those who are interested in participating in the group need to be screened to determine if they meet the selection criteria and then parental consent to attend should be obtained.

Preparation

When preparing people for the group, if group members have more understanding of what is expected from the onset, then the group tends to be more effective. Preparing people for participation can include discussing group goals, how the group works, how the group is structured, general expectations, as well as potential problems. This can be explained to a degree while recruiting group members. However, the preparation is essential during the first group session. Participants should know they can drop out at any time and are not required to participate. By having good preparation from the beginning, people are less likely to discontinue attending the group.

Feedback

It is helpful to know whether a group was beneficial to the participants. Sometimes, leaders will ask members to share their perceptions about the group before all the sessions are completed. Leaders may also wait until the group has concluded to ask group members to provide feedback. Adults, such as a parent or teacher, can be asked whether they have noticed changes in the child, especially changes that relate to the target problem. Obtaining feedback can help the leaders know what worked, what did not work, what the group members liked or did not like, as well as suggestions for future groups. If group members are asked in a nondefensive way, they will be more likely to be open to giving both positive and negative information. Asking for feedback is a way to obtain valuable information that leaders can use to improve the group in the future.

Conclusion

Group counseling is an effective form of treatment for children and adolescents who are suffering and in need of psychological services/treatment. Positive outcomes in group counseling can be attributed to the 'therapeutic factors' in a small group (also known as small group processes), formal change theory, leader characteristics, group member characteristics, and structural aspects of the group.[42] There are therapeutic factors that are unique to group counseling, as opposed to individual counseling. Part of the benefit to group counseling is the sense of belonging and acceptance that comes from being in a group. Formal change theory also can have an impact. Formal change theory essentially refers to a theory, or theoretical orientation that the counselor adheres to and which explains how people change. (Examples of theoretical orientations include behavioral, psychodynamic, and humanistic.) Characteristics of the group leader are important, namely, the ability of leaders to develop a positive alliance with group members. Characteristics of the group members are important, as it is important to have some commonalities between group members for it to be successful. Not all people who are interested in a group are suitable to participate. Finally, the structure of a group is important and has a bearing on the effectiveness. When a group is designed well, it has a greater potential of benefiting the group members.

Group counseling manuals have been designed that outline how to carry out a group. Manuals can assist counselors by having a format and plan to follow that has already been used with success. One example of a counseling manual for groups of adolescents, written by Herod and Briant, outlines how this has been done in an international context and provides detailed information for group leaders on how to develop and run a group. It is an example of a structured, open group. It was designed to assist refugees who had endured trauma and were in transition, and was intended as a supportive/psychoeducational type of group for adolescent boys. There is a theme for each session, focusing on positive mental health messages. Stories were included as they were culturally accepted ways to convey information. Suggestions are provided for group leaders so that the lessons can be altered. The group may be adapted for working with girls, with children of younger ages, with other cultures, and with a group who has experienced other kinds of trauma. It is easy to understand, and lay counselors have been trained in the use of this manual to assist healing in traumatized individuals.

PART III

SPIRITUAL ASPECTS OF COUNSELING

EIGHT

FORGIVENESS and RECONCILIATION
in the
HEALING PROCESS

Stephanie Goins

Forgiveness and reconciliation, at first, appear to be concepts that are quite easily understood and described by most anyone. The assumption is that when these words are used, "we all know what we are talking about." As well, the assumption often is that "we should all forgive." In reality, there are many ways to talk about forgiveness and reconciliation, to understand, justify and enact these processes. This is mitigated by various factors, such as the more interpersonal considerations of culture, tradition and religion, or the more intrapersonal considerations of age, gender, personality and so on. Obviously, these factors are not mutually exclusive.

What exactly is forgiveness? How does it work itself out in relationships? And how does forgiveness differ from reconciliation? Is there an obligation to forgive? Could forgiving or receiving forgiveness enable and support effective action in and intervention for children? Could forgiving have direct implications for resilience, the capacity of individuals to not only survive but also to overcome and even flourish despite, or even as a result of, the difficulties that have severely challenged them?

In literature, we find sharply contrasting views and conclusions about both forgiveness and reconciliation, but particularly about forgiveness. Even from a theological perspective, there is disagreement over what forgiveness or reconciliation means, or what is required for these to be realized. We have various assumptions about what forgiveness or reconciliation looks like, what value one or both hold and what conditions might enhance either process. Add the age factor or degree and/or longevity of abuse, and the discussion can get quite divisive.

As those who work with children in crises, we ourselves need to understand and be convinced of the merits of forgiving. Understanding what we are working toward and trying to lead children into it is crucial. The idea in this chapter is not to presume what may be best for the child, but to examine and think through how to work toward their healing and restoration. Therefore, before discussing practical ways to address forgiveness with children in crises, we will examine some specific ideas about forgiveness and reconciliation. Following that, we will then examine how these might contribute to the healing process for children in crises.

However, let us begin with a statement foundational to any understanding and discussion on forgiveness: Forgiveness begins with the recognition, by at least one of those concerned, that a wrong has been done. The identified wrong is understood to be one in which the wrongdoer is responsible, in some sense or to some degree, for having done it. If there is no recognition of a wrong, there can be no enactment of forgiveness. Hence, forgiving would not be the same as condoning or excusing. This would imply the offense was justified, permissible or excusable, which would mean there was not actually a wrongdoing to consider.

How Shall We Describe Forgiveness?

As a Shift in Attitude

Forgiveness is often described as a shift in attitude *toward* or feelings *about* the offender. From a psychological and philosophical perspective, forgiveness is a process of overcoming negative emotions and attitudes toward the offender, such as anger, avoidance and vengeance, and working toward an attitude of compassion and/or love.

One of the most frequently mentioned attitudes associated with forgiving is resentment. Resentment could be described as an attitude, an action or both, which moves the offended away from the offender. There are associated bitter or angry feelings about something that has happened. The etymology of the word resentment is quite revealing. Re-sent, with Latin and French roots, literally means to feel (*sentire*) again (*re*) or feel again and in a different way. To resent is to feel again, sometimes again and again. It is easy to imagine how maintaining an attitude of resentment would be a significant obstacle to forgiving.

Empathy is another way of understanding forgiveness as a shift in attitude, but one that moves toward the offender. Empathy has to do with entering the world of the other and responding accordingly. Forgiveness that comes about through empathy is really about discovering the similarities we have with others. Some talk about empathy as entering God's point of view. This may happen through prayer and/or through a realistic assessment of one's own self and one's weaknesses. Empathy is even said to reduce the injustice gap by helping victims to see themselves as less innocent and their offenders as less evil. Thus, to be forgiving is to have an attitude of empathy or compassion for the offender. The forgiver feels deeply, in an emotional and physical sense, compelled as suggested by the Greek word *splanchnizomai*, meaning "to feel sorry for" or "have compassion on."[43] Empathy can be a powerful influence in the forgiveness process for both adults and children.

As a Release

Forgiveness is often described as <u>release</u> from a debt or liberation from a burden, both of which may benefit the offended and the offender. With this release, the account is closed, the offense is canceled and has been absolved. It could even be said that there is the release from retributive justice.

However, there is another way to talk about release, and that is in the sense of freedom from a burden. Release means to set free. It is liberation from what has bound one to the past. In the New Testament, *aphiemi* means "to send or let off or away; to release or discharge," but can also be translated as liberation.[44] The *aphiem* kind of forgiveness is the kind that removes the marks left from sin, so that there is no trace of the offense for the parties concerned.[45] This is about liberation at the deepest personal level, not just from moral shortcomings. When Jesus lifts the burden off both offended and offender, he is enacting a liberating forgiveness. He liberates from the past and its effects, and makes a way to live as holy people.

Shame and/or guilt associated with an offense is a burden experienced by both offended and offender. It has to do with humiliation at being the object of offense, feelings of hatred toward the offender, the awareness of moral shortcomings or failures in one's own and others' eyes, the loss of status and reputation, to name a few. Shame and/or guilt relates to public and private behaviors, to violations that are physically abusive and vary in cultural interpretation, to self-accusations and justifications, to shameful hiding or guilt-ridden avoidance. Forgiveness that liberates takes on the burden of shame and guilt, and makes changed relationships possible. This liberation makes way for hope, an important construct in forgiving. This hope gives permission to live, unencumbered by the past, and hopeful for a better and different future.

Forgiveness as a release can also be letting go of a memory, which is not the same as forgetting. Forgetting suggests a disconnection with a past in which people may be held captive, particularly in the kinds of offenses discussed in this book. In the case of forgetting, and therefore disconnecting, there is no healing possible. Forgetting has its proper place, but before there can be forgiveness, the offense must be examined. Though the past cannot be changed, our relationship to it can. Therefore, "remember and forgive" so that the memory may be released.[46]

As a Transcendent Process

Some consider <u>transcendence</u> very significant to forgiveness, in that it may facilitate freedom from shame, guilt and anger. This transcendent quality is "a spark of courage to open up, that moment of daring and trusting which causes the heart to jump over the fence. It is this surprising energy which lays down the dividing walls between us."[47] Often, this transcending ability is attributed to God or "close to the divine," and indeed it feels like it when we see we have forgiven something very hurtful. It is likened to an "empowering grace," a "generosity of spirit," which seems to be a similar concept to *aphiemi*. Generosity of spirit is characteristic of God, who empowers human beings to be generous with giving the gift of forgiveness to one another. Thus, for some, the divine is not only evident, but indispensable because the power to forgive seems beyond one's ability. Yet, at the same time, there is an act of the will to make that leap.

In summary, the defining quality of forgiveness is that it is a process, not an event. Changes in attitude and behaviors take time, and unless the offense is quite minor, neither of these is accomplished all at once. As obvious as this is, it is frequently a source of confusion, accusation and condemnation to those involved in the process of forgiving. We believe we have forgiven someone, only to once again be confronted with those same negative attitudes and emotions associated with the offense and the offender. Or, we believe someone else should have been able to forgive an offense and just get on with life. This applies even more so to those struggling over heinous abuses. In many situations, it may be better to think of forgiving, rather than having already forgiven, indicating the process nature of forgiveness.

What Is Required for Forgiveness to Be Realized?

In order for forgiveness to be realized, there are certain elements that some consider integral to the process. One is repentance, derived from the Greek word *metanoia*, meaning a change of mind or attitude. This is a renewal of the whole psyche or person, which is the "morally regenerative" work of repentance.

However, repentance is more than a change in attitude or behavior, renewal, regeneration or self-transformation. Repentance signifies not only a turning away from the offending behavior, but also a turning back to the offended one with hope. It is what enables the offender to "face" the offended. Thus, repentance works on behalf of both offender and the offended as an interpersonal process. It can be especially empowering to the victim, as it requires that the offense be named and acknowledged. Further, acts of restitution reinforce the forgiveness process, enabling the victim to move beyond the offense, and the feelings of anger and powerlessness. Children are more likely to forgive when there is some form of apology, or expression of repentance or regret. Typically, these expressions are said to help the offended feel some sort of empathy with the offender, as long as the expressions are sincere.

Obviously, forgiveness given in response to repentance is reliant on both offended and offender. But what happens when there is no repentance? Here, forgiveness involves letting go of resentment and anger, independent of his or her response. It is an invitation for forgiveness to happen. Because it does not depend on the wrongdoer's acknowledgement, it is unconditional. We could view this as a gift awaiting reception. Nelson Mandela was one who extended invitational forgiveness, not for his own benefit or sake, but as an invitation for response from the South African whites.

Another defining quality of forgiveness is that it is an active rather than passive process. To forgive, one must work on changing attitudes, even if the process remains an intrapersonal one. To repent, one must acknowledge the offense through confession. To invite repentance, the forgiver must initiate and extend an attitude of goodwill toward the offender. To acknowledge one's need for forgiveness, as well as, forgive another, requires initiative toward the other, as well as (again) work on one's attitude toward the other. These are all steps of action.

At this point, we can make a helpful distinction between forgiveness and reconciliation, for they are not one and the same. "Reconcile" has its roots in *reconcilare*, Latin for "to bring together again," or *concilare*–to make friendly—*re*—again".[48] For some, the wrongdoer's acknowledgement of the offense—repentance—is essential to reconciliation. Acknowledgement signifies that the offender sees his or her wrong, hurtful behavior, and commits to not repeating the offense and to a change in behavior.

For others, reconciliation is not contingent on acknowledging the offense, but is the agreement to live in harmony and cooperation with the other. Both scenarios require a degree of trust before people are truly reconciled. While there is very little in any of the literature focusing on children, forgiving and reconciliation, some research suggests "young children define forgiveness via reconciliatory behaviors."[49] This puts the understanding of forgiveness parallel to the understanding of reconciliation. Often, the end and outworking of both processes is restored relationship.

Having briefly examined the forgiveness process and what is required for it to be realized, let us now shift to a more practical approach to forgiveness. What does the forgiveness process look like? What kinds of actions might help it, move it forward? How do we apply the forgiveness process to the issues surrounding children who have been through or are going through crises?

How Do Children Understand and Speak about Forgiveness? How Can Forgiving be Facilitated?

We will now turn our attention to the way children understand and speak about forgiveness, and how we, as their caregivers/counselors, can help them in the process. We will begin each subsection with their understandings and words about forgiving, following with some suggestions as to how to facilitate forgiveness.

Children typically do not articulate the forgiveness process in ways we have just done. Rather, they are quite practical in their approach to this process, though their descriptive words and phrases exemplify what has been previously examined through the literature.[50]

A Shift in Attitude

"When you forgive someone, you don't feel bad towards them." "Forgiving makes me feel happy." The child feels happy himself and feels happy towards the forgiven person. Feeling happy, here, alludes to the opportunity for a restored relationship. There is a change or shift in attitude toward the other, which then helps the forgiving process move toward reconciliation.

Forgiveness is active, rather than passive, so that it can be seen, as this child said: "When you forgive you don't point out when someone has done something wrong." Another primary school child illustrated the practical action involved in forgiving. She said that a former boy soldier showed he was sorry about his past. Because of that, she took the initiative. She encouraged her friends to stop taunting him with name-calling, which made him cry, and to include him in their playtime. This child helped others act in a forgiving way.

When children talk about "feeling sorry" for someone or "having mer-cy," they are speaking of a kind of empathy or compassion for the other person. Putting oneself in the other's place can be helpful for stirring up feelings of empathy or compassion. Children may experience these feelings when the offender exhibits a sorrow for his or her actions, such as in the ex-ample above where the offending boy was being called names. Empathy or compassion may be compromised in forgiving someone who has a history of abuse, where the "apology" may have been sincere at the time. Without the sincerity that would come through in changed behavior, the feelings of empathy or compassion will be short-lived.

Children said, "When you don't forgive, you get bad feelings." You "don't want to see the person." You try to avoid the person. One child said, "When I see that person coming, I will pass another way… I will not look at that person and I don't want him to see me anywhere." Where forgive-ness encourages openness and welcoming toward the offender, unforgive-ness makes you "feel like taking revenge and returning the offense." Some children said thoughts of revenge "kept them alive." Anger, resentment and hatred do have a powerful, emotional momentum, as was expressed through this child: ". . . I feel so angry that . . . if I have a gun at that time I would gun down that person."

Unfortunately, repetitive offenses and particularly those offenses that have left a permanent visible or physical reminder, fuel resentment and re-venge. Children talk about feelings of resentment and taking revenge every time they see or experience something that reminds them of the offense(s). The very interesting juxtaposition to this is that children often believe being resentful and/or revengeful is not who they truly would like to be; in other words, the "ideal self" is one who forgives.[51] Some children said that if you took revenge, "you will be more in the err . . . and your (act of) revenge would be the bigger one."[52] It seems better to forgive.

As a Release

Children speak about forgiveness meaning "you don't hold a grudge to-wards the other person." "You move on." Liberation from offense implies that you live differently, as this child said: "You be glad together, and share things in common. You love the person and share things." Letting go of the offense makes room for positive feelings and purposeful, helpful actions. In a sense, it is the forgiver who is paying the price for releasing the offense, and choosing to have an attitude of goodwill and generosity toward the other person.

Some children understood the biblical story of the prodigal son in terms of release. Though the son had deeply hurt the father, the father let the offense go, forgiving generously, lovingly and unconditionally.[53] Some children talked about this kind of forgiving as a way to acknowledge the importance of a relationship. Obviously, this serves both the offender and the offended. To paraphrase what one child said, you are able to accept the other and to be yourself. In this case, the father is free to love his son as a father would. The son is freed from the burden of his offenses, restored into his sonship and able to live a different life.

When there is unforgiveness, children say you "keep the offense and the offender in your heart" and "you never forget." However, when forgiving is pursued, "forgetting" could be understood like this:

> We came together and [they – the boy soldiers] asked us to forgive them . . . for [all] the things that they have done to us and so my father and mother accepted this and say they forget about everything and we too forget about it.

Though there is an offense that both acknowledge, both offender and offended are released because the offense is "forgotten."

Shame and/or guilt over an offense are heavy burdens. Releasing these burdens gives both parties an opportunity to have a different identity and future. In the process of forgiving, they are released from their pasts and freed to live a different life. Children talked about shameful acts and wanting to be free from them. One child talked about bringing things out in the open and revealing his participation in (for him) the most shameful acts. In one instance, he was caught between wanting to apologize and make amends for something that was not really his fault. In another instance, he could not bear to confront the victim of another shameful act he was forced to commit.

Especially when there is sexual violation involving a child, the shame and guilt associated with that significantly affects self-esteem and recovery of well-being. At the same time, sexual violation and resultant shame is complicated by culture and tradition. In countries where females and children are typically marginalized, sexual violations stigmatize the child and may result in a kind of isolation and/or rejection by family and community. One girl talked about her sister who became pregnant due to rape. The girl's father made the pregnant sister leave the house. While this may seem highly inappropriate to those who live in industrialized nations, it is not unusual in other countries whose cultures are shame-based.

The Supreme Deity and Transcendence

Children often link their desire and/or ability to forgive with God. One child said, "I want to forgive because God sent his holy son to die for us." Another child said, "My reason for forgiving is that my God is a God of forgiveness." Other children elaborated, as in the following:

In the Bible, Jesus said that if person do bad you have to forgive. I agree with that statement because if you don't forgive you still feel bad towards that person. I forgive when a person does me wrong because if I don't forgive, if I do some wrong things, I won't be forgiven. That's why I forgive.

From the day that our mother gave birth to us, we . . . have sinned different times against God and God is still continuing to forgive us. He has never recalled about things that have passed so because of that character in God, we should try to keep that in us and try to use it.

Clearly, children can understand forgiveness in terms of the Supreme Deity and as a religious duty. They also link forgiving to hope, as this child said: "I will forgive because I know I have a hope in Jesus."

Depending on religious background, children may understand the link between the Supreme Deity and forgiveness quite differently. "If we forgive, God will fight for us" can mean that the Supreme Deity will take revenge for the offense.[54] Children who link forgiveness with leaving the outcome to God may see this process as a source of comfort. However, some children feel they have no choice in whether to forgive or not, which can be an indication of the powerlessness they feel. This is when applying a religious directive is not helpful.

That said, it is clear from both my own research and others that children are very open to a Supreme Deity and/or transcendence as a part of everyday life. Psychologically, God can take almost any form with children. As well, they do not easily forget Jesus' ability to perform miracles. From what children said to me, they actually long for these miracles to happen in their own lives. Without putting pressure on the child, the caregiver could explore with the child his perceptions of the Supreme Deity. As was previously noted, this can be a source of hope for children.

Facilitating Forgiveness

In light of the discussion up to this point and what children themselves say, how can we facilitate forgiveness? Below are some suggestions that may be helpful.

1. **The obvious: Ask!** A psychologist named George Kelly once advised with these words of wisdom: "If you want to know what is wrong with someone, ask them. They will probably tell you. If we, as adults who care for children, want to know what forgiveness means to children, ask them. Ask them what it would feel like to forgive someone. Ask them if they think there is a difference between forgiving and being reconciled, and what that difference is all about." As has already been shown, children have some definite ideas about forgiveness, and they are usually less rigid in their approach to forgiving than adults.

2. **Using metaphors:** It may be helpful for children to visualize what forgiveness could look like. For example, forgiving someone might look like an embrace. In the child's mind, who should initiate this embrace? Forgiveness, moving toward reconciliation, could take the form of sitting together and having a fun snack or a nice meal. What would the child choose and why? These are some suggestions, but it's better to ask children to describe their own metaphor. They could do so verbally, through a song, a drawing, a game or vignette.

3. **Telling one's story:** We repeatedly hear the benefit of telling one's story. This is an empowering process. It allows for reframing of the experience on various levels. However, timing is critical. A child's story may be deeply buried as a way to cope. At the appropriate time, ask the child to tell his or her story, describing what happened and how he or she felt. Telling one's story helps in regaining the dignity and value lost due to abusive violations. This is particularly important in collective cultures, where a person's identity and value is affirmed through the group's acceptance, and where storytelling is naturally a part of that culture.

   The presence of significant others can be a positive addition to sharing one's story, depending on the particular situation or circumstances surrounding offending events. Significant others could be family. They could also be people with similar experiences who can relate, supply additional facts or help reinterpret events. That is not to say a child's experience and perspective should be subject to critique, but that there may be other details that would help him or her see things differently.

4. **Encouraging compassion/empathy:** In recalling the offense, ask the child questions that will draw out the humanity of the offender. Some suggested questions are the following: "Can you imagine being that person?" "How do you think that would feel?" "How do you think the other person(s) is feeling now?" Questions like these may help the child discover if there is another way to think about the offense and the offender. Despite the abuses that children may have suffered, they are

surprisingly open to humanizing the other, to discovering similarities rather than demonizing.

5. **Restitution:** When a child has been wronged, what would feel right to that child in terms of restitution? This is a good discussion to have, individually or with a group. Simply asking, "What would make you feel better about this situation" can be very insightful in terms of what is important to children. For instance, saying "sorry" may be very meaningful, particularly if the offender is an adult.[55] On the other hand, spending time together may be all the "words" a child needs to hear.

6. **Other practices:** For some children, certain traditional ceremonies or rituals facilitate forgiveness and even reconciliation. In every culture, there are specific practices that denote a kind of transition from one state to another. For instance, in some religious practices, dunking or bathing in water signifies a kind of cleansing and forgiving. It can make a place for the offender to be reconciled. In another culture, burning particular items associated with the offense denotes forgiving and starting anew. Writing in a journal can help with the forgiving process. There are many ideas such as these that could be explored.

What Conditions Make Forgiving Easier for Children?

Children are usually quick to forgive. However, there are some conditions that make forgiving easier for children. One of the most frequently mentioned is having their basic needs met. Here I am speaking of physical and emotional needs. Having these met, at least to some degree, boosts the forgiving process.

Helping children identify what they are currently thankful for may be linked to the forgiveness process. This was the case for children in Sierra Leone who had suffered tremendously, yet managed to be grateful for what they had. There was a direct link between what they were thankful for and what abuses they felt able to forgive. Going back to having their needs met and having someone to care for them, was the basis for this. Thankfulness is liberating and encourages hopefulness.

Resilience is closely linked to this. Resilience for children is strengthened through relationship, particularly with the primary caregiver(s). When a child has the benefit of a close relationship, he or she feels secure and able to trust. These factors contribute to the forgiveness process. Interestingly, some research on children has linked a lower level of resilience to harboring unhelpful emotions against the abusers, nurturing feelings of bitterness, hurt and anger.

Resiliency is also linked to forgiveness and hope. Hope and self-efficacy are characteristic of a resilient nature. Hope and optimism are effective in promoting and supporting forgiveness. Thus, resiliency is a significant aspect of the forgiveness process. There seems to be a circular relationship with resiliency, forgiveness and hope or optimism.

Depending on the circumstances, forgiving one's self may or may not be a consideration for the child. Culture and religious practices speak into how self-forgiving is understood, as does the nature of the abuse or offense. Bringing things into the light is key to dealing with shame, guilt and forgiving self where or when relevant. If self-forgiveness is not a relevant concept, it could be more appropriately interpreted as being released from shame and guilt. Sexual violation serves as a good example, where there is a deep sense of shame and guilt associated with the offense. Though the child cannot be faulted for the abuse, he or she will often take on the responsibility for its occurrence. While shame in particular makes one want to hide from or deny the offense, exposing it—in most cultures—is essential in the restoring process. However, this should be approached in whatever ways are culturally, gender and age appropriate, all the while respecting the individual's location in the healing timeline.

There is debate as to whether all offenses are forgivable and whether forgiving these offenses means that justice is forfeited. Aside from one's moral or religious values, it is important to distinguish between the offense and the offender. We do not want to "fuse the criminal with the crime." They are not one and the same. Additionally, every person has the opportunity for transformation, to be a different person. Just as the victim or survivor wants to begin anew, it is the case with most offenders. Therefore, on the basis that a person's behavior is not the person's fixed identity, forgiveness is justified.

At the same time, forgiving does not suggest that reconciliation with the offender is either appropriate or desirable. In fact, reconciliation may be dangerous, uncalled for or impossible. As well, it is important to remember that in forgiving, justice can and should still be met under most circumstances. However, there is release that comes with forgiving for both the offended and offender, apart from their being reconciled to one another.

A Final Word: Hope

Forgiveness is liberating, and this liberation engenders hope. Where there is hope, there is belief in the possibility of change. Forgiveness helps separate the offense from those associated with it, changing one's relationship to the past. One of my interviewees, Father Chema, made this profound statement with which I will end this chapter:

> . . . a focus on the person, respect and love for the person despite past records, no running away from ourselves but reaching ourselves within at the deeper level, self-acceptance and responsibility, repentance and forgiveness, . . . yes all that you can find in Jesus' Gospel and that is the ideal far ahead of me.

NINE

FROM SPIRITUAL HARM to SPIRITUAL HEALING

Christa Foster Crawford

As humans, we are made up of body, mind and spirit. All of the things that we experience in life affect us physically, mentally, emotionally and spiritually. Good things, such as encouragement from a friend in a time of trouble, cause our heartbeats to slow down, our thoughts to clear up, our emotions to settle and our spirits to soar. By contrast, bad things, such as trauma or crisis, cause our hearts to pound, our minds to race, our emotions to unravel and our spirits to plummet. Children and youth in crisis are no different. When they face traumatic events and experiences, it impacts all aspects of their development: physical, mental, emotional and spiritual.

The Nature of Spiritual Harm

It is often easy to observe and address the physical impact of traumatic events on a child's body. For example, children who are abused bear tangible wounds like bruises and broken bones. It is also easy to see—though often harder to address—the emotional and mental impact of that abuse: the sadness and depression, or the changes in concentration that showed up after the abuse began. But it is often difficult to recognize—and easy to ignore—the impact of abuse on the child's spirit. Identifying the spiritual impact is made even more difficult by the fact that spiritual harm can look very similar to, and overlap with, the other types of harm. In fact, "many physical, mental, emotional and behavioral problems are actually spiritual problems."[56]

And yet, we must not fail to recognize and address spiritual harm if children and youth in crisis are to find true healing. A person's core is made up of the spirit. Spiritual harm injures us at the very depth of our beings. While the damage to the spirit may be harder to see than damage to other parts of a person, the impact is just as real and the failure to address it can be devastating.

The Impact of Spiritual Harm

Now that we understand the nature of spiritual harm, we must understand the impact of that harm on children and youth in crisis.

Spiritual harm distorts the way children and youth view themselves, others and God.[57] This is true of spiritual harm caused by all kinds of trauma and crisis, but in the case of sexual abuse or sexual exploitation, the effect is especially devastating. We will look at the impact of spiritual harm in the context of sexual abuse and exploitation, keeping in mind that these distortions also occur with other types of trauma and crisis in varying degrees.

Distorted View of Self

First, spiritual harm causes a distorted view of self. The personal violation of sexual abuse and exploitation mars the ability of children and youth to see their true identity as created in the *imago dei*, or the image of God. Instead of being secure in who they are in Christ, they are bombarded with a barrage of lies in four primary areas: low self-image, self-contempt, shame and loss of self.

Low Self-Image

A low self-image makes children and youth feel unlovable and unworthy:

"I'm unlovable."

"There's something wrong with me."

"I'm not worth anything."

"I feel so insecure."

Because they do not value themselves, they experience lack of self-esteem, feelings of inadequacy, low self-worth and value, and feelings of insecurity and helplessness.

Self-Contempt

Ultimately this low self-view causes them to feel contempt and self-hatred:

"I hate my body."

"I hate myself."

"I hate my life."

They feel angry with themselves, and are self-condemning and unable to forgive themselves. They may blame themselves for the abuse and exploitation, and for failing to stop it.

Shame

The reason for this self-contempt is rooted in shame:

"I'm dirty."

"I'm ruined."

"I'm no good."

The very nature of sexual abuse causes them to feel tremendous shame, guilt and humiliation. The degradation and stigma of sexual exploitation cause them to lose their sense of dignity and self-respect. Though it is not true, they feel "dirty" or violated, like "damaged goods." Their sexuality is damaged and they feel like they have lost their innocence.

Loss of Self

When the shame and self-contempt are too much to bear, they become disconnected from their emotional or "true" selves, resulting in a loss of sense of self:

"I don't matter."

"My life has no meaning."

"I'm better off dead."

These false but powerful beliefs lead to a profound sense of grief and regret, the loss of hope and faith, and ultimately, resignation and despair.

Distorted View of Others

Second, spiritual harm also causes a distorted view of others. The sense of betrayal and violation from sexual abuse and exploitation sends children false messages about how they should perceive the world around them, and damages how they relate to others. These lies take root in three primary areas: disconnection from others, loss of trust and harmful self-protection.

Disconnection from Others

Sexual abuse and exploitation make children and youth feel disconnected from others:

"Nobody cares about me."

"I'm all alone in the world."

"I'm an outcast. No one will ever want me again."

Sexual abuse and exploitation can cause pain and wounding so deep that children and youth lose their ability to give and receive love. Often, the wounds come from family members, which means, children lose their sense of belonging. They feel neglected, abandoned, orphaned, rejected and outcast. They may even be rejected by others because of what happened, leaving them feeling isolated and alone. Or, their own feelings of shame and self-rejection may cause them to separate themselves from others. Finally, they have often been hurt in ways that seem "unforgivable." Unforgiveness makes them bitter, further isolating them from love and connection with others.

Loss of Trust

All trauma and crisis, but especially those of a sexual nature, cause children and youth to lose trust in others and question the goodness of all people:

"All men are bad."

"People are just out to hurt me."

"I can't trust anyone."

Sexual abuse and exploitation often entail a betrayal of trust from people whom children were supposed to be able to trust. They lose their ability to trust in others, including those who were supposed to protect them, but didn't. They may become unable to trust men and have a bad view of fathers or father figures. Ultimately, their trust in humanity itself may be shaken. Unable to reconcile the senselessness of the abuse and exploitation, they begin to doubt their fundamental beliefs about goodness and justice.

Harmful Self-Protection

This loss of ability to trust in others leads children to feel like they must protect themselves from others, often at the cost of connection to other people:

"I have to rely on myself."

"I'll never let anyone hurt me again."

These beliefs cause them to be suspicious of others and engage in harmful, self-protective behaviors, including isolation, hardness and erecting emotional walls to keep people away. Unforgiveness and bitterness further cement these walls, and ensure their continued isolation from others. Sometimes, self-protection takes the form of antisocial behaviors, with the motivation that "you can't hurt me if I hurt you first."

Distorted View of God

Finally, spiritual harm causes a distorted view of God. The horror of sexual abuse and exploitation undermines children's deepest beliefs and calls into question the very nature of good and evil. They are assailed by lies about God's existence and God's nature, and may even experience a spiritual crisis.

God's Existence

Sexual abuse and exploitation cause children and youth to question the existence of God:

"There is no God."

"How could this happen if there really is a God?"

Some children and youth in crisis have never believed in God at all. But even for those who do, the overwhelming evil of sexual abuse and exploitation can cause them to doubt whether God really does exist. Resignation, fatalism and despair are common replacements for the loss of belief in something greater than themselves.

God's Nature

Even if they do believe God exists, the only way they can reconcile the evil they have experienced with the existence of God is to question God's nature:

"God is not good."

"God can't be trusted."

"God doesn't love me."

"God is not able to take care of me."

If God does exist—they think—He must not be good, He must not be powerful or He must not care. These false beliefs about God reinforce the false beliefs they hold about themselves and others. They feel unloved and unacceptable, abandoned and alienated, and experience loss of trust, as well as disbelief, blame and anger.

Spiritual Crisis

This questioning of everything they have ever held to be true, including the nature of good and evil, as well as the existence and nature of God, impairs children's spiritual formation and often leads them into a spiritual or existential crisis:

"The world is against me."

"Nothing matters anymore."

"Life stinks."

This crisis can ultimately result in a fundamental lack of meaning and purpose in life, a complete loss of hope and faith, and a sense of utter hopelessness, resignation and despair. Moral development may begin to crumble and they may become more entangled in the effects of sin and being sinned against, with spiritual bondage and oppression as the result. Often, suicide or nihilism seem to be the only options available.

From Spiritual Harm to Spiritual Healing

It is clear that children and youth in crisis experience spiritual harm from which they are in desperate need of spiritual healing. Now that we understand the impact of spiritual harm, what can we do to bring spiritual healing?

The most basic spiritual need that all people have is for reconciliation with their Creator, which God has made possible through the sacrifice of Jesus Christ. This saving relationship is the ultimate source of forgiveness, healing, power, grace, freedom, deliverance, restoration and every other thing that is necessary for spiritual healing to occur. As caregivers, we should offer this to the children and youth in our care in a way that does not pressure them and respects them where they are.

In addition, because the impact of spiritual harm is distortion of the truth, the key to spiritual healing is the replacement of those lies with God's truth. Spiritual healing brings truth to the distortions about self, others and God. But it is not enough for children and youth merely to have the knowledge of the right answers in their heads. As caregivers, we must help them to be able to experience and be transformed by these truths at the very core of their being. Romans 12:2 promises that we can be transformed by the renewing of our minds. Spiritual healing involves the process of God renewing their minds from these distorted thoughts to the truth, so they can experience transformation in every part of their being: body, mind and spirit. Our role is to consistently model these truths—in word and in action—so they can learn to truly believe them and begin to live as if they are true.

Renewing the View of Self

As we have seen, spiritual harm causes a distorted view of self that stems from lies in four primary areas: low self-image, self-contempt, shame and loss of self. Spiritual healing must counter these lies with the truth God has to say about them:

"You are special."
"God created you."

"You are not a mistake."
"You were made in the image of God."

"God loves you no matter what."
"God treasures you so much He died for you."
"Nothing can ever separate you from God's love."
"Your sins are washed whiter than snow."
"God created you for a purpose."
"God has a plan for your life."

From Low Self-Image to Infinite Worth

We must help children and youth in crisis replace the lies they believe about themselves with the truth of what God says about their value and worth: They have been created in the image of God (see Gen.1:27; James 3:9). God himself formed and made them (see Ps. 139:14-18; Isa. 43:1; Jer. 1:5). This means they have infinite value and worth (see Matt. 10:29-31; Luke 15). We can help build their self-image and self-esteem in practical ways by giving them affection, affirmation and approval, and by being generous with sincere praise and encouragement.

From Self-Contempt and Shame to Unconditional Love, Acceptance and Forgiveness

We must also help children and youth in crisis replace feelings of self-hatred with the truth of God's love: God loves them unconditionally and unceasingly (see Rom. 5:8; Jer. 31:3-4). There is nothing they can ever do—or can be done to them—that will separate them from God's love (see Rom. 8:35-39; Ps. 103:8-12). They are accepted and acceptable (see Eph.1:4-5; Rom. 8:1-2). Instead of self-condemnation and self-blame, they can be assured God forgives them of all their sins (see 1 John 1:9; Ps. 103:12). They do not have to earn God's love, but are worthy of God's love because of who God is, even when they feel unworthy (see Rom. 8:33-34). Because God loves, accepts and forgives them, they can love, accept and forgive themselves, as well. We can help them to learn about God's love through showing them human love in tangible and consistent ways.

From Loss of Self to Significance

Finally, we must help children and youth in crisis replace the lie that they don't matter with the truth that their life has significance (see Ps. 139:1-18; Matt.10:29-31). God has chosen them and created them for a purpose (see Jer. 1:5; 29:11; Eph. 2:10). We can help them realize their significance by helping them discover the ways God has gifted them and helping them discern the plans He has for them.

Renewing the View of Others

We have also seen that spiritual harm causes a distorted view of others that affects three key areas: disconnection from others, loss of trust and harmful self-protective behaviors. Spiritual healing must counter these lies with the truth of how God has designed children and youth in crisis to relate with others:

"You are not alone."
"You do not have to rely on yourself."
"Not all people are bad."
"Some people are trustworthy."
"Forgiveness is possible."

From Disconnection to Belonging

Belonging is one of the most basic needs of all human beings.[58] Unless a child or youth belongs to someone, he or she cannot survive. This is true, both on a physical and emotional level. Belonging provides safety, security, identity and significance. An essential part of the spiritual healing process is giving those in our care a sense of belonging. The most important One they need to belong to is God. We can also help them to reconnect with their family and community in ways that protect them from additional physical, emotional or other harm. Where this is not possible, we must create new communities to replace the natural connections that have been lost.

From Loss of Trust to Restoration of Trust

Trust is essential for a person's sense of safety and value, and forms the basis for all relationships.[59] We must help children and youth to rebuild the trust that has been destroyed through trauma and crisis. We must help them learn how to trust again. Those who have been harmed or failed by others are right to question the trustworthiness of others. However, they must learn to trust appropriately. We can help them do this by being trustworthy ourselves. We can also help them to learn proper boundaries that protect them from harm without closing them off from healthy relationships with others. Most importantly, we can help them to learn to trust God, who is the only One who is perfectly trustworthy.

From Harmful Self-Protection to Healthy Forgiveness

Without forgiveness, complete healing and wholeness is impossible. Without forgiveness, we are forever tied to those who have wronged us. Without forgiveness, bitterness will eat us away. We must help children and youth in crisis learn to forgive in order to release the barriers they have erected to protect themselves from others. First, we must help them forgive those who have harmed them. This means, helping them understand what true forgiveness is and what it is not. Forgiving is not excusing the wrong or remaining in a place of harm. What true forgiveness entails is discussed in greater detail elsewhere in this book. Second, we must help them to forgive themselves. Often, children and youth in crisis experience self-blame and self-condemnation. They must learn to release false guilt, as well as to repent from, take responsibility for and receive forgiveness for any wrong behaviors. Finally, they must learn to release God from ways in which they have blamed Him.

Renewing the View of God

Finally we have seen that spiritual harm causes a distorted view of God that questions God's existence and nature, and may even lead to spiritual crisis. Spiritual healing must counter these lies with the truth about who God is:

"God is love."
"God is good."
"God is trustworthy."
"God is sovereign."
"God is a rescuer."
"God is a healer."
"God is a good father."
"God cares for you."

From Doubting God's Existence to Enjoying His Sovereignty

Crisis and trauma can cause children and youth to believe God does not exist. We must help them learn the truth that God does exist and He is sovereign, regardless of what may happen. God has created them for a purpose (see Jer. 29:11; Eph. 2:10). The fact that bad things have happened to them does not thwart God's plan and purpose for them; in fact, even those bad things can be used to further God's purpose, just as they did with Joseph (see Gen. 50:20). While crisis and trauma are never God's desire for children and youth, we can reassure them with the truth that "in all things God works for the good of those who love him, who have been called according to his purpose" (see Rom. 8:28).

From Questioning God's Nature to Experiencing His Care

Crisis and trauma can also cause children and youth to believe God does not love them or care for them. We must help them learn the truth about God's character: God is love and He is loving (see 1 John 4:16; Ps.103:8). God is good and does good (see Luke 18:19; Ps. 86:10). God is all powerful and gives us strength (see 1 Cor. 1:25; Isa. 41:10). He cares for us (see 1 Pet. 5:7). He protects us (see Deut. 33:27). He rescues us (see Ps. 72:12-14). He comforts us (see Matt.11:28-29; 2 Cor. 1:3-4). He is a good Father who provides for our every need (see 1 John 3:1, Matt, 7:9-11; Acts 14:17; 1 Tim. 6:17).

From Battling Spiritual Crisis to Encountering Redemption, Restoration and Hope

Finally, crisis and trauma can cause children and youth to lose meaning and hope. We must help them learn the truth that God redeems, God restores and God gives hope. God is a God of redemption. With God, nothing is wasted. He promises to redeem the senseless pain of the past for His own perfect purpose (see Ps. 103:1-6; James 1:2-4). What the devil has wrought for evil in their lives, God plans to redeem into something that will make them stronger and their lives more beautiful, bringing glory to God's name (see Gen. 50:20). God is also a God of restoration. He promises to restore their personal losses, relational losses and spiritual losses (see Joel 2:25; Ps. 71:20-21). He offers a restored sense of childhood, a restored sense of innocence and a restored self-identity (see 2 Cor. 5:17; Isa. 43:18-19). Finally, God is a God of hope. He restores lost hope, for both their present and their future (see Titus 3:7; Ps. 25:1-3). He promises beauty in exchange for all of their ashes and covers their shame with joy (see Isa. 61:1-7; Ps. 30:11). He has great plans for them: to give them hope and a future (see Jer. 29:11).

Barriers to Spiritual Healing

The key to spiritual healing is applying God's truth to lies. Unfortunately, trauma and crisis cause people to disbelieve God and His truth. Overcoming this barrier is essential to spiritual healing.

Our view of God is based on our experiences with people. "Our concept of God is a composite of theology (what we believe about God and what we believe God thinks about us), and our experiences in interpersonal relationships (what we believe about ourselves and what we believe others think of us)."[60] Therefore, our experiences with others determine and can also distort what we believe about God.

The devil uses crisis and trauma, including sexual abuse and sexual exploitation, as powerful tools to disrupt children's spiritual development. Children are not born with an automatic, clear perception of God; their concept of God must be developed.[61] Ordinarily, childhood is a period in which parents and other adult figures contribute to the child's spiritual development through modeling God's love and care in their own behavior. But when "parents abuse or neglect their children, those intended 'agents' of God's grace not only reinforce the child's fallen perception of God, but actually become tools of destruction."[62] We have seen how this destruction impacts how they view themselves, others and God.

Sexual abuse is especially devastating to a child's concept of God. In particular, incest by fathers and father figures damages the child's ability to understand God as a loving Father. The fatherhood of God is an essential part of His nature, and a powerful part of His healing and redeeming relationship with us. If we cannot trust that God is the good Father He says He is, it becomes nearly impossible to believe the other truths about His existence and nature. Children and youth in crisis need for their image of God to be lined up with God's true character in scripture, rather than the false image drawn from their experience with parents and other authority figures who have neglected, abused, failed or disappointed them.

Overcoming Barriers to Spiritual Healing

If appreciating the fatherhood of God is an integral part of spiritual healing, then how can we help those who have been abused or exploited by parental figures have a correct view of God as a good father? We cannot begin with the image of God as a father because the negative associations that fatherhood carries for them translate to lies about God's true character. Instead, we must start with an image that is not rooted in their brokenness. Once they are able to understand God's character in that non-threatening image, we can help them bridge those qualities to the image of God as the Good Father. The image of God as a Good Shepherd can provide that bridge.

Meeting the Good Shepherd

In Scripture, each member of the Trinity is compared with many roles: comforter, advocate, judge and king, to name a few. One comparison that is especially helpful for children and youth in crisis is that of a shepherd.

God as Shepherd throughout Scripture

Several of God's titles in Scripture refer to him as a shepherd: "Shepherd of Israel", "Shepherd and Overseer of your souls", "Chief Shepherd", "good shepherd" and "great Shepherd of the sheep" (Ps. 80:1; 1 Pet. 2:25; 1 Pet. 5:4; John 10:11, 14; Heb. 13:20). So, what is the role of a shepherd? A shepherd is one who is committed to caring for his sheep:

> The shepherd is the first to see the lamb at its birth, and not one day goes by but he visits it. So needful and merciful a work is it that it has no Sabbath, but as on the day of rest the shepherd feeds his own children so he cares for the lambs of his flock, sees that no harm is befalling them, remembers their dependence on him, observes their growth, [and] removes what hinders [them].[63]

In the same way that a shepherd cares for sheep, God cares for children and youth in crisis. Scripture contains numerous examples of God's shepherding care for His people. For instance, we learn in Isaiah 40:11 that God tends us, gathers us in His arms, carries us close to His heart and gently leads us. In Psalm 78:53, we learn God guides us to safety and makes us unafraid. In Jeremiah 31:10, we learn God watches over us. Most famously, in Psalm 23, we learn God leads us beside quiet waters, makes us lie down in green pastures, restores our soul, comforts us, makes us not be in want, guides us in paths of righteousness and helps us not fear evil, even in the shadow of death because He is with us.

In addition to these general descriptions, Scripture provides several extended passages that vividly illustrate aspects of God's character that are particularly meaningful to children and youth in crisis. A first example is found in John 10, and demonstrates God's care and concern as a *Good Shepherd*. A second example is found in Luke 15, and illustrates God's pursuit, love and acceptance as a *Seeking Shepherd*. A final example is found in Ezekiel 34, and reveals God's deliverance, provision and restoration as a *Saving Shepherd*. Let's look at each of these examples in more detail.

The Good Shepherd, John 10:11-15

> "I am the good shepherd. The good shepherd lays down his life for the sheep. The hired hand is not the shepherd who owns the sheep. So when he sees the wolf coming, he abandons the sheep and runs away. Then the wolf attacks the flock and scatters it. The man runs away because he is a hired hand and cares nothing for the sheep. I am the good shepherd; I know my sheep and my sheep know me—just as the Father knows me and I know the Father—and I lay down my life for the sheep" (John 10:11-15 NIV).

In John 10, Jesus twice calls himself the "Good Shepherd." What does it mean to children and youth in crisis for Jesus to be a good shepherd?

First, as a good shepherd, Jesus is responsible for their care; they no longer have to struggle to take care of themselves:

> "'I am the Good Shepherd'—here is guidance, guardianship, companionship, sustenance—all responsibility laid upon His broad shoulders, and all tenderness in His deep heart, and so for us simple obedience and quiet trust."[64]

Second, as a good shepherd, Jesus can be trusted to care for them because they belong to Him. They can be secure in His care because He is not merely a hired hand who will abandon them when trouble or danger comes. In fact, not only will He not run away, but He will even lay down His own life to save them:

> "'I lay down My life for the sheep.' . . . So, then, in some profound way, the shepherd's death is the sheep's safety. . . . We read, 'Smite the shepherd, and the sheep shall be scattered,' but here, somehow or other, the smiting of the Shepherd is not the scattering but the gathering of the flock. Here, somehow or other, the dead Shepherd has power to guard, to guide, to defend them. Here, somehow or other, the death of the Shepherd is the security of the sheep."[65]

Finally, as a good shepherd, Jesus knows His sheep. This means children and youth in crisis can experience unconditional love, acceptance, belonging, significance and freedom from shame. He doesn't just know "about" children and youth in crisis; He knows each one of them personally and individually:

> "'I know My sheep.' That is a knowledge like the knowledge of the shepherd, a bond of close intimacy. But He does not know them by reason of looking at them and thinking about them. It is something far more blessed than that. He knows me because He loves me; He knows me because He has sympathy with me. . . . [U]nless the Shepherd's heart was all love He would not know His sheep. The Shepherd's love is an individualised love."[66]

Jesus also knows them intimately:

> I know them; their inmost hearts. I know their sins and their follies: but I know, too, their longing after good. I know their temptations, their excuses, their natural weaknesses, their infirmities, which they brought into the world with them. I know their inmost hearts for good and for evil.[67]

Although Jesus knows them intimately, He accepts them unconditionally—even in their deepest and darkest parts. In fact, those things they are most ashamed about do not drive Him away from them, but instead draw them to His side:

> When they can see nothing but their own sin and weakness, and are utterly ashamed and tired of themselves, and are ready to lie down in despair, and give up all struggling after God. I know their weakness—and of me it is written, 'I will carry the lambs in mine arms.'[68]

Jesus is indeed a good shepherd to children and youth in crisis.

The Seeking Shepherd, Luke 15:3-7

> "Then Jesus told them this parable: "Suppose one of you has a hundred sheep and loses one of them. Doesn't he leave the ninety-nine in the open country and go after the lost sheep until he finds it? And when he finds it, he joyfully puts it on his shoulders and goes home. Then he calls his friends and neighbors together and says, 'Rejoice with me; I have found my lost sheep.' I tell you that in the same way there will be more rejoicing in heaven over one sinner who repents than over ninety-nine righteous persons who do not need to repent." (Luke 15:3-7 NIV)

In Luke 15 (and again in Matthew 18), Jesus describes a shepherd who leaves behind his other sheep to find and bring home the one that is lost. What does it mean to children and youth in crisis for Jesus to be a seeking shepherd?

As a seeking shepherd, Jesus goes after the sheep that are lost and carries them home. They do not have to find their own way back or return in their own strength. "He does not put them on their own legs to go alone; nor does he lead them, and much less drive them before him; but he takes them up in his arms, and lays them on his shoulders."[69] Even when children and youth in crisis are weary, worried and worn away from their wanderings, Jesus tenderly brings them back into the fold."[70]

As a seeking shepherd, Jesus loves, treasures and cherishes each one of His sheep. The reason He goes after them is "because of his love to them, and the relation between them as shepherd and sheep."[71] In the same way, every child and youth in crisis has individual value, worth and significance to God. They matter to Him.

As a seeking shepherd, Jesus cares for them not because of their worthiness, but because of their worth to Him. Even when children and youth in crisis are lost or wander away, Jesus still loves them:

> They were the objects of his Father's love, and of his own; and he took delight in them, as he saw them in the glass of his Father's purposes, as they were chosen in him, and given to him; and this joy in them still con-

tinued, notwithstanding their fall in Adam, and their own actual sins and transgressions.[72]

As a seeking shepherd, Jesus does not reject or give up on those who are lost. Even when children and youth in crisis have been soiled by the sins of others and by their own sins in response, Jesus still accepts them:

> That great seeking Shepherd follows us through all the devious courses of our wayward, wandering footsteps doubling back upon themselves, until He finds us. Though the sheep may increase its distance, the Shepherd follows. The further away we get the more tender His appeal; the more we stop our ears the louder the voice with which He calls. You cannot wear out Jesus Christ, you cannot exhaust the resources of His bounteousness, of His tenderness. However we may have been going wrong, however far we may have been wandering, however vehemently we may be increasing, at every moment, our distance from Him, He is coming after us, serene, loving, long-suffering, and will not be put away.[73]

In fact, Jesus seeks out the one that is lost, "following it, enquiring after it and looking about for it, until he finds it."[74] And when He does find it He rejoices over it, "not upbraiding them with going astray; nor complaining of, or groaning under the burden; but rejoicing in a kind of triumph, and carrying them as a trophy of victory, and a spoil obtained."[75]

What does it mean to be found by the Seeking Shepherd? For a child or youth in crisis, it means so many wonderful things:

> Finding them dead in sin he speaks life into them; he calls them by name, and asserts his property in them; he takes them out of the pit of nature; he rescues them out of the hands of Satan; he washes them from their filthiness, and heals all their diseases; he feeds and refreshes them; he covers them with his robe of righteousness; he beautifies and adorns them, and brings them home in the manner after described.[76]

To be found by the Seeking Shepherd is to be both saved and safe.

The Saving Shepherd, Ezekiel 34:11-31

Scripture provides a poetic example of what it means to be found by the Shepherd in Ezekiel 34. While this passage was written about God saving Israel, it has remarkable relevance for and offers tremendous comfort to children and youth in crisis, especially those who have been exploited or abused.

As a saving shepherd, God delivers His flock from danger. He brings back the lost and rescues them from harm:

> "For this is what the Sovereign LORD says: 'I myself will search for my sheep and look after them. As a shepherd looks after his scattered flock

when he is with them, so will I look after my sheep. I will rescue them from all the places where they were scattered on a day of clouds and darkness. . . . I will search for the lost and bring back the strays.'" (34:11-12, 16 NIV)

As a Saving Shepherd, God repairs His flock from damage. He heals what was broken, restores what was lost and rectifies injustice:

"'I will bind up the injured and strengthen the weak. . . . I will shepherd the flock with justice . . . I will save my flock, and they will no longer be plundered . . . They will know that I am the LORD, when I break the bars of their yoke and rescue them from the hands of those who enslaved them.'" (34:16, 22, 27 NIV)

As a saving shepherd, God makes His flock secure. He establishes them in a place of safety and provides for all their needs.

"'I will bring them out from the nations and gather them from the countries, and I will bring them into their own land. I will pasture them on the mountains of Israel, in the ravines and in all the settlements in the land. I will tend them in a good pasture, and the mountain heights of Israel will be their grazing land. There they will lie down in good grazing land, and there they will feed in a rich pasture on the mountains of Israel. I myself will tend my sheep and have them lie down,' declares the Sovereign Lord."(34:13-15 NIV)

"'I will make a covenant of peace with them and rid the land of savage beasts so that they may live in the wilderness and sleep in the forests in safety. I will make them and the places surrounding my hill a blessing. I will send down showers in season; there will be showers of blessing. The trees will yield their fruit and the ground will yield its crops; the people will be secure in their land. They will no longer be plundered by the nations, nor will wild animals devour them. They will live in safety, and no one will make them afraid. I will provide for them a land renowned for its crops, and they will no longer be victims of famine in the land or bear the scorn of the nations.'" (34:25-29 NIV)

God, the Saving Shepherd, offers the hope of salvation for the present, the past and the future.

Mending the distortions

Seeing God as a saving shepherd, a seeking shepherd and a good shepherd brings truth to the distortions of spiritual harm. The image of the shepherd enables children and youth in crisis to renew the distorted view of God. God demonstrates His sovereignty as a saving shepherd, expresses His care as a good shepherd, and delivers redemption, restoration and hope as a seeking shepherd. The image of the shepherd also enables children and youth in crisis to renew the distorted view of self. God, the Good Shepherd, demonstrates they have infinite worth and value because He is willing to look after their needs, search for them when they are lost and rescue them when they are troubled. God shows they are loved, accepted and forgiven because He is willing to bring them back even when they have strayed away. He affirms their significance by knowing them personally and willingly sacrificing Himself for them.

Moving from the Good Shepherd to the Good Father

Seeing God as a Good Shepherd not only brings truth to distortions, it also reveals the truth of God's character, including His love, care, concern and devotion. Many of the qualities that describe God as a shepherd are also qualities of God as a father. As such, the image of God as the Good Shepherd is an excellent bridge to the image of God as the Good Father. In Luke 15, Jesus gives a trio of parables beginning with a shepherd and ending with a father. In the same way, we can begin with the image of God as shepherd, and bridge those qualities and truths to the image of God as a father.

There are many similarities between the shepherd and the father in these stories, including their acceptance, pursuit, deliverance and restoration. Once children or youth in crisis are able to accept God's truth through the neutral image of God as a shepherd, we can help them to be able to see the truth through the image of God as a father, as well. We can teach them to transfer the qualities they have learned about God, the Good Shepherd to God, the Good Father.

Moving from the Good Shepherd to the Good Father allows children and youth in crisis to successfully move from spiritual harm to spiritual healing. God, the Good Shepherd, is good news for children and youth in crisis, indeed.

TEN

HEALING PRAYER for CHILDREN

Irma Chon

"Everybody gets their heart broken sometimes, but now I know how to mend mine."

These were the words spoken by a little girl who was sexually abused by a trusted family friend when she was only eight years old. On her graduation day from counseling, her counselor reminded the little girl that she would always remember her courage in facing her feelings, getting through the fears and becoming a confident young girl. The counselor told the little girl she was inspired by her faith and courage.

Far too often, many children do not find the healing for which their hearts are crying. The success of the little girl who could say, "Now I know how to mend mine," is doubtless related to the fact that she was led by her parents and her counselor to know and to hear God's voice. Through the intimate friendship she had with God through prayer, she was able to make a connection with Jesus, not only as her Savior, but also as her Helper through terrible memories.

Parents and spiritual caregivers of children have the most direct impact on a child's spiritual formation. Our underlying assumptions about a child's spiritual capacity will be the greatest factor in determining how we lead them. Children need adults who see their potential to connect with and receive from God, and who will stand with them in the process. We need to guide children who have been entrusted to our care to know and recognize the voice of the One who loves them, and wants to heal their souls.

Healing Prayer is Listening Prayer

Listening to God and learning to hear His voice is an important part of the training children need in order to heal. God is speaking to His children all of the time, but just like adults, children need help understanding how to tune into God's voice. They need to be taught, as Eli taught Samuel when he told him: "Samuel, that voice is God speaking; go and lie down and if He calls you say, 'Speak Lord, for your servant is listening'" (see 1 Sam. 3:8-10).

Healing prayer is an effective way in which Jesus speaks to the brokenness in a child's heart. In all cases, healing prayer is accomplished through listening prayer. In this process, we never deny the feelings the child is experiencing, we affirm those feelings. The following comfort questions can be asked after a child tells Jesus what has happened to cause his or her pain:

- What is Jesus doing?
- Can He come closer?
- Can He hold you?
- What is He saying?

Brad Jersak in his book *Children, Can you Hear Me?* says, we need to be convinced of the reality and necessity of treating prayer as a real meeting with a living friend. Jersak believes children can and should be trained to know Jesus as their best friend, and trained to meet with Him in a variety of meeting venues. Jersak suggests the following questions to get them started:

- Jesus lives in your heart. What does it look like? If He could meet you anywhere at all, what would that place look like? What is He doing there? (You may want to have the child draw or paint that place.)
- Jesus is with you in the house, the bedroom, the backyard, at school, everywhere. Where is He right now? What is He up to? What is He saying?[77]

Parents or spiritual caregivers can then ask the child to invite Jesus to come, to take action, to lift burdens, to speak truth, to comfort pain or to heal memories. It is our role as parents or spiritual caregivers to simply come alongside children as they invite Jesus into their lives, empowering them to hear from and see Jesus for themselves. When children begin to recognize the voice of God, they will be able to come before Him, finding Him in the situations that have brought them pain and sadness.

A Spiritual Practice for Children: Time With Abba (TWA)

Time with Abba (TWA) is an effective and meaningful spiritual practice that can be taught to children. It is based on Jesus' intimate relationship with the Father: Jesus called God the Father, *Abba*, which is Arabic for "Daddy."

While ministering on earth, Jesus also "often withdrew to lonely places and prayed" (Luke 5:16 NIV).

The practice, at its essential core, includes giving God one's full attention and spending uninterrupted time with Him. When children spend time with Abba, talking and listening to Him, they will begin to:

- Know Him
- Love Him more as He shows them His love
- Receive His strength to help them through tough times
- Gain His wisdom to make right decisions
- Grow to be more like Him[78]

Learning to Recognize God's Voice

Before children can hear God, they must learn to recognize the sound of God's voice. The Bible says God's voice is like a gentle whisper (see 1 Kings 19:11-12). Usually, it is not a whisper we can hear with our ears, but the Holy Spirit speaks directly to our spirits through spontaneous thoughts. "Spontaneous" means these thoughts seem to just appear in our hearts. They are not something we are already thinking about. When God puts His thoughts in our hearts, we often feel peace, faith, conviction or a special excitement. God can speak to children by putting a thought, a word, a picture, an idea, a feeling, an impression or even a vision in their hearts.

Psalm 46:10 says, "Be still, and know that I am God." Often the heart of a child is so broken it may be hard for him or her to hear God's whisper. We need to lead the child to focus on Jesus, to express the child's love for Him. This can be done by listening to worship music and asking the child to find a quiet place, and taking a moment to close their eyes and invite Jesus to meet with them.[79]

Disciplining children to hear and recognize God's voice can become an integral part of every day. As children practice this spiritual discipline, they will begin to talk to God about their troubled hearts. Children can and will receive the healing they need as they begin to recognize and hear God's voice.

Reading God's Word

Reading God's Word is important for children because God's Word is alive and active, sharper than a double-edged sword (see Hebrews 4:12). It can renew their minds and restore their wills. As children "eat" God's Word, it changes them from the inside out. There is nothing more powerful than the Word of God—the Truth—to replace the lies children have been told and currently believe about themselves.

As children begin to spend time with God's Word, either reading it or listening to it read aloud, they begin to feel more comfortable talking to Him about anything and everything in their lives: "And because we are his children, God has sent the Spirit of his Son into our hearts, prompting us to call out, 'Abba, Father'" (Gal. 4:6 NLT).[80] God's Word is powerful in quieting children's hearts and dispelling fears. As children begin to hear God's loving voice, healing thoughts will come to their hearts and produce positive change.

Writing and Drawing God's Thoughts

As we model and teach children the discipline of healing and listening prayer, it is often helpful to allow children to record the thoughts that come from God's heart. Ask the children to write down or draw pictures of the thoughts they are having. Instruct them to try not to discern if their writing or pictures are from God until they are done, as our doubts and judgments can often inhibit the voice of God speaking to us. After the children are done drawing or writing, they can go back and compare what they wrote to God's truth in the Bible. Encourage them to continue to write down or draw pictures of what God speaks to them from the Bible or His answer to any other questions they ask Him.

Bedtime Prayers

For children who are suffering with brokenness, night time is often a time where they are tormented with nightmares and night terrors. Converting bedtime prayers into listening prayers can bring healing while they sleep. Jersak encourages parents and spiritual caregivers to walk their children through a three-way conversational prayer between them, the child and Jesus. The adult can ask the question and the Lord can provide the answer, then the child can report it back to the adult. In *Children, Can You Hear Me?*, Jersak suggests the following starter questions:

- Jesus, is there anything today that we can thank You for? Why?

- Is there anything that we need to say sorry for? Will You forgive me?

- Is there anything You want us to pray for? How?

- Are there any burdens we are carrying that You want to lift for us? If so ask Jesus where the burden came from, what it is, and if He would please remove it.

- Jesus, do You have any promises or blessings for me before I go to sleep?

- Jesus, what was the best part of Your day? What made You happy?

Conclusion

Let us remember the little girl who said, "Everybody gets their heart broken sometimes, but now I know how to mend mine." On her graduation day from counseling, she also went on to say: "Having God in your heart does not mean nothing bad will happen to you. It does mean that even if bad things happen, God is with you, God loves you and God will strengthen you. He will make good things happen out of the bad."

PART IV

SKILLS FOR EFFECTIVE COUNSELING

ELEVEN

PEACE EDUCATION and CONFLICT RESOLUTION

Delores Friesen

As a counselor and teacher, I often meet victims of abuse, ignorance and suffering who are so discouraged they want to give up. In training others to work in the healing ministries of counseling, teaching and evangelism, I try to give at least as much attention to prevention and justice ministries as I do to the healing and caring ministries.

It is appropriate to feed the hungry, heal the wounded and rescue the perishing, but one also must ask why these persons are hungry, wounded and dying. A person cannot go on carrying out rescue operations without trying to find out why people keep falling into the river of despair and suffering.

If there is abuse, what can someone do to stop the violence? If there is war, how can the two sides come together in peace? If there are no options for growth and learning, how can anyone open up such avenues? This chapter focuses on prevention and healing by describing some resources for peacemaking and reconciliation, and detailing some basic conflict mediation and resolution skills.

Peace education and conflict resolution: Tools for meeting trauma

Previous chapters have described the kinds of emotions a traumatized child or person goes through: panic, exhaustion, guilt, rage, shame, protest, anxiety, denial, intrusive thoughts, numbing, hypervigilance, fear, confusion, impaired functioning and flashbacks. The next stage includes working through the trauma, helping the person to discover meaning, mourning and making new plans. In order to survive and grow beyond the crisis, a person needs to recover the ability to work, act and feel. One helpful tool is to give traumatized persons skills in resolving or meeting crisis and conflict, so they can face the future with some practical coping skills, and a sense of hope and personal power.

In crisis intervention work, a caregiver rapidly establishes connections and relationships, so the expression of painful feelings and emotions can happen. In discussing the events that have taken place, it is important to assess what has happened and form ideas of what you can do to restore some sense of well-being and safety. You will need both knowledge and skills to help resolve a crisis. Peacemaking and conflict resolution skills are useful both in processing trauma and pain, and in working toward the prevention of violence and war. If a person has concrete ways to respond to threats and oppression, this lessens the sense of helplessness and victimization. These skills can bring hope, empower the weak and restore relationships.

If you are working in a religious setting, there are many passages and stories in both the Old and New Testaments that illustrate and illuminate these concepts. The Beatitudes in Matthew 5; Psalms 34 and 85; Jeremiah 8:11-15; Luke 1:46-55, 68-79 and Matthew 18 are particularly helpful.

Children have most of their problems in one of the following areas: conflict with others, conflict with self, lack of information about self, lack of skill and lack of information about the environment. As individuals, we often have conflict with others. We may also have internal conflict with self, lack of information about self or lack of information about the environment. These areas account for most of the problems human beings encounter. Learning conflict resolution and peacemaking skills is a very significant way of meeting both personal and interpersonal needs.

Healing through story

Storytelling is a very important way of releasing internal feelings and conflicts. In the Liberia conflict, adults and children often recounted what it meant for them to "walk the road." Verbalizing the terrors of seeing persons killed, scattered and lost became part of the healing process, for both the speakers and the listeners. Poetry, story writing and drawing may also serve as outlets for feelings and experiences that are unspeakable or difficult to share.

One storytelling technique that may help to give support is to have a group of people form a circle. Two to four persons go into the center of the circle to tell their story, and then exchange places with others in the outer circle until all who wish to tell their story have done so. This "fishbowl" method makes the speaker feel listened to and surrounds the speaker with a circle of caring persons.

The other person or persons inside the circle may wish to hold hands or otherwise physically touch the speaker, or respond with encouraging gestures or eye contact. This is not a time for discussion, however. Simply let the speakers tell their stories in an environment of support and affirmation. This will encourage the listeners to make peace by grasping the depth of pain and suffering experienced by others. Those who share their stories often experience some release and healing.

If there are other sources of stories, life experience and history available in your setting, use them to dramatize and illustrate the principles that follow. For example, in my religious tradition there is a large book called *Martyrs Mirror*, which contains thousands of stories of persons who were martyred for their faith from the time of Jesus through the seventeenth century. When I was a child and young adult, these stories were shared in many settings at home, church and school. They served as an inspiration and example of what it means to follow the way of Jesus in life and death. One of the more famous stories is that of Dirk Willems.

In 1569, Dirk Willems was jailed because of his religious beliefs. He managed to escape, but a prison guard observed him and pursued him across an ice-covered pond. As he reached the opposite side, Willems turned and saw that his pursuer had fallen through the ice. Dirk turned back and saved the man's life. Willems was recaptured, jailed and burned at the stake. Despite his heroic rescue of his enemy, the authorities still killed him. He had the kind of commitment it took to love an enemy and give up his life for doing good. These historical examples help motivate us to exercise faith and learn skills of peace. Nelson Mandela and Mother Teresa are two notable examples whose stories you can tell or dramatize.

You can also create and stage biblical dramas. A biblical drama created in Ghana grew out of a South African sermon on the first Adam and the second Adam. As the preacher told it, the first Adam—the ancestor of all humankind—went to heaven and held a place of honor there. But he had to bear the consequences of his sin. Therefore, from his seat in heaven, he had to watch all the hatred and killing, lying and cruelty that resulted from his sin. He watched Cain kill Abel, Joseph's brothers sell Joseph into slavery, King David with Bathsheba and Uriah, and many other events in biblical history, finally leading up to the events surrounding Jesus' crucifixion.

As each event unfolded, the first Adam hung his head, beat his breast and said, "Oh, my God, my God, what have I begun? The weight of my sin and guilt is too much to bear," or "My guilt, my guilt . . . isn't there anything that can be done?" When, finally, the second Adam walks into heaven declaring He has won the victory over sin and death, the sermon and drama close with the powerful words, "And the first Adam had peace."

"Solomon's Wisdom" is another powerful biblical drama created by some participants in the healing and reconciliation workshops in Liberia. They simply portrayed the dilemma of the two mothers who both claimed that one child was theirs and linked that story to that of their country's civil war. It provided a very powerful and spiritual moment of truth and insight.

Language, drama, music, dance and art are media for the expression of feelings, dreams, vision, hope and despair. It is important to allow the telling of both negative and positive experiences. Healing and reconciliation come only in the acknowledgment of darkness and terror. When in trouble, allow the full, free and total expression of laments. Pouring out a lament is not an expression of a lack of trust. Consider the place of lament in the Psalms, in Job's experience, in literature and music. It is also helpful to engage in illusory thinking, "I would that there were . . . ," as a way of moving beyond present despair.

Stories acknowledge the deep human needs for love, safety, shelter and warmth. Listening to and telling stories help us to belong, to love and to survive. A storytelling circle or community is interconnected, balanced and purposeful. It processes pain, lays the foundation for seeking solutions to problems, and encourages and strengthens a sense of solidarity and understanding. The Lord God asked the children of Israel to recount His marvelous deeds, lest they forget how they survived the wilderness, the Red Sea, and the plagues and oppression of Egypt.

Memorials of stones, places, altars and events can also serve as sacred reminders of the experiences of inhumanity and grief. Remember Job, who wished that his words were engraved in a rock so that no one would forget what he had suffered (see Job 19:24)? Part of peacemaking within may require some outward symbol or sign of acknowledgment. Naming those who have died, bringing symbols of suffering or healing to a worship table, planting something to symbolize new life or composing a song are some signs that come to mind.

Defining community and conflict

A warm and caring community needs these five qualities:

- Cooperation
- Communication
- Tolerance
- Positive emotional expression
- Conflict resolution

Things that work against such a peaceful atmosphere include competition, intolerance, poor communication, inappropriate expression of emotion, lack of conflict resolution skills and misuse of power. Situations charged with bad feelings, lack of trust, unresolved or suppressed conflicts, irrational or impossibly high expectations, inflexible rules and an authoritarian use of power create an atmosphere of fear and mistrust. Conflicts tend to fall into three areas: 1) Conflict over resources—two or more parties want something that is scarce; 2) Conflict over needs—needs for power, safety, food, self-determination, friendship, self-esteem and achievement; and 3) Conflicting values and beliefs. The last area is the most difficult type of conflict to resolve. Challenging a person's values threatens a person's sense of self, and people cling to positions with a tenacity that other types of conflict do not inspire. Goal conflicts are also value conflicts.

Most of us know only three ways to respond to conflict: 1) Respond aggressively, that is, physically, verbally or in some other way to defeat our opponent; 2) Appeal to a higher authority or someone stronger to battle for us; or 3) Ignore the situation.

These are ineffective ways to resolve conflict. Instead, they increase both internal and external stress and tension. Everyone needs to develop peacemaking skills, and learn how and when to apply them most effectively.

Conflicts *escalate* (grow bigger and more serious) if:

- There is an increase in exposed emotion, such as anger and frustration
- There is an increase in perceived threat
- More people get involved, choosing sides
- The children were not friends prior to the conflict
- The children have few peacemaking skills at their disposal

Conflicts *de-escalate* or are more easily resolved if:

- Attention is focused on the problem, not on the participants
- There is a decrease in exposed emotions and perceived threats
- The children were friends prior to the conflict
- The children know how to make peace or have someone to help them to do so
- One person cools the conflict, keeping it from spreading and becoming more violent, and channels it along positive rather than negative lines

This is very different from the aggressive and passive ways most of us use to handle conflicts. Physical or emotional hurt, humiliation and suppressed anger accompany passive and aggressive responses. Such responses also tend not to solve problems, are ineffective and leave us at the mercy of a conflict, feeling overwhelmed by it and powerless to respond effectively. "Either the other person wins or I win." This locks persons into a behavior pattern with no apparent way out.

Teaching children to be peacemakers

Preventing conflicts is the work of politics; establishing peace is the work of education. - Maria Montessori

Conflict resolution and peace education means learning a whole range of responses that lie between aggression and inaction. It is looking for constructive alternatives and acting on them. Losing and winning are not the only options.

Instead, a person tries to generate solutions or come to new understandings of the situation: "Let's talk." "Let's look for a solution." "What are the underlying needs and wants?" For example, a fight is a concentration of physical and emotional energy. Anything you can do to divert this energy will help cool the situation. What are the needs of the two persons who are fighting? Does someone feel disrespected? Made fun of? Put down? Are there inadequate resources to go around? The simplest way to deal with a fight is to:

- Break it up
- Cool it off
- Work it out

We can summarize problem-solving techniques as defining the problem, producing solutions and choosing and acting. It is not easy to identify problems in terms of needs, but it is an important first step in working toward a solution or an "I win, you win" stance.

William Kriedler suggests considering the following four things when you need to choose a conflict resolution technique:

1. Who is involved? How old, how mature, how angry are they? What are their needs?

2. Is the time right? Do you have enough time to work things out now or should you wait? Do the participants need to cool off first? Is it too soon to talk things out?

3. How appropriate is a particular resolution technique?

4. Should the resolution be public or private? Would the persons involved be embarrassed or would others benefit from seeing the conflict resolved? Could these other beneficiaries help with the resolution?[81]

There are many skills that facilitate the smooth management of conflict. Some of these are cooperation and communication skills, the ability to express feelings constructively and tolerance of diversity. Learning to tolerate and appreciate diversity is another aspect of peacemaking that we should not neglect. Conflicts often arise out of a lack of acceptance or understanding. Learning about other cultures, languages and religions, and noticing the pluses and minuses of having different customs, inheritances and values will help to open the door to fruitful conversation. We need to confront, acknowledge and understand prejudice or it will undermine attempts to resolve conflict and make peace.

A conflict resolution technique simply provides a safe, structured way to air grievances, feelings and differences of opinion so that a conflict can serve a useful purpose. Some useful techniques include: cooling off, mediation, smoothing, reflective listening, storytelling, time-out, written fight forms for children to report problems, role-playing, role reversals, the problem puppets and the three "R" strategy: resentment, request, recognition.

There is also the "fight fair" method: State the facts as calmly as possible and refer only to the present situation, not to the past or future. Express how you feel. Talk about your feelings without making negative remarks about the other person. Find out what you can do about the situation. Try to think of a solution that will satisfy all the participants.

Advocacy and action

Too often we give children answers to remember rather than problems to solve.
- Roger Lewis

Peacemaking includes internal processing, external action and witness. Persons whose way of life has been destroyed by violence or trauma often need persons to advocate for them. They also need to learn the skills of advocacy and political action. Four of the steps that bring change are: 1) becoming aware, 2) gathering resources, 3) developing models and 4) challenging structures.

Paul Tournier says "the key to the problem of violence is to be found in that of power: that benign violence is that which is put at the service of others, protecting the weak, healing the sick, liberating the exploited, fighting the injustice of the powerful; and that improper violence is violence on one's own behalf, aimed at securing power for oneself, violence which is inspired by the fascination of power."[82] He goes on to suggest that a major difference between power and violence is that power is accessible to reflection, while violence is unleashed passion, a kind of rage that suspends all reason.

Violence has short-term, immediate objectives in mind. Empowerment works out a whole strategy, weighs dangers, sets limits and develops all the stages of progress. Conflict resolution and peace making skills are tools to empower and engage persons in settling differences and meeting needs.

Teaching students and others to be peacemakers

The following are several lists of issues and topics to discuss in the process of learning to be peacemakers.

A global perspective: global awareness; basic facts and comparisons; global connectedness; global interdependence; trade relations; resources; religion; social, political and economic interrelations between nations; crosscultural understandings; and an appreciation and respect for diversity, while emphasizing similarities—finding common ground.

Conflict resolution skills, ranging from a personal to a global level: defining conflicts; understanding the causes of conflicts; gathering information; examining facts and feelings; generating and choosing solutions; and using critical thinking skills.

Peacemaking strategies: a study of and participation in strategies resulting in a just and peaceful world, including cultural exchanges and networking; use of nonviolence and pacifism; religions; respect and empathy for human rights; economic, environmental, scientific and other cooperation; force and deterrence; and a historical review of peacemakers.

A conflict resolution model

Although it is not the only way to organize conflict resolution skills, the SIGEP models (Stop - Identify - Generate - Evaluate - Plan) may be one of the easiest to remember.[83]

Stop

When you find yourself being drawn into a conflict, the first step is to stop and decide how you want to handle the conflict. If you decide to negotiate, the first step is to calm down enough to negotiate.

Identify the problem

Sometimes the problem is straightforward, at other times it is not. State concerns in terms of "needs" rather than "solution." A need is the underlying concern. A solution is one way to meet the underlying need. Make sure both parties agree to what the problem is about. It may be necessary to look at things from the other party's perspective to correctly identify the problem. Stating the problem in terms of needs instead of solutions, increases the possible ways to get what someone wants. This also increases the chances of finding something that works well for both parties.

Generate (Gather) ideas

The more ideas you have, the more likely you are to find ones on which you can agree. Try to come up with at least twenty ideas. When you generate ideas, include some "crazy" ones, as well as practical ones. This helps everyone get past the one-sided, typical, too-easy answers. If you cannot move forward, you can return to the problem and review it or look at the "idea starters" below. Remember that this is the time to free your imagination. You can evaluate the ideas after you generate them.

Idea starters: Who else can do it? Where else can we do it? What else can we use to do it or solve the problem? What can we add to make it easier? What can we remove to eliminate the problem? How would an expert solve the problem? What would Jesus do about this? How would God handle the problem?

Evaluate the ideas

Read the list of ideas one by one and check on how everyone feels about each idea. Put a star by each idea for every person who finds the idea acceptable. During this process, people will often object to particular ideas. Jot those objections down, as well. If you have several ideas that everyone likes, you can go on to making a decision. If no idea has everyone's approval, then consider the ideas with the most supporters and see how you can modify them to make them acceptable to the others. Remind yourselves that you are committed to finding an idea that works for everyone. When you have evaluated all the ideas and at least one idea is acceptable to everyone involved in the conflict, you can then make a decision and implement it.

Develop a plan

Many good ideas falter because there is no plan for implementation and evaluation. Differences arise in people's expectations when there are many issues to resolve. When you make a decision, consider how to implement it. Consider, also, what could go wrong with the decision, and if there is an alternate or "backup" plan that everyone finds acceptable. Plan how you might handle the situation. Unexpected problems rarely cause major difficulties if there is a structure for dealing with them. If things do not work out, go back to the beginning and start again or return to another idea you generated in step three.

Mediation

Sometimes it is necessary to have a third party or outside mediator come in to help with the process. Mediation is simply a process by which the parties to the conflict consult with a neutral third party to settle the areas of disagreement. The mediator does not dictate or decide the solution, but helps both sides listen to each other and work together to find a mutually agreeable solution.

This often reduces the anxiety, anger and communication problems, and it can help to clarify the areas of agreement and nonagreement. A mediator may take several roles: educator or expert, translator, message carrier, discussion facilitator, summarizer, rebuilder of relationships, agent of reality, face-saver, lightning rod or idea generator. In other words, a mediator may be able to listen to both sides *when hostility or tension is too high for either party to speak directly to the other.*

See Matthew 18 for some biblical guidelines for when and how to use a mediation process. A mediator keeps a balance between control and participation, makes sure the issues are identified and clarified, points out areas of agreement and disagreement, and summarizes.

The process of mediation is very similar to the SIGEP model, but it can often identify blocks or why the process does not work. Mediation usually includes: 1) Introduction—who is there, what will happen, ground rules, clarification of the mediator's role, expectations, what happens if the parties cannot agree; 2) Gathering information—presenting problems, safety concerns, availability of resources and support; 3) Isolating issues and finding hidden agendas—underlying causes, communication blocks, motivations, power differences; 4) Development of alternatives—brainstorming, suggestions, recommendations; and 5) Decisions and production of agreement.

A mediator needs the following skills and techniques:

- Ability to build and maintain trust and confidence
- Ability to clarify issues, ask questions, summarize
- Ability to break deadlocks or impasses
- Ability to help the parties save face
- Ability to keep emotions under control
- Ability to identify power differences and hidden agendas
- Ability to separate needs from motivations and wants

Other roles and methods

Some other roles that may be needed in conflict resolution and peace-making are that of *observer* (helps to discourage violence, documents what is happening), *sustainer* (helps locate resources and support so the parties will not give up), *legitimizer* (helps establish the credibility of the weaker party's needs, may also verify legal rights), *advocate* (a sustainer and legitimizer who speaks for the weaker party, may represent persons to government or others who hold power), *resources expander* (helps persons access the system and network, so everyone stands to win more) and *activist* (arouses energy that can be channeled toward constructive change).

Another way to think of the conflict resolution process is: introduction, storytelling, problem solving and agreement.

In the *introduction* stage, you want just the parties involved present (as few people as possible). Establish guidelines for the process.

In the storytelling stage, persons or sides describe their feelings, talk about when-who-what caused the situation or problem, then try to get to the root cause or "why" questions, before turning to solutions. Listen for facts, feelings, demands, possible solutions and needs to reflect what you are hearing or encourage more detail to clarify the situation. Some examples of what you might say are: "Tell me more about that." "So you felt that was really unfair?" "What would you like to have happen next?" "Could you explain that?" "What do you mean by____?" "I am not sure I understand that." "Could you elaborate?"

In the *problem-solving* stage, list areas that need resolution and focus on issues of both agreement and disagreement. Ask such questions as: "What will it take to resolve these issues?" "Where does common ground exist?" "Where or from whom can I get what I need to make agreement possible?" This stage may take a lot of patience. It helps to brainstorm solutions, list solution criteria, evaluate the solutions against the criteria established and then develop the best or most acceptable answer. Resolution is based on: satisfying needs, saving face and self-respect. You may need to recognize and express anger, but do so with "I" messages rather than "you" messages. Ask questions in order to learn and to generate possible solutions, rather than to accuse or blame.

In the *agreement* stage, summarize the process and solution clearly and in detail, so everyone understands what it is they have agreed to: "Each of you has agreed to do certain things." "You have agreed to do____. Is that right?" Establish ownership of the agreement. Sometimes a written or symbolic form is helpful at this point. Follow up to see if the solution reached is still satisfactory.

What if all attempts fail?

If the parties do not reach an agreement, then it is important to stay in contact with them. Over time, more trust may develop, or there may be new information or developments that will help to soften attitudes. New events tend to work in favor of compromise and resolution. Sometimes parties weary of the frustration and expense of continued discord and fighting. Spiritually and emotionally wounded people may need time to heal and open up to God's grace.

When there is no resolution, agree to meet again. Recognize and help individuals express anger and hurt in safe and appropriate places and ways. Use "I" messages to further define the problem and ask questions to learn more about the needs of each person involved.

When everyone negotiates in good faith, the goal is resolution. A win-win solution preserves the dignity of both parties. It helps to be specific and open to facts. The ability to initiate conversation and maintain a humble spirit that thinks the best of people are two other very valuable peacemaking skills. We can see conflict as a tool that helps us to understand and meet needs. *It can be constructive, if it helps to identify evil and stops violence from happening.* Conflict resolution leads to healing and restoration. It also ensures that needs are met, at least in part, or that people are willing to continue the conversational process.

System adaptability depends on leadership, rules and roles, negotiation, organization and values. System cohesion—how to balance autonomy and separateness with mutuality and togetherness—depends on how individuals deal with closeness, support, decision making, commonality and unity. In order to move from victim to survivor to peacemaker, people must be adaptable and maintain both separateness and connectedness.

Peacemaking and conflict resolution skills are invaluable in developing flexibility in the face of crisis. Individuals have to take responsibility for their own future and emotional well-being, yet remain emotionally engaged with others in the system, even if they are enemies. Resist focusing on changing others, do not get too anxious and keep clear boundaries of safety and self. Jesus, Martin Luther King, Mother Teresa and Nelson Mandela are individuals who have been able to live out these principles in powerful and life-changing ways that have enabled many others to find hope, salvation, healing and *shalom.*

TWELVE

THE JOURNEY of CROSS-CULTURAL COUNSELING

Leah Herod and Harvey Payne

Before going on a journey, a person will make preparations. They find out about the destination, anticipate what they will need, pack their bags, begin the travel, and finally arrive and settle in. In a similar way, a lay counselor can prepare for working cross-culturally with children. The Christian lay counselor can consider how much experience he or she has with children and with counseling, as well as determine his or her knowledge of counseling principles and biblical principles. If there are gaps in experience or knowledge, it is beneficial to discern that and work to remedy it prior to departure. He or she should recognize these preparations will be helpful, but there will inevitably be adaptations in the new culture, and the lay counselor will need help in making the adjustments. The lay counselor's attitude will be critical in how well he or she adjusts and is accepted in the culture. Humility is key. Entering the culture with the attitude of being a learner, rather than an expert, will likely serve to foster relationships. These relationships may facilitate the awareness of counseling to people in the community. Ultimately, the lay counselor will know he or she is at home in the new culture when the counselor is able to relate to children in that culture naturally, while demonstrating the truth of the gospel in a caring and culturally appropriate way.

Preparing

My Bags Are Packed!

A traveler will get ready for a journey by gathering clothing and basic necessities into a suitcase. A lay counselor who is going to work cross-culturally with children will pack one bag with experience and one bag with knowledge. It is important to have experience with children and experience with counseling before setting out. In addition, knowledge of counseling principles and biblical principles are necessary. The next section will outline key aspects of experience and knowledge.

Suitcase One: Experience

Experience with Children

Besides the fact that we were all once children, our experiences with children vary widely. Some have had a lifelong involvement with children, perhaps have had their own children; and some will have had little experience with children, but will see the need to minister to children in a new context. Regardless of the amount of experience with children, few have taken the time to simply be with children. To watch, listen and really hear their inner experience. We, too often, view children as simply short adults who have limited knowledge and experience. In some sense, children are aliens who think, feel and respond in very different ways than adults.

Although they grow up to be adults, children start out and develop in ways that most adults have forgotten. Lay counselors must go back and learn about this forgotten time to truly help children. If children are treated as if they were adults, a profound opportunity to minister effectively to them will be missed.

Adults are mostly verbal in perceiving and understanding. Actions are usually (not always) filtered through a process of reasoning. Adults have a sense of who they are, the life experiences that have shaped a sense of self, and filter life—consciously and unconsciously—through this viewpoint. We understand ourselves and others out of a sense of being able to observe, think and respond. Children are not so.

From birth to around the age of eighteen to twenty-four months, infants' and toddlers' responses are primarily unfiltered reflexes to sensory information (smell, taste, touch, sound, sight and movement) and especially to pain and pleasure.[84] Experiences of distress and joy are not remembered consciously, but become embedded within the infant and toddler. The emotional tone of numerous interactions over time either increases or decreases the child's ability to trust, relax and enjoy his world. In a sense, the child "incorporates" the world around him into his soul without knowing it.

The experience of a warm and nurturing mother, in a stable environment with minimal stress, creates an emotional tone and response style of relaxed trust for most children. However, some children are born with a high-strung, untrusting temperament that makes it harder for the mother and child to connect and bond. Likewise, a mother with little nutrition for herself living in a chaotic and threatening world communicates this emotional distress to her child. Some children incorporate this emotional tone into a hypersensitivity and hyperarousal response, where they are easily agitated, frustrated and hard to soothe.[85] Others may develop a dulled or blunted response, regardless of the stimulation provided. Sometimes, children respond with a mix of both extremes, and sometimes, by God's grace, some children are born with a highly resilient temperament that appears little damaged by the stress of the outside world. Around eighteen to twenty-four months, with the mastery of walking and running and the development of language, children begin to have a slow, developing sense of control of their impulses and perceptions. If you will, they experience their world and self as many fragments or puzzle pieces, but no sense of a coherent whole picture of their self or their world. They cannot comprehend the whole. They have little ability to make sense of significant events—good or bad—and they thus often misinterpret much of what happens around them.

God has made us with an innate desire to create meaning out of life (see Prov. 25:2); and yet, imagine a situation in which you only understand 20 percent of what you hear and only 25 percent of what you see. What misunderstandings and distortions you would make! This is the life of a young child, fully experiencing life, but comprehending so very little. Part of the foolishness of a child in Proverbs is not rebellion but developmental. A child who believes his father can do anything and then watches his father do nothing while his mother is dying, can easily believe his father chose to allow his mother to die. The child who believes she is the only one being abused by a trusted adult can mistakenly believe she is being abused because there is something dreadfully wrong with her compared to the others who are not abused.

This developmental process of primarily unfiltered reflexes to the world of sensory input, incorporating the emotional tone of their world into their soul, and slowly developing fragmented and often inaccurate concepts of themselves and the world, lasts much longer than most adults realize. We mistakenly assume increased verbal language with accurate and realistic understanding. Without positive support, instruction and guidance, many children carry these affective tones, thinking distortions and response patterns into adulthood. With sensitive responding and counseling, these emotional and thinking distortions can be healed.

Somewhere between the ages of five to seven, children begin to perceive and understand their self and world in a different way. They develop an understanding of their needs, interests and desires in a more clear and coherent fashion. Children begin to develop a sense of their role in their family and community, learn to follow the rules (communicated both directly and indirectly) they are expected to live by and practice the daily rituals that make up their life. This period lasts from this transitional period of five to seven years of age until puberty or adolescence.

Children who have had secure, loving attachments with sensitive, age-appropriate explanations of life tend to develop realistic, fulfilling roles; follow rules as a means of pleasing others and gaining positive recognition; and live out daily rituals that bring meaning, a sense of security, and a growing recognition of their God-given significance in the life of their family and community. Children living in traumatic, chaotic and/or abusive situations develop survival and "masked" roles, struggle to make sense of and follow rules that are often contradictory and random, and find rituals often meaningless or overly rigid.

Not until adolescence do children really begin perceiving and thinking much like adults, and even then in immature and limited ways. They begin to use their rational and verbal abilities to better understand and reframe their life experience. However, their more basic, unfiltered reflexes to sensory and emotional responding continues to break through long into adulthood. For the adult with secure, loving childhood attachments these emotional breakthroughs are experienced as positive, authentic reflections of their self. For the adult with a traumatic, chaotic and/or abuse history, these emotional breakthroughs can be experienced as intrusive, conflicted and even painful.

The lay counselor who has experience with children and who is aware that they experience the world differently, will have a better chance of relating to a child in a cross-cultural setting.

Experience with Counseling

Some people are natural healers, and others come to them for advice and comfort. These natural healers may not be aware they already possess some of the qualities research has demonstrated to be vital when counseling others. Counseling research has shown the most important factor in change is the relationship between the counselor and the counselee (person seeking counsel). When looking at characteristics of the counselor, characteristics of the counselee, and the type of treatment offered, the most important part is the relationship between the counselor and counselee. Within the relationship, effective counselors provide empathy and acceptance, while being genuine.

Some of the natural healers, although they may not have had formal training, have skills that enable them to connect easily with others. Some of these skills can be taught to enhance the relationship. Some of the fundamental counseling skills include attentive listening and the attunement to nonverbal cues. Attentive listening has been divided into components that include summarizing, paraphrasing, asking appropriate questions and reflecting. The lay counselor who has worked only with adults may not realize counseling with children requires modification of these basic skills and expectations. With an adult, it may be typical to discuss an issue or concern for an hour or more. It has already been established in the first section of this book that children are not miniature adults. They process and interact differently from adults. Children cannot be expected to talk for an extended time like an adult might.

Children "show" you what is wrong more than tell you. Children may not have the verbal skills or attunement (awareness) to know and verbalize what they are thinking and feeling. They may demonstrate what they are feeling through facial expression; indirect means, such as creative expression (art, drawing); and play interactions with toys. The counselor should pay attention to how they interact with toys, what they say and how these expressions change during play. Through creative outlets, such as art and play, they may reenact things that concern them. The counselor, rather than asking a question, may simply reflect or comment on what the child is doing. The lay counselor who has experience with counseling has probably already developed a template or framework for interacting with children and for discerning what is typical childhood behavior or development. This experience will be important as the counselor enters another culture, in that there are commonalities between cultures in how children react and interact.

Suitcase Two: Knowledge

Knowledge of Basic Counseling Principles

It is beneficial for the lay counselor to have a framework, or paradigm, for understanding how people change. This is like a road map of where you are going, how to get there and what to expect. Whether articulated or not, all people have developed a model of how the world and people in it are to act. Recognizing, understanding and evaluating your model in light of Scripture and basic counseling research can help increase your effectiveness in working with children.

Children may be in a difficult situation where the context is unlikely to change. For a child who is in a troubling situation, it is important to give him tools so he is less likely to feel like a victim, with no ability to change or alter his situation. One way to assist the child is to guide him toward grasping his resources. The lay counselor can focus the child's attention on what he does have, who he is or what he can do. In other words, the counselor is promoting a sense of security, good self-concept and self-efficacy. These are sources of resilience.[86] researched resilience in cross-cultural settings and demonstrated it can be promoted. The table below is taken directly from Grotberg's work and lists phrases within each category that were used in working with children:

I HAVE	I AM	I CAN
People around me I trust and who love me, no matter what	A person people can like and love	Talk to others about things that frighten or bother me
People who set limits for me so that I know when to stop before there is danger or trouble	Glad to do nice things for others and show my concern	Find ways to solve problems that I face
People who show me how to do things right by the way they do things	Respectful of myself and others	Control myself when I feel like doing something not right or dangerous
People who want me to learn to do things on my own	Willing to be responsible for what I do	Figure out when it is a good time to talk to someone or to take action
People who help me when I am sick, in danger, or need to learn	Sure things will be all right	Find someone to help me when I need it

(Grotberg, 1995, p. 9-10).[87]

Not only can the lay counselor promote resilience in children, but he or she can teach parents and community members to do so, as well. This simple technique is easy to convey and can have a powerful impact. In addition, it can be taught quickly and there is less concern of doing harm if the counselor is only working for a short time with the child or family.

Knowledge of Biblical Truth/Principles

For Christians, it is essential to know general biblical truths and principles. The Christian lay counselor recognizes that the Bible is the foundation of counseling, prayer is an integral part of counseling and dependence on the Holy Spirit is crucial. The lay counselor will rely on these three aspects regardless of the culture or the counseling issue.

First, the Bible is the foundation through which any theory must be filtered. It is helpful to realize that there are general truths in the Bible that can be applied in any context, regardless of the religion of the counselee. Proverbs has many of these truths as guidelines for living. Beyond that, however, there are truths that do not necessitate a scriptural reference. There are truths about a person's worth and purpose. Life has meaning. The counselee can contribute something to the world. They are unique. There is someone (actually Someone) who cares about them.

Second, the Holy Spirit guides the believer. It is important for the Christian to be attuned to the Holy Spirit. The Holy Spirit may lead the counselor to speak a certain truth or may lead the counselor to be silent. The Spirit may prompt a certain activity that will enable a child to grasp the concept the counselor is trying to convey. The Spirit not only provides this wisdom in counseling, but also the power that makes counseling effective.

Third, prayer is vital for the Christian counselor. This does not mean the prayer is spoken aloud and it does not mean the counselee is even aware the counselor is praying. Since the Lord hears at all times, the counselor can pray silently while counseling.

As noted above, it is not uncommon for a child (or adult) to have beliefs that are not true. These lies can be confronted with truth. Some examples are as follows:

Lie	Truth	Biblical Basis
I am worth nothing	You are valuable	God the Father created each person with infinite value in His image.
Nobody cares about me	I care about you(name others)	Jesus Christ so loved each person that He died for us.

Nothing will get better	Things change, there is always hope	Hope does not put us to shame, because the Holy Spirit pours God's transforming love into our hearts.
I have no purpose	There is a purpose for you	We are God's workmanship created for good works.
I cannot do anything	You can do something	I can do all things through Christ.

Just like a traveler will evaluate whether he or she has what is necessary for a journey, the lay counselor can evaluate if she has what is needed for cross-cultural counseling with children. The lay counselor may realize she has a light bag of knowledge, and may work to increase her knowledge by talking with others, reading books and researching relevant topics. Alternatively, she may realize her bag of experience is light and may work to increase it by volunteering/working with children or by finding a counselor to mentor her. It is beneficial for the counselor to evaluate whether she has adequate experience and knowledge prior to departure.

While biblical truths must be introduced and discussed in culturally sensitive ways, these truths and the practiced faith of Christians can actually provide real advantages in relating to people from other cultures. These advantages are outlined in the article "Christian Counselors' Resources for Multi-cultural Understanding and Counseling."[88] As believers, we have a viable way of knowing truth that is compatible with many cultures—an authoritative source of knowledge, the Bible. We believe God speaks and acts in powerful and healing ways within the community of faith. Although Christianity has a focus on individual responsibility (see Ezek. 18), the responsibility of the community is an equally strong concept, as in many non-Western cultures. We have amazing stories from Scripture to tell that all fit within the great universal story of God's process of redemption. Especially in oral-tradition cultures, stories can be very powerful and transforming. Consistent with many cultures, Scripture teaches a spiritual and supernatural reality that is more than just the physical world of sensory experience. In addition, this spiritual world is understood on three levels: the Supreme Spirit (God), intermediate spiritual beings (angels and demons) and earthly spiritual beings (humans). The concept of forgiveness rooted in sacrifice is an ancient and almost universal concept. The use of symbols, especially religious symbols, is appreciated and found to be healing in different cultures. For many Christians, being a minority in their own culture can help with understanding and connecting with other minority groups in another culture. The apostle Paul found common ground in other cultures with biblical Christianity to use as a bridge in communicating God's truth, such as when he addresses the Areopagus in Acts 17.

Planning

Map for the Journey

Generally, when visiting a new place, a person will take a map and have a plan. With cross-cultural counseling, it is helpful to plan for entering the destination country. Many people think they are ready when their bags are packed. However, there is an additional preparation that can help prior to boarding the plane. Knowing about the place and people before arriving will save time and speed adaptation. Research can be done by searching on the Internet and talking with people who have been to the destination, or who are from there. It is particularly beneficial to find out about typical attire and recent geopolitical events.

The lay counselor does not want to offend simply by what he or she wears, since this is an easy thing to avoid. In some countries, women only wear dresses while men wear pants. Only children are allowed to wear shorts in some places. T-shirts may be acceptable, but the logo or message on the shirt may be offensive. Medical personnel in North America may wear scrubs, but that might be offensive in some cultures because it is seen as disrespectful (if the culture is more formal). In some cultures, it is OK for women to show their midriff, while in others they cannot show their ankle. The clothing a lay counselor wears can immediately alienate him or her and reveal the counselor as different, or can immediately show respect of the local culture.

A second aspect the lay counselor can research is recent events in the country. It is important to have an idea about national events, such as natural disasters, wars, political controversies and so on. By being informed, the lay counselor can anticipate some of the concerns of the locals. For example, a year after the 2005 tsunami in Indonesia, people were still living in temporary housing such as tents and barracks. They had access to food and water, but the living conditions were crowded. Therefore, there was an issue of privacy and conflict ensued from being unsettled. Immediately after a natural disaster, there is concern for safety, shelter and nourishment. The counselor may help by problem solving and being directive immediately after a disaster, while later on, the focus may be on coping and adjusting to the new reality.

If the counselor is informed about who she plans to work with, then she can anticipate what type of issues might be related to that group. For example, there are a number of challenges that might be particularly relevant when working with refugees. When working with refugees or displaced people, it is beneficial to be informed about the conflict that led to the people fleeing their home. The lay counselor may be able to find out the facts prior to arrival, which will speed the process of learning about the impact on the people. And, the counselor can anticipate what issues might be relevant. In the case of a refugee, the lay counselor can expect there may be grief, due to leaving one's home suddenly—even possibly leaving family behind. Or, there may be extreme stress and worries due to witnessing violence. Refugees will likely have some issues with adjustment, since they are in a new culture and likely fled their home due to fear of harm, rather than simply a desire to move. In addition, the host country of the refugees may not like their presence and the refugees could experience discrimination, which could also cause stress. In essence, the response and intervention by a lay counselor will be different based on recent events. If the counselor researches recent events, she may be able to anticipate the needs and challenges of the people/children with whom she desires to work.

Arrival

Unpacking

When the counselor arrives in the new culture, she will begin to notice she cannot use everything she brought with her in the same way. Her suitcase, filled with knowledge and experience, was useful in her home country, but may not be adequate, or may need to be modified in their new setting.

A counselor must consider what is normative, or typical, for the culture she has entered. "Culture influences what gets defined as a problem, how the problem is understood and which solutions to the problem are acceptable."[89] Research demonstrates people vary in the following: their experience of pain, beliefs about the origin of pain, what is labeled as a symptom, how the symptom/pain is conveyed[90] The lay counselor may notice people complain about somatic (bodily) pain rather than emotional pain, either because it is more acceptable or because they do not recognize the emotional pain. For example, a child may complain about having a stomach ache every day at school. It might be the child is anxious and is having a tummy ache because he or she is worried. There may also be cultural differences as to the origin of pain or trauma. The interpretation of why a trauma occurred could vary from scientific to supernatural explanations. The culture may see trauma or pain being accidental, bad luck, punishment from God, an evil spirit, "God's will," a curse from others, failure in a parent or due to a scientific reason. The lay counselor should be cautious in the message she gives to the child about the trauma, as it may directly contradict the cultural message. It can cause conflict with parents for a lay counselor to undermine their authority and give a message to their child that is not acceptable in that culture.

Counselors are often unaware of the beliefs held within a different culture and may inadvertently behave inappropriately. They may use illustrations that are, at best, not understandable and at worst, have the opposite meaning. In a culture where hierarchy is important, leaders are experts. Individuals from that culture may perceive they have less power and are likely to be reluctant to correct mistakes by the counselor. Subsequently, the counselor may fail to effectively deliver an understandable intervention without realizing it. It is a case of "not knowing what you do not know" that causes these problems.

In addition, what seems to be the normal procedure, or even a necessary procedure, may be inappropriate in a given culture. For example, with any suspicion of child abuse in the United States, counselors must report their concerns to the appropriate state agency (Department of Social Services, Department of Human Resources). The department is responsible for investigating and taking action. When in another country, there will be different procedures for reporting abuse. Even the definition of abuse may be different. What is defined as abuse in one context may not be considered abuse in another context. Corporal punishment in a school setting may be acceptable in one place and not acceptable in another. In some cases, there may be lack of capability (due to limited resources) to respond. Therefore, the lay counselor should seek guidance from local respected guides (see below) and seek God's wisdom in how to proceed.

Using A Guide

The counselor may be surprised her electronics (i.e., computer, hair dryer, cell phone) cannot simply be plugged into the electrical sockets of the new country. The items may need an adapter or transformer in order for them to work. In a similar way, the counselor in a new country will need an adapter or transformer for her counseling to work. Travelers often ask a local guide for help and advice. In a similar way, the lay counselor can use a local guide, or cultural helper, to discover how to adapt and learn how to do things in an appropriate way. The cultural helper is a person in the community who has an awareness of cultural norms and is able to convey them. If possible, it is best to communicate directly with the cultural helper. This would require that either the counselor or the cultural helper share a common language. It is important to use wisdom in selecting a cultural helper and develop a relationship so that the helper is comfortable giving accurate information. Over time, the lay counselor will see how her prior knowledge and experience can be adapted to the new culture. This will not happen immediately, as it is a process to develop cultural competence.

Cultural competence involves having awareness, knowledge and skills in order to function naturally in a culture different from your own. In developing cultural competence, it is beneficial for a counselor to be aware of her own values, biases and assumptions about human behaviors. As the counselor works with the cultural helper, she can develop an understanding of someone else's worldview. Then, hopefully, she will begin to develop appropriate, sensitive and relevant ways to counsel in the new culture.[91] It is more likely for people to have a positive outcome if the counselor makes adaptations. Positive outcomes (for the child or his family) are more likely if the counselor makes adaptations in a culturally sensitive way.[92]

It is vital for the lay counselor to have a learner stance in this process of developing cultural competence. An experienced counselor may think she has a better way to do things, but this attitude will be conveyed subtly and can alienate others. Having humility is biblical. Entering a culture with an expectation of being a learner can benefit the lay counselor, as well as those with whom she intends to counsel. People are more receptive to what is offered if the counselor shows respect and willingness to learn, rather than coming in to impose the counselor's perspective.

Adapting

Some areas in which the counselor may need to adapt expectations or behaviors relate to confidentiality, gender roles, physical touch and value conflicts.

Ethical standards for professional counselors stress confidentiality. Confidentiality refers to the information disclosed by the counselee being kept private from others. A professional counselor informs the counselee that information will not be disclosed to others unless there is a concern the counselee will harm his or herself or others, or if child abuse is suspected. For a lay counselor, there may be similar expectations for maintaining confidentiality. However, in a different culture, this may not always be possible. For example, in some countries neighbors might look in the window during counseling. The counselee might not view this as a problem, as it is 'normal' to have less privacy in his culture. Notions of independence are not as valued in some countries as they are in the West. The lay counselor may need to work out an acceptable way to have some confidentiality, while adapting to the culture that does not stress privacy in the same way

Another consideration is the gender roles held by that culture. Many cultures have strongly defined gender roles. Certain topics are taboo to discuss with a counselee of the opposite sex. It may also be inappropriate for a counselor to meet alone with a person of the opposite sex. In addition, women are often lower than men in the social status hierarchy. This can cause difficulties if a female counselor is working with a child and requests the father change his behavior. The counselor should find out how acceptable it is for girls and boys to be together for a counseling activity. In some cultures, boys and girls play and interact together when they are young, but at a certain age (usually prior to puberty), they are separated. Group activities can be beneficial for children. However, working with a mixed-sex group is unusual in many cultures where the norm is to have the genders divided, often only with the exception of the family group. The cultural helper can assist in determining what is appropriate and possible.

Somewhat linked to gender roles are the cultural practices or norms for physical touch. In the Middle East, it is common for both girls and boys to hold hands, even in adulthood. Males hug tightly in greeting. People of the same sex greet with a series of two or three kisses to the cheek, alternating between left and right cheek. However, it is unacceptable in some of those same cultures for a husband and wife to have a public display of affection, such as a kiss. It is OK to touch a baby on the head in some cultures, while in others it is taboo. The counselor would be wise to discover what forms of physical touch are accepted and which are offensive or taboo. The lay counselor may feel uncomfortable if the expression of physical touch is significantly different from her home country and will have to find ways to maintain her personal boundaries while adapting with the new culture.

An area needing God's wisdom and the sensitive leading of His Spirit is when the values of the lay counselor conflict with the values of the local culture. For example, spanking or corporal punishment may be the norm in the new culture. However, in her home country, the lay counselor may have defined certain forms of corporal punishment as abuse. The counselor who enters a culture and immediately imposes her values by trying to teach other ways to discipline, may lose the opportunity to influence the culture entirely. The counselor may not be welcomed or respected. If the counselor dismisses the values and beliefs of the local culture, there is a good chance her values and beliefs will be dismissed. For example, this author worked at a school where it was common practice for the teachers to carry a small rope. For discipline, the teachers would hit the misbehaving or unruly child with the small rope. This was not allowed at the school by the administrators, but was a common practice, nevertheless. After working in the school for months and developing friendships, this author gave a short presentation to demonstrate alternative forms of discipline. Several of the teachers implemented these methods, such as brief time-out from the classroom activity, and found they were successful. They saw they could be effective using a different form of discipline. These other forms of discipline probably would have been rejected if the initial focus had been on the "badness" of the rope practice, especially if presented immediately upon entering the school. However, with the development of positive relationships and focusing on alternative solutions, real change was possible.

In adapting, the lay counselor may feel she is not being herself as she conforms to the local standard. For example, a counselor who is friendly, smiles at strangers and engages in direct eye contact may discover it sends a message of interest to a person of the opposite sex. If the counselor does not change what she is doing, she may discover the community views her as promiscuous. If the counselor changes, she may feel like she is changing her personality. In the new culture, there will be personal challenges, such as this, and the counselor will have to find how she can adapt to the culture while remaining true to herself.

Counseling Concepts

It is helpful to know what people do to seek help when they have concerns and problems in daily living/psychological problems. In many cultures, counseling may be an unfamiliar concept. There may not even be a word for counseling. To introduce counseling, it can be associated with a parallel type of service offered in the community. Or, a comparable word may need to be used such as advisor. Then, similarities and distinctives will need to be explained so the concept is grasped.

Even if there is a word for counseling, there may be a stigma associated with seeking counseling services. It might be viewed as something reserved for crazy people. Some cultures hide those individuals who have a disability because it is shameful to have an obvious physical problem. There may be a similar stigma for emotional or behavioral problems. The person with psychological problems may be sent to an institution, or may be locked up or restrained in the family's home. Therefore, counseling may be associated with severe mental disorders and people may want to keep their distance. In many post-Union of Soviet Socialist Republics (USSR) countries, counseling was predominantly a form of political abuse to "reform" individuals.

Another stigma may be held by Christians who view counseling as something that is unbiblical. This is particularly true if the Christians base their conclusions on what they have learned about early contributors to the field of psychology (such as Freud who dismissed religion). Some Christians see psychology and counseling as a threat to biblical truth, having a foundation that relies on scientific methods rather than the Bible. And, some secular counselors do ignore the spiritual dimension, so there is some justification in that bias. Therefore, some Christians are unlikely to seek counseling from someone other than their spiritual leader or pastor, viewing counseling and psychology with suspicion.

In most Western psychotherapies, the counselor is cautioned to not disclose too much personal information. However, in many cultures trust is built not on your "expertise," but on your relationships and level of personal knowledge. Positive counseling relationships can be increased by culturally sensitive self-disclosure. For example, parents in pain can form quick bonds with other parents who disclose they also have been in pain. Self-disclosure of the counselor's own parenting struggles, or having a child with developmental or behavioral issues can help speed up and close cross-cultural divides for more effective counseling relationships.

Again, most Western psychotherapies recommend a role of facilitator for the counselor and caution against giving direct advice to counselees. Some nationals may look to the counselor to tell them what to do. They may view the counselor more as an expert who will direct them. Lay counselors can feel caught between wanting to simply give advice and be seen as the expert, and wanting to help the counselee learn how to better understand, process their thoughts and emotions, and develop more effective coping and problem-solving skills. This slower process leads to more growth and resourcefulness for the future, and the possibility of the counselee to help others down the road. God's wisdom is knowing when an individual simply needs to have a fish to eat right away, and when he needs to learn how to fish for himself and others.

The challenges of unfamiliarity, stigma and different models of counseling may be overcome if the concept is introduced well, with sensitivity to the cultural issues involved, and conveyed by a trusted individual in the community. The cultural helper may be able to help break down some of the barriers that would prevent non-Christians and Christians from seeking/receiving and understanding counseling.

Gatherings

Over time, the traveler discovers how to get around and begins to participate in local events. He learns where he can find good music, food and shopping bargains, as well as where the locals hang-out. As the lay counselor finds her way around, she may begin to notice how the community works together in ways that could facilitate counseling. There may be structures in place through which a counselor could convey a message of healing, or provide mental health messages or services. In some cases, there is a gathering place, such as a community center. For example, Indonesia has community centers that were built after the 2004 tsunami. There is a children's preschool program in the morning where children learn traditional dance, songs and prayers, and play together. It is an ideal place for working with children, since it is already a part of the community. A second example would be Rwanda, where there are mandatory community work days once per month. Everyone in the village, actually in the whole country, is required to participate in the work day. The community comes together and works on a project. Although not the focus, it is a time for building relationships and socializing. In addition, there is a time during which community leaders disseminate information. This could be an ideal time for announcing counseling services that are available, and possibly incorporating a positive mental health message through information or a shared activity

In many cases, the lay counselor may need permission to participate in the community activity. This permission may be granted by a community leader. The community leader could be a government official, a village leader, a religious leader or a "man of peace" (essentially, a respected person who does not have an official title). In some communities, it is inappropriate to even enter a village without approaching the leader to explain the purpose of being there. Having a relationship with a community leader provides access to the community and acceptance. If the leader accepts the presence and services of the lay counselor, then the community members will likely be more receptive to receive counseling services by the lay counselor.

Settling In/Being at Home

The lay counselor brings many positive experiences and knowledge with them. How helpful this will be for those in a different culture will be based on the counselor's humility to be a learner under God's guidance and His provision of local "guides" to help unpack the counselor's experiences and knowledge in culturally sensitive ways along the journey. Learning and adapting while maintaining one's sense of authentic self and biblical values (not just learned values of one's home culture) is no easy task. The apostle Paul's wisdom still rings true,

> For though I am free from all, I have made myself a servant to all, that I might win more of them. To the Jews I became as a Jew, in order to win Jews. To those under the law I became as one under the law (though not being myself under the law) that I might win those under the law. To those outside the law I became as one outside the law (not being outside the law of God but under the law of Christ) that I might win those outside the law. To the weak I became weak, that I might win the weak. I have become all things to all people, that by all means I might save some. I do it all for the sake of the gospel, that I may share with them in its blessings. (1 Cor. 9:19-23 ESV)

You will know that you are at home when you have placed your own cultural bags in storage, have become comfortable in your different cultural clothing and surroundings, and are finding joy in new ways to live out God's grace and truth with children in that culture. God's blessings on the journey!

THIRTEEN

INTEGRATED CHILD PROTECTION in CHRISTIAN MINISTRY

Wendy Middaugh Bovard

This chapter examines child protection from two perspectives: 1) protection through engaging in advocacy for children and 2) protection through children's programs that implement policies that provide for their safety and protection.

Filandie: A Child Without Protection

Filandie was born in southern Haiti near Jacmel. There were seven children in her family and no school anywhere in the vicinity. One day, when she was ten years old, some missionaries from Port au Prince came to her village and her mother asked the missionaries to help with her daughter's education. Filandie traveled with the missionaries to the capital city. Soon after, the missionaries left the country for some rest, so Filandie stayed with a Haitian neighbor family who was given money to send her to school in the coming year.

Filandie missed her family, but was excited about being in the big city and going to school. She woke early, helped with all the household work and the family was nice to her. It was crowded in the tiny two-room house, so she really did not have a good place to sleep. When a relative of the house mother came by to visit and offered to have Filandie live with them, the neighbor family quickly agreed. The new family seemed kind at first, but Filandie soon found it to be a very strange and frightening environment. The family had three young children and Filandie became busy with their care. She was given so much work to do that she collapsed every night from

219

exhaustion. Because there was no place for her to sleep, she ended up sleeping under the table on a pile of rags most nights. She then awoke early to prepare food for the family and clean the house. When the other children went to school, she was told there was too much work to do so she could not go to school. She was required to help sell boiled eggs on the street to help the family pay for her upkeep.

Morning after morning, Filandie helped prepare the other children for school and walked them safely to their classes. One day, when she returned to the house, the "Auntie" was very angry because Filandie had not finished her work well. The next thing she knew, the lady was beating her with the very wooden spoon Filandie used to prepare the food. As Filandie began to shout and cry, an uncle of the woman passed by; he stopped and tried to comfort her. She went with him to his house to wait for the woman to settle down. She started feeling very uncomfortable with the way the man was touching her. He told her to remove her clothes and before she could run away, he began defiling her.

The "Uncle" told her he would protect her from the mean "Auntie" if she would come and visit him. Because Filandie was often beaten by the "Auntie", she found herself escaping to the "Uncle's" house often. Soon, the poor girl was pregnant. When the "Uncle" realized this, he became angry and threatened to kill Filandie if she told anyone. He was desperate to keep his secret from his family and his church, so he bought some herbal tablets and gave them to Filandie, telling her the pills would solve all of her problems. Later that night, Filandie began bleeding heavily. "Auntie" did not want the girl to die in front of her, so she took Filandie to the bus station and put her on a six-hour bus trip back to her home in Jacmel. By the time Filandie arrived in Jacmel, she was too weak to walk anywhere, so a "good samaritan" took her—by motorcycle—the rest of the two-hour trip to her home. When she reached her home, her father called for a health worker but before help could arrive, Filandie bled to death. She was able to tell her father what had happened to her just before she died; the entire family was so sorry to hear her terrible story. They said it must have been from the result of a bad spell that had been put on her by a local voodoo priest.

Nelson Mandela once said, *"There can be no keener revelation of a society's soul than the way in which it treats its children."* Any nation that allows its children to suffer abuse, including various forms of child slavery, cannot expect to be anything but the poorest nation in the world. According to a recent study conducted in Haiti, there are currently an estimated 250,000 children who suffer as child domestic slaves. These children are without a voice and without a future. Most of these children are sent to the cities by their own families hoping the child can bring them some luck or economic advantage by exchanging a little house work for the opportunity to go to school. Years ago, this system became popular because some children actually did get to go to school and found good families to work with. However, the system is now known as *restavek*, and it has become increasingly violent and abusive for the children who seldom ever see the door of a school.

Worse yet, the *restavek* system became such a culturally accepted part of Haitian society that even pastors and bishops would rise to preach on Sunday and go home to a meal cooked by a *restavek* child, who did not get to hear his sermon, attend Sunday school or sing in the children's choir. Many of these children live isolated from their families and communities, and begin to ponder whether God could love some people so much and despise others so much.

Since my first mission trip to Haiti and my subsequent years in Africa, I have seen some of the most terrible trauma and crises that children face. I have seen children who live in refugee camps having to run for their lives; child slaves afraid to even look at me for fear of smiling; children die of Aids-related illness in my arms; street children so high on glue they did not even know where they were; children devastated by the loss of their parents in the terrorist attack on the US Embassy in Nairobi; girls disfigured by the Lord's Resistance Army; children unable to speak after watching their mother raped until dead in Rwanda; a child shot multiple times by Ugandan forces; a fourteen-year-old boy who was a well-trained killer in the Congo; rejected *restavek* child slaves who were devastated by rape and physical abuse.

It was difficult and overwhelming for me and for the precious people with whom I worked. And about the time I was ready to join the many others who have asked, "Where in the world was God when all this happened?" I became acquainted with Gary Haugen of the International Justice Mission. I realized I certainly was not alone in my passion for helping the hurting children and giving a voice to the voiceless. I soon discovered Gary also had seen very difficult things, including genocide in Rwanda, child slavery and sexual exploitation. He said he also had asked those questions of God, but had come to realize the real question was not, "Where was God?"; the real question was, "Where were God's people?" The Creator of the universe gifts His children with all kinds of love and compassion and skill to do what is required. However, many times when good could have easily won, it lacked one voice, one hand or one call.

This thought strengthened me, and gave me courage to enlist and train everyone I could in Africa and around the world to equip God's people to not only care about children in crisis, but to do something about it. God calls Himself "a father of the fatherless" in Psalm 68:5, a defender of "the poor and fatherless" in Psalm 82:3 and in Lamentations 2:19, God says, "Arise, cry out in the night: in the beginning of the watches pour out [your] heart like water before the face of the Lord: lift up your hands toward him for the life of your young children that faint for hunger in the top of every street." God's people are to arise, cry out (speak up), pour out their hearts to God for the children, and lift their hands and take action to save them. These children have no voice and no one to advocate for them, unless the people of God hear their cry and stand up and speak out for their freedom and protection. If we do not speak for these children, who will?

Safety Nets and Social Systems

We have all heard it said that "it takes a village to raise a child." In the case of Filandie, the village failed, her family failed, missionaries failed and civil authorities failed. In the communities of developing countries, it takes an entire community to protect a child. It takes the community being aware of the issues related to child abuse, and knowing how to respond and care for children who have been survivors of such abuse. What can we as Christian workers around the world do to prevent abuse and even death for children like Filandie?

Children are born to be loved, nurtured and protected from the violence of this world, but in many cases they simply are not. Churches sing and preach, pastors lead the lost to salvation, but children in their own communities suffer. In some extreme cases, leaders and members of the church and its ministries become the predators. All too often we, as a church, are a part of the problem of child abuse instead of being a part of the solution. While we have abundant resources and opportunities as the church of Jesus Christ to make a difference in the lives of these children, we must ask ourselves what we can do to protect our children and respond to their needs.

There are several natural "safety nets" within most cultures that help prevent an even wider spread of the pandemic of abuse that we see. The first level of the system of safety nets is the immediate family, which is the frontline of defense against child abuse. The Bible is clear that the ultimate responsibility for the safety and security of children are their parents. Of course, most of this world falls very short of the ideal family that is described in Genesis, in which a man leaves his parents to marry and the couple bears children and cares for those children until they are old enough to start a family of their own. Parents are responsible for their own children, whether they are rich or poor.

One of the most disappointing situations in Haiti and many countries around the world is that children with living, capable parents are put in orphanages because parents say they cannot afford to care for them, or they want them to be given the educational advantages of the orphanages or child centers. The fastest way to get into an orphanage in Haiti is to just slip the manager a few dollars and promise to bring him something when you can. In many cases, parents who return to take their children back are issued huge bills they are unable to pay.

These are the kinds of problems that perpetuate child slavery in Haiti. Parents send their children to work in cities closer to schools so they might get an education and be able to help the family out of their abject poverty. The problem then arises of the child being abused by the "host" family. A child is more likely to experience life-threatening abuse when living with someone other than his or her biological parents. While it may be true that some well-meaning Christian people help orphans and vulnerable children by taking them into their home and caring for them, this relationship is primarily focused on domestic servitude; the children are seldom treated as well as the other biological children in the family. Giving a child to an orphanage is not the answer and neither is sending them into work so they can help the family, but this is the belief of many of the world's poorest countries.

The second level of the safety net is comprised of the extended family and friends who usually know the child from birth, and feel a part of the development of the child. They are happy to see the child and as the child grows, he or she becomes more familiar with the extended family members and is able to trust them in a similar way as they do the mother and father.

The third level of the safety net is the community where the family lives, whether it is rural or urban, rich or poor. Every group of families that form communities do so for one reason or another. Some communities come together because they are a part of a particular clan or tribe. Others come together because of friendship or common interests. Community carries a number of definitions, but for the most part, it refers to the nonfamilial group.

Every community has civil institutions such as churches and schools, which are the fourth level of the safety net. When a family joins a local church, relationships are developed with a smaller group of people within the family's community who may have a similar belief system. They can work together for their Christian ideas, and share the blessing of giving their children biblical lessons and encourage them in Christian living.

The fifth level of the safety net for children includes the governmental and nongovernmental organizations, such as Christian missions and agencies that stand in the gap when the other levels of the safety net cannot function because of natural disasters, war or family crises. These organizations and Christian ministries must work with the government to ensure children are protected.

The aforementioned safety measures are the support systems for children that can promote their healthy development and general welfare. Strengthening these systems and encouraging them to all work together will certainly promote resilience in difficult times because the child will have the bonding and the interaction with peers that will guide him or her during difficult times. The problem comes when these natural systems for the safety of children deteriorate and gaps develop. This is when the church, the government and other community institutions have to step in and provide services to ensure children's rights to survival, development and protection are not being denied.

We must be aware of the realities of the terrible situations and that which creates these great gaps where children fall through the natural safety nets. Children need families, communities, churches, schools, health services, nutritious foods and clean water; but they need even more. The United Nations has developed a program called *A World Fit for Children,* which identifies ten goals for the protection of children. These goals are not anything new to those in the Christian community who have served children their entire lives. These are basic goals that most of us from developed countries take for granted. In this program, children's rights are divided into three very basic rights:

- **Survival rights, which include such basics as** adequate food, water, shelter, health care and an adequate standard of living.

- **Development rights** in education that provides children with special disabilities special care and the right to play.

- **Protection rights, which include the right to** a name and nationality, protection from armed conflict, protection as a refugee, protection against torture and death penalty, juvenile justice, protection from exploitative work, protection from exploitation and abuse.

Additionally, the *A World Fit for Children* program summarizes what are considered the millennium goals for children worldwide, including the following:

1. **Put children first**–the best interest of children should always be considered.

2. **End poverty by investing in children**–stop child labor and invest in kids healthy growth and development.

3. **Leave no child behind**–every boy and girl is born free and equal; end all kinds of discrimination.

4. **Care for every child**–the survival, protection, growth and development of healthy and well-nourished children so they can learn and be physically, mentally, emotionally and socially healthy.

5. **Educate every child**–all boys and girls should be allowed to complete a primary education that is free. Boys and girls should have equal access to primary and secondary education.

6. **Protect children from harm, exploitation** and discrimination, also from terrorism and hostage taking.

7. **Protect children from war,** including children living in areas occupied by another country.

8. **Combat HIV/AIDS**

9. **Listen to children and ensure their participation**–respect children's right to express themselves and be involved in all things that affect them, according to their age and maturity.

10. **Protect the earth for children**–protecting children from the effects of natural disasters and environmental problems.

These goals are extremely important and are being used worldwide as a basis for the improvement of living conditions for children and help to facilitate their holistic development.

Some nations of the world have taken these protection measures seriously, and have implemented and enforced specific laws in regard to the protection of children. More and more children are being protected from the worst forms of child abuse, including sexual exploitation. However, this has resulted in child abusers leaving their countries in the name of tourism to have sexual encounters with children in countries where the laws are not so strictly enforced. This has been the case in both Asia and Africa, where poverty and the AIDS pandemic have forced children into the workforce, including the sex trade. This is most unfortunate and is being combated at every level.

Biblical Model for Rebuilding the "Jerusalem" of Our Children

Nehemiah was called upon to lead and facilitate the rebuilding of Jerusalem, which was in ruins following years of conflict and domination by the enemies of God. This situation sounds familiar because this is the very task we are given as Christian ministers in the world today. Children are the greatest victims of war, disease and exploitation. It is our responsibility as Christians to "do justly, to love mercy and to walk humbly with our God." Our children must be protected from the things that will devastate them for life. When terrible things happen, we must walk with them through the process of rebuilding their lives for the glory of God.

In the first chapter of the book of Nehemiah, we see that Nehemiah had an open heart and open ears. He listened to the report and was gripped by the pain of his own people, and their need to rebuild their lives and their city.

1. **Nehemiah heard the cry—open your ears, eyes and heart (1:1-3)**

2. **Nehemiah prayed for wisdom in how to respond (1:4-11)**

3. **Nehemiah assessed the actual situation (2:11-16)**

Nehemiah did his homework before making his plan. He confirmed the report by conducting a community assessment of sorts. He looked to see what others were doing about the issues in that area and found the need was genuine.

We must learn everything we can about child abuse and how to prevent it. It is important to know the children you serve by learning about their culture, and understanding their temperaments and the way they think.

4. **To Nehemiah, a call to serve was a call to prepare and to plan (Chapters 2 and 3)**

Train Your Team

Building the capacity of your church or Christian ministry members should follow a very basic model of providing information so the church can understand the reality of the issue. Raising awareness in the church and community of the problem will make them all more open to cooperation, as the church makes an effort to help children in crisis.

Education about these issues can be accomplished in many venues, including large open forums in which community members discuss the basic issues and its impact on the community, as well as small focus groups of specific community leaders who have the necessary qualifications or work experience. A deeper understanding of the issues is achieved by these small groups that then can support and guide the volunteers who will be trained in the communication section.

Communication is the core of the children in crisis program and it includes the training of child workers who can do the assessments, basic interventions, referrals and follow-up for the children. It also involves a more individualized approach by training the volunteers who then are able to work with up to twelve children.

5. Nehemiah created awareness of need and made it personal (2:17-20)

When I carried the first HIV-positive child into my house in central Kenya fifteen years ago, the children's home staff ran straight out the back door. Community elders sat down to discuss the wretched looking baby that we had rescued from death's door and the teachers refused to come to school if any of my orphans had AIDS! At one point, villagers threatened to burn our house down, but what they could not dispute was that I had taken the disaster of HIV in our community personally.

When that baby died four years later, we sat around a fire of *mombolezi* (mourning) and I listened to our neighbors say, "We have heard the gospel many times, but this is the first time we have seen the gospel so clearly demonstrated." That was the beginning of years of work with HIV orphans and children that culminated in the production of a twelve-module educational series called "Let Your Light Shine." It was used by frontline caregivers in Africa who work with children affected by HIV. It is not enough to see the problem and talk about it; we must own it. We must take it personally and model the kind of love and care we are talking about.

Minimum Standards for Christian Ministry

How do we make the protection of children a "personal concern?" How do we ensure children have a voice and they are not simply "seen and not heard?" How do we prevent them from being hidden away behind concrete walls and high fences, forced to burn bricks, cook and clean for large families, and sleeping under the table or bed of their owner? The first thing we need to understand is God's heart for children.

The truth is that every child is uniquely and specially made in the image of God, and is greatly valued by Him. God's design is for every child to grow and flourish, becoming that entire person God created them to be (see John 10:10, Jer. 29:11). Also, every person has a unique and important

God-given calling to impact the world around them. Thus, every human child is essential to the healthy development and well-being of his family, community and nation.

Therefore, the church must recognize that abuse and exploitation of children is a very real and growing worldwide problem. As Christian ministries work for the well-being and development of children, it is of the utmost importance for us to take the steps necessary to prevent and respond to this abuse in whatever capacity we can.

The Christian community must be committed to the prevention of child abuse and provide a clear response to children who suffer this abuse. Churches need to help families and communities create safe and positive environments, where children can live and grow safely and happily. Every person who works with us, including our partners, representatives and volunteers, need to value the rights of children and make sure they understand child abuse, and how to prevent and respond to it.

In recent years, Christian organizations have begun to develop child-protection policies and codes of conduct so everyone who works for them understands their "zero tolerance" for child abuse or child trafficking. In Appendix A, you will find a child-protection policy all WEC International workers must sign. The need for such a policy is clearly stated in the organization's opening paragraph:

> We in WEC USA recognize the value and priority of children in the heart of God, seen throughout Scripture and demonstrated in the life of Jesus. We also are burdened by the fallen world in which we live, the potential harms to children, and the severity of Christ's warnings to those who have a negative impact on these "little ones" (Matthew 18:6). Therefore we pledge ourselves to a lifestyle of care and protection of children described in the policies below, for their good and the honor of Christ.

The policy summary is in Appendix A of this book. Children-in-crisis workers will find the principles and concepts in this policy helpful in formulating a child-protection policy for their organizations.

Protection Principles and Core Values

Every church and every Christian ministry must recognize that child abuse has physical, emotional/mental and sexual dimensions. Most Christian ministries have a firm commitment to biblical values and will ensure the promotion of human rights, and specifically protection from unintentional harm, as well as deliberate abuse. A child-protection policy should demonstrate an awareness of child abuse, and will serve as a reminder to all staff and beneficiaries that organizations working with the vulnerable have been and will continue to be susceptible to harboring abuse until the issues are brought into the open.

Children have the right to be happy and live safely in their communities. All children, including those living with AIDS and disabilities, should be free from harm, and treated with dignity and respect. Their educational, developmental and protection rights should be observed at the highest level, in every organization that engages in community development and transformation. The churches they attend should be safe churches; the communities they live in should be safe communities; and the Christians who work in their communities should do so with the highest regard for their human rights and safety.

Churches and parachurch organizations and ministries can lead the way in the protection of children by following some basic steps recommended by the United Nations and Christian organizations alike. These basic steps are summarized below:

a. **A protection focal person** who leads the assessment, training, and monitoring of women and child safety in the organization globally. This includes the training and supervision of protection focal persons in every field of work and monitoring their progress.

b. **A clear protection strategy** that includes policies and protocols of conduct, consequences, systems of reporting incidents, and physical and psychological support of the victim, and referral systems for additional needs.

c. **A clearly written plan of action** that outlines the steps to be taken to safeguard women and children, how this will be completed and a time frame for the completion.

d. **Internal and external regular and effective information, communication, and education** on the policies, protocols and practices of child protection, including orientation, training, and information sharing that creates an atmosphere of learning and responsibility for the safety of every woman and child by all staff, volunteers and partners of the organization.

e. **A monitoring system** to review and evaluate the safety of the environments on a regular basis. It includes the implementation of protection systems that are reviewed annually.

f. **Networking and linkage to the government, available public services, the community-based church and community leaders are vital components in the protection system for vulnerable children.** The moment you think you are the only one working for the sake of these abused and abandoned children, think again. There are thousands of God's people standing for freedom all over the world and giving voice to the voiceless. Work with them to add value to other ministries by sharing learning points and challenges.

What are We Protecting our Children From?

Child abuse involves the physical, sexual or emotional abuse and neglect of children. UNICEF describes it as "any harm to a child that results from human action or inaction."

Sexual abuse of minors, which includes child molestation, is a serious moral failure and illegal activity that is subject to criminal charges in even developing societies. Child abuse is simply the misuse of authority that breaches ethical principles by misusing a trust relationship to exploit a child for sexual or other gratification. Child sexual abuse and exploitation is against the law of God and causes deep emotional, spiritual and psychological wounds.

Physical abuse involves actions that inflict pain on the child and is capable of causing harm to the body, i.e., child battering, corporal punishment, exposure to war and conflict, child labor, etc. Physical neglect happens in cases where the child is abandoned or deprived of basic necessities that are necessary for his or her normal development.

Sexual abuse includes incest, sexual exploitation, rape, use of children for pornography, child prostitution, child sex trafficking, etc. Emotional/Psychological abuse includes verbal insults and comparison of children based on performance, etc. Christian ministries must ensure staff, volunteers, board members and all other persons that serve our children:

- are aware of the problem of child abuse
- safeguard children from abuse through good practice
- report all concerns about possible abuse
- respond appropriately when abuse is discovered or suspected

6. **Nehemiah built a team and gave them work based on their ability (Chapter 3)**

Choose the team, train the team, supervise them and celebrate their accomplishments.

It takes tremendous teamwork to protect children today. No counselor or ministry should ever stand alone in this work. It takes the work of both a church that is aware of the needs of children and willing to keep their children safe, and government authorities and similar organizations to effectively protect children.

7. Nehemiah participated in the work as a servant leader (Chapters 3-6)

Nehemiah modeled what he wanted his team to be like. There are countless books today telling us how to be leaders and managers and great people. However, the most critical need is to be of the same mind as Christ, by being a servant and a leader.

8. Nehemiah was very misunderstood in his effort (Chapter 6)

It is strange to me that the global effort to protect children was not initiated by the church of Jesus Christ.

9. Nehemiah managed well and monitored the progress well (Chapter 4)

Every effort needs to be documented. Always do a baseline survey so you can assess your progress in meeting your goals. Choose your goals and ask yourself how you will reach them. Write down the indicators of your success. Remember that you cannot monitor what you cannot measure. Use pre-test and post-test evaluation tools before and after trainings, so you now whether your training efforts are actually equipping the volunteers.

Develop good monitoring and evaluation tools that make it easy for you to report success and challenges. Do not be afraid to identify those efforts that did not go well or what you may do differently next time. Always be open about the lessons learned.

10. Nehemiah praised God for the victories and took responsibility for the mistakes

How can we walk in the light when we work in the darkness? When I was in junior high school, I went to summer camp. When they called for volunteers—being my competitive self—I quickly raised my hand. I was then blindfolded and found myself being guided through a heavily forested area by a girl who did not seem to know her right hand from her left. Since the first team to reach the other side of the forest would receive some tremendous prize, I began moving quickly, and my guide became more and more confused. By the time we finally reached the other side, I had hit so many trees that I was black and blue. I had to be taken to the doctor for a minor concussion.

That experience gave me some very good observations which have helped guide me through the dark forest of working with child slavery, neglect and abuse. The most important lesson I learned was that running in the dark when you have no idea where you are going is very dangerous. When God calls us to serve Him, He calls us to prepare for that service. A lack of preparation makes the darkness so much worse and makes us so much more fearful. Prepare yourself well for the ministry to which God is calling you. Read all related materials possible; meet everyone you can who has experience in the field and build a great team of people around you that clearly knows their right hand from their left. Here are some additional points to consider:

- We learn so much more about ourselves when we stand in total darkness—when we cannot see exactly what is ahead. I think it is true that "our character is who we are when no one is looking."

- One of the most difficult things to do is to not only move through a forest in the dark, but also to lead others through the same darkness. The Bible calls it, "the blind leading the blind and they all fall into the ditch." (see Matt. 15:14)

- Natural disasters, terrorist attacks, war and genocide all make crisis care for children very difficult. You actually share the darkness with the children you are trying to help. For that reason, it is important to have the necessary support. Being in the dark is bad enough, but being in the dark alone is really difficult. Building strong teams that can work together even in the darkness is what the International Justice Mission has done for years in rescuing children from slavery.

- Even caring touches or attempts to help can be rejected.

- Darkness has a way of driving us toward even the smallest light, especially when it has been dark for some time. We are so thankful for the smallest ray of hope.

- When we see light it makes us thankful.

- Darkness clarifies our fear and sharpens our focus and our message. Nehemiah took responsibility for the results and mistakes. Constantly evaluate and reevaluate the relevancy of your caring programs. Good leaders see farther down the road than others and they apologize when they are wrong. Good leaders have compassion, courage, and clarity in the purpose and work of their organizations. They give clear direction to the team and leave the results to God.

The church has a very important role to play if children are to be safe in the world in which we live. Stop asking yourself, "Where was God?" and ask yourself, "Where were God's people?" We all have a role to play and by following the example of Nehemiah, we can rebuild the lives of our children, strengthen their safety nets and close the gap when children begin to fall through the cracks. May we be a shining light to the darkest area and may the reflection of our nations' souls be happy children living up to their God-given potential.

Part V:

SUPPORT TOOLS FOR CHILDREN AND COUNSELORS

FOURTEEN

The IMPORTANCE of FAMILY and PARENTAL SUPPORT

Rosemary Sabatino

*"Unless the LORD builds the house, They labor in vain who build it;
Unless the LORD guards the city, The watchman stays awake in vain."*
(Psalm 127:1 NKJV)

He was just six or seven years old when he took to the streets of Dakar, Senegal, West Africa. Some months prior, due to poverty and dysfunction at home, he was given over to an Islamic priest called a *marabout*. His new home was called a *dara*—a small, shabby room shared by dozens of other boys in the same situation. Their ages ranged from four or five to twelve or thirteen; many were malnourished and visibly ill. Each morning at sunlight, they were forced to take a tomato can in hand and go to the streets and beg. Upon their return in the evening, the *marabout* would take inventory of their cache for the day. If certain quotas were not met, harsh consequences would follow. Most often there would be severe beatings accompanied by a withdrawal of food.

With such abuse, it's not hard to see why he left the *dara* for life on the streets. However, the streets held new and different cruelties—abuses and exploitative situations too horrible to mention here. Although it wasn't an option, he longed for home, dysfunctional as it was. It was at this point that he met the missionary.

He had encountered Christians before, but this was different. Usually they would give him a piece of candy or bread and a piece of paper saying, "Jesus loves you." The missionary just sat and talked to him, like a friend. He came back several times, and the boy was always happy to see him. One day, the missionary asked the boy to come to his house, the House of Hope, to see if he would like to live there. Guardedly, the boy said yes.

When he got to the House of Hope, he couldn't believe his eyes. It was clean and neat. There were four or five other boys there who had come from the streets as well. They had on clean clothes and they didn't look hungry. He decided to stay. That was ten or twelve years ago. Today, the boy is on his way to university, where he will study to be a teacher. What he found at the House of Hope was more than just a shelter. It was a real home and family, with respect and responsibility, where the love of Jesus was experienced, not just talked about. The boy found it to be a place of healing, where, over the years, through many ups and downs, the missionary and his wife remained strong, consistent parental figures in his life.

There was one incident that I remember well. When the boy was about fifteen, he needed a serious eye operation and he asked the missionary if perhaps his biological father would come to see him in the hospital. After talking with the boy about possible outcomes, the missionary agreed to contact the father. The reply was stinging, hurtful and discouraging: "I didn't want him then and I don't want him now." This was a devastating blow that could have set the boy back into depression and despair, but it didn't. Hard as it was, he got through it in the loving arms of his surrogate parents. They were with him then and they are with him now as he takes the next step into adulthood at the university. His heart's desire is to be the kind of godly parent that his new "mom and dad" have been to him. Their display of godly family life and unconditional, consistent love made all the difference in his life, and he wants to pass it on!

Family: God's Design

It has been said the family is the essential building block of human society, and as such, it must be nurtured and protected.[93] The health of any society depends on the physical, emotional, cognitive and psychological health of each family system. Yet, beyond its importance to the well-being of every civilization, the Lord has a much more significant purpose for family.

God created man and woman to fulfill His desire to have children, a family created in His very own image (see Gen. 1:26-27). The first man and woman were to be "fruitful and increase in number [and] fill the earth" (1:28 NIV) so that the earth would "be filled with the knowledge of the glory of the LORD as the waters cover the sea" (Hab. 2:14 NIV). Through procreation, God would "build His house," a dwelling where His Spirit and glory would live with and in His people. The family was designed to be a safe and healthy environment where children—new glory-bearers—would be nourished and encouraged as they grow into the unique masterpieces God created them to be.

Through the fall, the enemy's intent was to destroy forever the glorious household of God. Yet, what he meant for evil the Lord turned to a marvelous good. Through the redemptive plan of the cross, beautiful aspects of God's glory are made known through the lives of the redeemed people of God: kindness, compassion, mercy, forgiveness, justice and unconditional love. As the people of God in the world, we must continue to strengthen the families within our communities and to affirm the significance of each new child. As we do so, the kingdom and household of God will flourish.

God: Builder of the Household

Solomon, the author of Psalm 127, which opened this chapter, was commissioned as a youth to build the house of the Lord (see 1 Kings 3:7; 1 Chron. 28:6), a daunting task for one so young. Yet, he was encouraged to move forward, believing it would be the Lord Himself who would build the house *through* him (see 1 Chron. 28:20).

The first two verses of Psalm 127 describe a house (temple) that will endure beyond one made of brick and mortar. The word "build" is translated from the Hebrew *banah*,[94] which means to establish something that would continue; to establish a family. And the word "house" is taken from the Hebrew *bayith*,[95] a derivative of the word *banah*, which means "a household." The only family that will endure throughout eternity is the one built and kept by the Lord. In the next verse of Psalm 127, the Lord discloses the means by which He will build His family or household.

Children: A Heritage from the Lord

"Behold, children are a heritage from the LORD, The fruit of the womb is a reward."
(Ps. 127:3 NKJV)

"Behold!" This word is translated from the Greek *hinneh*,[96] which almost always signals something very important will follow. Yes, children are a heritage from the Lord. Many translations interpret "heritage" as a gift, but the word heritage means much more. It is defined as something that comes or belongs to us by reason of birth.[97] The concept of heritage carries a past, present and future hope. It instills in us a sense of who we are, what we might become and what we are expected to transfer to the next generation.

Children Are a Responsibility

In Deuteronomy 6, The Lord gave His people, Israel, their mission statement and it stands for His church today.

> Hear, O Israel! The LORD our God, the LORD is one! You shall love the LORD your God with all your heart, with all your soul, and with all your strength. And these words which I command you today shall be in your heart. You shall teach them diligently to your children, and shall talk of them when you sit in your house, when you walk by the way, when you lie down, and when you rise up. (Deut. 6:4-7 NKJV)

Children were an integral part of Israel's mission. The Lord made it clear that the onus to nurture the precious promise of the Kingdom, which lay in the hearts of the children, was a preeminent responsibility. The role of parents was to model the ways and statutes of the Lord in every area of their lives. This mission and role is still in effect for parents today. And, where parents are absent, as is the case for so many children at risk and in crisis, the responsibility belongs to the church. We are to be as God is: "A father to the fatherless . . . is God in his holy dwelling" (Ps. 68:5 NIV).

Children Have Been Given a Ministry

"Like arrows in the hand of a warrior,
So are the children of one's youth.
How blessed is the man whose quiver is full of them;
They will not be ashamed
When they speak with their enemies in the gate."

(Ps. 127:4-5 NASB)

In these verses, the Lord shows us that children hold an important place in the Kingdom. He has ordained a special place of ministry for them in the body of Christ—that of arrows against the enemy. The Hebrew word *dabar* translated as "speak" (or "contend" in many versions) literally means "to command, warn, threaten and put to flight."[98]

This ministry that children have been given is confirmed in Psalm 8 and quoted by Jesus in Matthew 21:16. "Out of the mouth of babes and nursing infants You have ordained strength, Because of Your enemies, That You may silence the enemy and the avenger" (Ps. 8:2 NKJV). What a tremendous ministry children have been given by the Lord—a ministry of prayer and praise—and for an important purpose, to silence the enemy and the avenger! It is no wonder that the enemy has waged a war against children in an attempt to eradicate the power behind their praise and hinder the future of the Kingdom.

Children Are a Target

For those of us who work with and for children at risk and in crisis, we are well aware that the enemy has targeted them for destruction. We see firsthand the tremendous damage inflicted on children today through the trauma of abuse, abandonment, neglect and exploitation. Such trauma can hinder children's emotional, physical and spiritual development, and can destroy their ability to have meaningful and healthy relationships, ultimately affecting their relationship with the Lord. How can we help them?

The most important factor of care for all children is the influence of parental support. Therefore, the most significant prevention and intervention strategy the church could employ, to mitigate the cause and effect of trauma-related injury to children, is to promote a healthy family lifestyle, which includes Godly parental support.

The Healthy Family: There is No Place like Home

"Nor need we power or splendour, wide hall or lordly dome;
the good, the true, the tender, these form the wealth of home."
Sarah J. Hale[99]

Growing up in the outskirts of New York, New York, USA, was a wonderful experience. The diversity of our neighborhood alone was a cultural education in itself. However, at times it could be tough going, even in school. I can recall instances when playing in the neighborhood or on the school yard could become emotionally hurtful and, at times, pretty scary. No matter how tumultuous my day seemed, it all melted away when I walked in our front door—there was no place like home!

Our home was a place of safety and security, of unconditional love and acceptance. It was a place where moral standards were encouraged and modeled by my parents. Home was where my sister and I learned kindness, forgiveness and commitment. For instance, my mom refused to engage in neighborhood gossip and would not tolerate "tattle-telling" or gossip. If I came home angry at a schoolmate, my mom would say: "Jesus forgave those who nailed Him to the cross, certainly you can forgive your friend." She had a compassionate heart, but she was also governed by wisdom. My dad was hardworking and loyal, always providing for our needs. There were times when he worked two jobs to support us. He did everything with excellence and expected the same from us. And, there was never a doubt our parents loved each other and would always be there for us. Lastly, there was joy in our home with lots of music and singing. Even though I did not grow up in a traditional Christian home, it was a healthy family atmosphere and I am grateful.

Defining a Healthy Family

> "A house is made of walls and beams; a *home* is built with love and dreams." Anonymous[100]

The first step in defining a healthy family would be to begin with the concept of "family." Family may be defined in the following ways: (a) a basic social unit consisting of parents and their children, considered as a group, whether dwelling together or not: the traditional family; (b) a social unit consisting of one or more adults together with the children they care for: a single-parent family; or (c) any group of persons closely related by blood, as parents, children, uncles, aunts, and cousins: extended family.[101]

While this is a good, but sterile start, Chuck Swindoll's definition better captures the essence of family:

> The family is where you put down your first roots, where you form your most lasting impressions, where you put together the building blocks of your character and where you determine whether you will view life through the eyes of prejudice or acceptance. Family is where you learn to laugh and where you are allowed to weep without losing respect. Family is where you learn how to share, how to relate, and how to treat other people. Family is where you learn how to interpret your surroundings correctly. It is where you discover how to draw the line between right and wrong, between good and evil.[102]

Characteristics of a Healthy Family

The following "composite of characteristics" comes from a cross-section of experts—counselors, psychologists, psychiatrists, researchers and authors—who have spent more than half of their lives working with children.

1. The members of the household are committed to one another. The family, therefore, is a unit with members dedicated to living their lives in support of one another with unquestioned loyalty.

2. A healthy family spends time together. A wholesome, healthy family believes that time together cannot have quality without sufficient quantity.

3. A healthy family enjoys open, frequent communication. No question is inappropriate, no opinion is disrespected and no subject is considered off limits. Important, life-determining subjects are naturally intermingled with the mundane.

4. The healthy family turns inward during times of crisis. Members of wholesome, healthy families work through difficulties together. A crisis brings them closer because they look within the family for strength rather than looking to something outside.

5. Members of a healthy family express affirmation and encouragement often. "Good job!" "I admire you for that!" "You mean a lot to me!" Notice that affirmation and encouragement are different. You affirm who people are, while you encourage what people do. Both are necessary to help others discover who they are and what they do well, which builds a strong sense of personal security. You are not born with a well-defined sense of self; you discover yourself through the influence of those important to you.

6. The members of a healthy family share a spiritual commitment. The family members are bound in unity by their shared relationship with God and they learn to nurture it as a result of mutual encouragement.

7. Each person in a healthy household trusts the others and values the trust she or he has earned. This trust is built upon mutual respect and a dedication to truth.

8. The members of a healthy family enjoy freedom and grace. Each has the freedom to try new things, think different thoughts, and embrace values and perspectives that may be new to the family—even challenge old ways of doing things. All of this is built upon grace. Everyone has the freedom to fail, to be wrong, and to have faults and weaknesses without fear of rejection or condemnation. In a grace-based environment, failure is kept in perspective so that members of the family have enough confidence to recover, grow and achieve.[103]

In addition, J. Bradley Wigger, in his book *The Power of God at Home*, portrays the healthy family as a place of learning where life skills and relationship building is a part of everyday life. In a healthy family, the goal of discipline is to teach, guide and direct; it is never to punish. Of course, all of this should be done in the context of a spiritual life in which both parents and children are guided by God's wisdom:

One of the hopes for the spiritual life is that, through it…we can find some guidance as well—guidance for ourselves as parents, but also a guidance that our children can learn and rely on when we are not around… Such guidance in the face of life's possibilities is called wisdom. The hope is that the spiritual life can help us be wiser parents and that our children can themselves grow in wisdom … Children need freedom and choices to open the way to discovering the wonders of existence, including the beauty of their own lives. But children also need down-to-earth guidance and a wise hand to lead them through the dangers and responsibilities of living.[104]

There is much written about what makes up a healthy family. However, there is one thing that a healthy family is not—it is not perfect. The Lord has chosen to use broken people, in the context of family, to build His kingdom here on earth. As a result, there will be stumbling, mistakes and failures. We must remember, however, that "Love covers a multitude of sins" (1 Pet. 4:8 NASB). Through the redeeming grace of our Savior, as we bring our failures to Him, they will not be fatal. Only He can transform them into memorials of forgiveness, compassion and growth opportunities for the entire family.

When all of this takes place in an atmosphere of love, where parents surrender to the Word of God and to their God-ordained roles, then healthy, godly family life will be the result.

Understanding the Dysfunctional Family

"He who brings trouble on his family will inherit only wind,
and the fool will be servant to the wise." (Prov. 11:29 NIV)

The unfortunate reality is that most child-experienced trauma takes place either in, or because of, dysfunction within the family. The first step in bringing healing and hope to the children living in this kind of environment is to understand the dynamics of a dysfunctional family.

A dysfunctional family is a unit of repeated and chronic malfunction. It is usually an environment of continued, regular conflict and misbehavior on the part of individual parents. Children can be subjected to neglect and/or physical, psychological or sexual abuse. Dr. Charles Swindoll explains:

Dysfunctional families blur that line [between good and evil], and boundaries become unclear. Solid, secure families have a clear view of the difference so that its members have little ethical confusion. Moral dilemmas will challenge you, but if you come from a healthy family, you are seldom unclear about what is right or wrong.[105]

Most families experience periods of stressful circumstances (death of a family member, disaster, serious illness, etc.). However, when the crisis passes, the healthy family returns to normal functioning. On the other hand, in dysfunctional families the problems are ongoing—many times stemming from conditions, such as mental illness, addiction and abuse—and children's needs go unmet. Without intervention, the ensuing psychological effects on children can be terribly destructive and continue into adulthood. One child of an alcoholic parent recalls:

> I can't remember a time when my mother didn't have a drinking problem. My dad abandoned us when I was twelve, leaving me to cope with my mother on my own. Weekends when my Mom wasn't out in bars, she brought strange men home, many of whom were sexually abusive to me. Now, as an adult, I feel emotionally unable to cope with the normal stresses and strains of life and my relationships with men always seem to turn into disasters.[106]

Adults raised in dysfunctional families frequently report difficulties forming and maintaining intimate relationships, maintaining positive self-esteem, and trusting others; they fear a loss of control, and deny their feelings and reality.[107] Growing up in a problematic, neglectful family environment, which was believed to be normal, can leave scars that last a lifetime.

Characteristics of Dysfunctional Family Environments[108]

The following are characteristics of dysfunctional family environments:

- Needs and desires of the child are usually neglected
- Lack of trust and absence of security
- Absence of the feeling of love and belonging
- Lack of understanding between family members
- Parents fail to nurture and support the children
- Verbal, physical or sexual abuse may be a part of family life
- Family member(s) create an "unpredictably unhealthy environment"
- Disputes develop on petty issues like money, love, work or almost anything
- Negative dealing of stressful situations
- Family values and rules are rigid and illogical
- Boundaries either do not exist or are violated repetitively

- In rare cases, overprotecting the child may cause an adverse effect

Examples of Dysfunctional Parenting[109]

Deficient Parents

Deficient parents hurt their children more by omission than by commission. Frequently, chronic mental illness or a disabling physical illness contributes to parental inadequacy. Children tend to take on adult responsibilities from a young age in these families:

> As a kid I was like a miniature adult. I cooked and cleaned and made sure my little brothers got off to school. My mom was always depressed and stayed in bed — she was in the hospital a lot. I guess I never really was a kid. Now, I work hard to get A's, take on lots of responsibility and put on this competent front. Inside, I still really feel empty.[110]

In these families, parental emotional needs tend to take precedence and children are often asked to be their parents' caretakers. Robbed of their own childhood, they learn to ignore their own needs and feelings.

Controlling Parents

Unlike the deficient parents described above, controlling parents fail to allow their children to assume responsibilities appropriate for their age. These parents continue dominating and making decisions for their children well beyond the age at which this is necessary. These children frequently feel resentful, inadequate and powerless. Transitions into adult roles are quite difficult, as these adults frequently have difficulties making decisions independent from their parents.

Alcoholic Parents

Families built around alcoholic parents tend to be chaotic and unpredictable. Rules that apply one day, do not apply the next. Promises are neither kept nor remembered. Expectations vary from one day to the next. In addition, emotional expression is frequently forbidden and discussion about the alcohol use or related family problems is usually nonexistent. Family members are usually expected to keep problems a secret, thus preventing anyone from seeking help. All of these factors leave children feeling insecure, frustrated and angry. Mistrust of others, difficulty with emotional expression and difficulties with intimate relationships carry over into adulthood.

Abusive Parents

Abuse can be verbal, physical or sexual. Verbal abuse, such as frequent belittling or criticism, can have lasting effects, particularly when it comes from those entrusted with the child's care. Criticism can be aimed at the child's looks, intelligence, capabilities or basic value. Some verbal abusers are very direct, while others use subtle put-downs disguised as humor. Both types are equally damaging.

Physical abuse has much to do with meeting the parent's emotional needs and nothing to do with concern for the child. Parents often erroneously justify the abuse as "discipline" intended to "help" the child. Physically abusive parents can create an environment of terror for the child, particularly since violence is often random and unpredictable. Abused children often feel anger. Children of abusive parents have tremendous difficulties developing feelings of trust and safety, even in their adult lives.

While parents may justify or rationalize verbal or physical abuse as discipline aimed at somehow helping the child, there is no rationalization for sexual abuse. Sexual abuse is the most blatant example of an adult abusing a child purely for that adult's own gratification.

Understanding the Children in Dysfunctional Family Systems

Psychological Impact on the Child

Living in a dysfunctional, neglectful environment, where distorted attitudes and unnatural relationships are presented as the norm, can have tremendous traumatic effects on children. While trying to adapt, children may display some of the following signs and symptoms:

- Feelings of loneliness
- Being too hard on oneself
- Finding it hard to relax and enjoy
- Difficulty expressing feelings
- Extremist responses and decisions
- Problems forming intimate relationships
- Failure in school, truancy
- Delinquent behavior
- Frequent physical complaints

- Abuse of drugs or alcohol
- Depression/suicidal thoughts
- Physical illness from improper nutrition
- Risk-taking behavior
- Lacking friends, withdrawing from classmates
- Attaching to abusive relatives or relationships
- More concerned in helping others; seeking approval
- Taking over more than they can handle
- Inappropriate displays of anger, frustration and hatred

Roles the Children Adopt[111]

Many children in dysfunctional family systems adopt different family roles in order to cope with their unhealthy situation.

Hero

These children try to ensure the family looks "normal" to the outside world. They often project a personal image of achievement, competence, success and responsibility. The cost of such success is often a denial of their feelings and a belief they are "imposters."

Adjuster

These children learn to adjust in inappropriate ways. They learn never to expect or to plan anything. They often strive to be invisible, and avoid taking a stand or rocking the boat. As a result, they often come to feel they are drifting through life and are out of control.

Placater

These children learn early to smooth over potentially upsetting situations. Consequently, they tend to take total responsibility for the emotional care of the family. As adults, many placaters choose careers as helping professionals—careers which can reinforce a tendency to ignore their own needs. Continuing in this role as adults, they often end up with codependent personalities.

Scapegoat

These children are identified as the "family problem," often getting into various kinds of trouble, including drug and alcohol abuse, as a way of expressing their anger at the family. They also function as a sort of pressure valve. When tension builds in the family, the scapegoat will misbehave as a way of relieving pressure, while allowing the family to avoid dealing with the problem.

Clown

These children use humor and antics to direct the focus away from family problems. This child is often hyperactive and usually seeks to be the center of attention. Their humor is often a mask covering their true feelings, which surface later in life in unhealthy ways.

Dysfunctional family life has tremendous emotional impacts, which many times cause the cycle of neglect and abuse to perpetuate to the next generation. How can we help these children heal when the crucial factor of care is a healthy family environment with loving parental support?

Planning Your Work with Children in Dysfunctional Family Systems

"Those from among you will rebuild the ancient ruins;
you will raise up the age-old foundations;
And you will be called the repairer of the breach." (Isa. 58:12 NASB)

As you think through and plan your work with children caught in dysfunctional family systems, it is important to keep in mind that the best intervention is prevention. Awareness and education go hand in hand in turning the tide of neglect and abuse associated with unhealthy family life. God has ordained the family to be the essential building block for the furtherance of His kingdom here on earth.

Working with dysfunctional families is not a short-term project—it takes a commitment bathed with prayer. Even in the hands of trained professionals, the success rate is less than staggering. The dynamics of the dysfunctional family are extremely complex and, therefore, usually require professional help. That being said, research has shown lay helpers can play a valuable supportive role.[112] Throughout your work, there will be disappointments, but if the cycle of dysfunction and neglect is halted and reversed for even one family it is worth it.

Begin with the Family

The most important factor of care for all children, including those who experience trauma, is the influence of parental support. Therefore, the most significant prevention and intervention strategy is to encourage and promote a healthy family lifestyle, which includes godly, nurturing parental support.

The following are a few things to remember when working with dysfunctional parents:

Identify and Strengthen Parental Weaknesses

From the onset, helpers and counselors should realize, in many cases, neglectful parents want to be good parents, but may lack personal, financial and/or supportive resources. All parents have strengths and weaknesses. The hidden strengths of the neglectful parent or parents should be identified, reinforced and built upon.

Know When to Respect and When to Challenge Culture

It is important for helpers and counselors to be culturally sensitive, showing respect for differences in life experiences, child-rearing norms and values that support responsible parenting. Look for respected elders and extended family members to be key resources in aiding the family.

If we truly want to see families and communities transformed for His glory, then it is imperative we engage in communicating and fostering godly, healthy family life. In some cases, this may mean challenging individual cultures and traditions. In many places, due to cultural traditions and beliefs passed down through generations, there is a lack of knowledge as to what healthy family really looks like. Instruction and modeling in this area are as essential in fostering a mature Christian community, as any other biblical truth.

Parenting the Parent

Neglectful parents are often psychologically immature, usually as a result of their own lack of nurturing as a child. Therefore, they may require nurturing themselves to enable them to nurture their children. We may have to help them recall and work through their own issues stemming from childhood—in a sense, we may have to "parent" the parent.

Set Healthy Limits and Boundaries

Setting clearly stated, limited, realistic and achievable goals that are shared and agreed upon by parents, can help to avoid dysfunctional dependency and foster more independent, responsible functioning.

Use Praise and Affirmation

Neglectful parents are empowered when incremental achievements are rewarded and praised. Even small efforts such as preparing a meal, making positive statements about themselves or their children, or keeping an appointment should be met with positive affirmation.

Strengthen Social Networks

The informal social networks of neglectful parents are often closed, unstable and tend to be dominated by often critical, nonsupportive relatives. They usually do not provide the guidance and emotional support needed, and it is here that helpers and counselors can make a huge difference. They can also help the parents develop new friends and positive networks of support through community groups, school, church and other avenues, and link the parents with supportive resources in the community.

Direct Families to Appropriate Resources

Due to poverty, many neglectful parents lack access to resources. Mobilization of outside resources may help to overcome the family's hopelessness, resistance and possible distrust. Community services that strengthen families include:

- Food/clothing bank
- Medical Care
- Parent Aids
- Job Training
- Addiction Counseling
- Home Skills Training
- Transportation
- Emergency Financial Assistance
- Low Cost Child Care
- Mental Health Assessment
- Parent Support Groups
- Temporary Foster/Respite Care
- Budget Counseling

The Best Interests of the Child

"Let the little children come to me, and do not hinder them."
(Matt.19:14 NIV)

There is an unspoken code of conduct applicable to those working with children, especially in the area of counseling: do no harm. The best interests of the child should always be in the forefront of our prevention and intervention strategies. The very best scenario for dysfunctional families is for the children to be able to stay with their parent or parents while they go through the process of healing and recovery. However, this is not always possible.

In the case of physical and sexual abuse, the best practice would be for the child to be removed from the location of abuse to a place of safety. We certainly have the responsibility to do all we can to help this occur. In some areas, where laws are in place to protect the child, it is not difficult to report the abuse and for authorities to take action. However, in other places where the laws are vague or simply not enforced, removal can be difficult and the child remains in the abusive situation. Similarly, in many dysfunctional family situations, parents deny their need for help and the child has no recourse but to remain at home.

Surrogate Parental Support

The most important factor to foster resilience in a child is to develop a close bond with trusted adults/caregivers as a form of parental support. This can be provided through youth centers, after-school programs or church activities.

> Children of dysfunctional families who rely on supportive adults have increased autonomy and independence, stronger social skills, better ability to cope with difficult emotional experiences and better day-to-day coping strategies. They need to know that there are safe people who care about them and who can help them.[113]

Surrogate parental figures can work with the children of dysfunctional family systems to:

- **Develop safe ways to explore and express their feelings** of anger, fear, hurt, guilt and shame.

- **Learn how to take care of themselves and stay safe**.

- **Establish routines** that lend structure and stability to their day.

- **Learn how to cope positively** with problems at home, such as parental fighting, verbal violence, broken promises and neglect.

- **Develop problem-solving strategies**, especially ways to explore options. One good way to do this is to play the thinking game: "What else—Who else," which encourages coming up with alternatives to a problem situation. Here's how it works: "My dad is drunk every time he picks me up at swimming on Saturdays and I am afraid to ride with him." What else? "I can say, 'no thanks' and go home with another parent." What else? "I can call my mom to pick me up." Who else? "My neighbor or . . ."

- **Build self-esteem and self-efficacy**. Gently encourage them to talk about life and just listen. Invite them to an outing or offer a quiet place to do homework (perhaps a tutoring program at church). Encourage the child to think of people who would be understanding and helpful in hard times—perhaps a teacher, friend, relative or neighbor.

- **Relax, have fun and enjoy just being a kid**.

Let the Church Arise

"A father to the fatherless...is God in his holy dwelling." (Ps. 68:5 NIV)

Working with children at risk or in crisis and their families is as much a spiritual effort as it is physical or emotional; it requires a holistic approach. There is a war against the family and against the children—a war that is not relegated to certain areas of the world, but has permeated every community and every culture.

Traumatized and hurting children and their families are well within the reach of every church and faith community, and the Lord has given us the responsibility to be fathers to the fatherless. May we, His church, recognize the tremendous value He places on these little ones, realize the powerful ministry He has ordained for them, and rise up in His strength to bring healing and hope to their hurting hearts. They are the heritage of the Lord!

FIFTEEN

STRESS, BURNOUT and SELF-CARE

Phyllis Kilbourn

As God's chosen people, holy and dearly loved,
clothe yourselves with compassion, kindness, humility,
gentleness and patience. (Col. 3:12)

During the early stages of responding to crisis, caregivers may have abounding energy and motivation. Their cognitive functioning, training and resilience make them important assets to children who have been deeply wounded emotionally, and who have lost hope through their experiences of broken trust, betrayal and abandonment. Day after day as caregivers enter the children's world of pain when listening to their tragic and emotionally difficult stories and identifying with them in their suffering, they soon realize their job comes with many inherit risk factors, including high levels of stress.

Although helping children and youth overcome the negative effects of trauma is deeply meaningful and rewarding work, it also can be very emotionally demanding and challenging. Caregivers are expected to be empathic, understanding and giving, yet they must control their own emotional needs and responsiveness in dealing with the children. Images of violence, despair and hardship, and/or continuous concern over possible danger also contribute to caregivers' trauma-related feelings of isolation and depression, particularly if they do not have an opportunity to process their reactions.

When this happens, caregivers run the risk of having their compassion dry up, leading caregivers into compassion fatigue, a term Charles Figley originally coined as "an experience in which exposure to the suffering of clients coupled with an inability to rescue them from their suffering, results in feelings of depletion, anxiety, depression, resentment and/or emotional withdrawal."[114], [115]

Dr. Conrad points out other terms found in professional literature to describe these feelings: secondary trauma is commonly referred to as "the stress resulting from helping or wanting to help a traumatized or suffering person." Vicarious trauma is the term used to describe the "cumulative transformative effect of working with survivors of traumatic life events."[116]

When on earth Christ, too, knew the pain of reaching out to the poor, the lame, the blind, the beggars, the exploited, the oppressed and down-trodden, some of whom were widows, orphans and outcasts. He knew all were in need of healing touches of compassion, kindness, humility, gentleness and patience. Jesus wove these attributes into healing garments for any who were willing to convey His love and compassion to the broken and the hurting.

Many caregivers have clothed themselves with these healing garments, giving hurting children those compassionate and gentle touches, kind words as they demonstrate humility, and patient responses to the children's need. What a contrast to the neglect, lack of love and care that far too often characterize a child's day. However, no matter how much one loves the children, compassionate caregiving can affect a caregiver's emotions negatively, as well as positively.

Feelings of anger over the children's situations, inadequacies when it comes to their care, and a sense of hopelessness can cause compassion to dry up and the caregiver's healing garments to start getting ragged around the edges. The stresses have simply become too overwhelming. Like Elijah, who, in spite of the tremendous victory he had just won over the prophets of Baal on Mount Carmel, ran away in fear from Queen Jezebel. Totally exhausted and discouraged, he lay in the desert and even prayed he might die. The angels came and ministered to Elijah saying, "The journey is too much for you." God did not berate Elijah for not trusting His care. Instead, God gave him what he needed most at that time, a freshly baked loaf of bread, cool water and rest. (see 1 Kings 18, 19)

God also knows when the journey gets too much for compassionate caregivers. He has many ways to invite them to "come with Me to a quiet place and rest awhile." (see Mark 6:31) Such are His invitations for caregivers to engage more fully in "self-care." Self-care refers to those decisions and actions an individual can take to cope with his or her stress, and remain emotionally healthy. Children need (and deserve) emotionally and spiritually healthy caregivers.

To achieve this kind of health while engaged in stressful work, caregivers need to understand what causes stress and burnout so they can engage in self-care practices that alleviate stress and prevent burnout.

Emotions and Stress

Emotions are the outlet for reactions to traumatic or stressful events, both for the child and the counselor. Feelings of sadness over the children's situations are often intertwined with anger, feelings of helplessness and other emotionally draining feelings. When strong feelings or emotions threaten to overpower the caregivers, their natural reaction is to defend themselves from being overwhelmed or incapacitated by their intense feelings. The emotions are there, but they are "frozen" for the sake of self-protection.

The defenses caregivers construct as survival strategies against their stress and emotional trauma, closely resemble the coping strategies children use to mask their intense pain. They either deny its existence or express an unwillingness to share their deepest feelings with others.

If compassionate caregivers are to play a crucial role in helping the children cope with their pain, they will need special care to maintain their own emotional health.

Defining Caregivers' Stress

Stress is the response of a person's body to all the demands being made on it. There are warning signs when a person's stress level is exceeding his or her ability to cope. Sandra Rankin[117] lists warning signs, including feeling irritated about clients (here, the children), experiencing a low level of energy, having problems develop at home, viewing the world and the people in it as unsafe, and losing one's sense of humor. Paying attention to the physical and mental symptoms of stress is as important as is taking action to alleviate those symptoms, instead of ignoring them and simply hoping the situation will fix itself. Learning to recognize the symptoms within oneself that indicate heightened stress is imperative to addressing, relieving and avoiding it. Stress unchecked will lead to caregiver burnout.

Numerous symptoms may indicate a caregiver is experiencing reactions to traumatic stress. In fact, the very qualities that make one an excellent caregiver, such as empathy, identification, safety, trust, intimacy and power, are the very qualities that can cause one to face high stress levels leading to burnout.

Whatever term is used, if the emotional reaction is left unchecked, it will lead to burnout. Understanding these terms highlights the need to be aware of the need for self-care, if counselors are to be effective in their caregiving while maintaining their own emotional health.

Stress warning signs include, but are not limited to, the following:

- Strong, unexpected emotional changes, such as being quick to become angry
- Easily moved to tears or quick to become frustrated
- Eating problems, including eating too much or loss of one's appetite.
- Interrupted sleep or chronic fatigue
- Racing heartbeat
- Confusion or loss of memory
- Inability to make decisions and/or express oneself either verbally or in writing
- Developing new health problems or worsening of existing chronic conditions
- An inability to stop thinking about the crisis, crisis victims and/or the crisis intervention
- Withdrawal from contact with co-workers, friends and/or family.
- Alcohol and substance abuse
- Impulsive behaviors

Unfortunately, many counselors use stress as an indicator of the quality of work they are doing, believing they are being ineffective if they experience even a hint of stress. What counselors need to remember is stress and the accompanying symptoms are indicative of how the work is affecting them.

Defining Burnout

Burnout is a special type of stress in which a person becomes physically, mentally and emotionally exhausted from the seemingly insurmountable pressures faced. Compassion fatigue is also recognized as a form of burnout—"a deep physical, emotional and spiritual exhaustion accompanied by acute emotional pain." Compassion-fatigued caregivers may continue to give themselves fully to the children they are caring for, while finding it difficult to maintain a healthy balance of empathy and objectivity. The cost of this imbalance can be quite high, in terms of ability to function effectively in the family, at work, in the community and, most of all, in one's personal relationships.

This kind of stress can negatively affect a person's motivation, energy levels and mental well-being. It comes from working in a situation that produces overwhelming emotional stress, such as working with children in crisis. Burnout is a gradual process that occurs over an extended period of time. It does not happen overnight, but, instead, creeps up on a person if he or she is not paying attention to the warning signals. The signs and symptoms of burnout are subtle at first, but they get worse and worse as time goes on. Burnout stems from several factors, including the workplace where a person encounters stressful work, often from too many responsibilities. Other factors include a person's lifestyle and certain personality traits. What you do in your free or leisure time, and how you look at the world can play just as big of a role in causing burnout as work or home demands.

Burnout occurs when a person feels overwhelmed and unable to meet the constant demands of meeting the children's needs. As the stress continues, caregivers begin to lose the interest or motivation that led them to take on a certain role in the first place. Having their energy drained, burnout reduces their productivity and leaves them feeling increasingly disillusioned, helpless, hopeless, distrustful, resentful and completely worn out. Eventually, such caregivers may feel like they have nothing more to give.

When one is burned out, problems seem insurmountable, everything looks bleak, and it is difficult to gather up the energy to care—let alone do something about the situation. The unhappiness and detachment burnout causes can threaten not only a person's work with the children, but also his or her relationships with family, friends and coworkers, and even a person's health. However, burnout can be healed. But since burnout is not an overnight occurrence, it is important to recognize the early signs and to act before the problem becomes truly serious. The key is learning to recognize the physical, emotional and behavioral symptoms of burnout. Counselors can regain their balance by reassessing priorities, making time for those priorities and seeking support.

Difference Between Stress and Burnout

Burnout may be the result of unrelenting stress, but it isn't the same as too much stress. Stress involves *too much*—too many pressures that demand too much of you physically and psychologically. Stressed people can still imagine, though, that if they can just get everything under control, they will feel better.

On the other hand, burnout is about *not enough*. Being burned out means feeling empty, lacking motivation and beyond caring. People experiencing burnout often do not see any hope of positive change in their situations. Just as excessive stress is like drowning in responsibilities, burnout is the opposite; it is being all dried up. Another vital difference between stress and burnout is that while you're usually aware of being under a lot of stress, you do not always notice burnout when it happens.

Stress versus Burnout	
Stress	**Burnout**
Characterized by overengagement	Characterized by disengagement
Emotions are over-reactive	Emotions are blunted
Produces urgency and hyperactivity	Produces helplessness and hopelessness
Loss of energy	Loss of motivation, ideals and hope
Leads to anxiety disorders	Leads to detachment and depression
Primary damage is physical	Primary damage is emotional
May kill you prematurely	May make life seem not worth living
Source: *Stress and Burnout in Ministry*[118]	

Stress that Leads to Burnout

There are many reasons for caregivers' traumatic stress that ends in burnout. Some of the reasons can be found in the warning signs that follow. If a person recognizes these warning signs of impending burnout, steps can be taken to get a person's life back into balance, preventing burnout from becoming a full-blown breakdown. If nothing is done to address the issues causing burnout, the situation will only get worse.

Other-Focused

As stated earlier, perhaps one of the main reasons for burnout is that those who care for others are more apt to be "other-focused," becoming so wrapped up in the children's or caregivers' needs, they forget their own physical, emotional and spiritual needs. If caregivers are not careful, they unconsciously will turn every relationship into a counseling one, leaving them without meaningful emotional or spiritual support.

Work Difficulties

In many cases, burnout stems from a person's job or work. Caring for children in crisis is one such job that has a high stress level that can lead to burnout. Especially in emergencies or major disasters, those seeking to comfort and counsel frightened, hurting children find themselves immersed in an excessively hectic and pressure-filled workload. The demand on their time and energies is enormous, and counselors simply cannot begin to meet all the children's needs. As they discover their limitations, feelings of helplessness, inadequacy and incompetency begin to affect them. Anyone who feels overworked and undervalued is at risk for burnout. Other work-related issues include:

- Unclear or overly demanding job expectations
- Doing work that's monotonous or unchallenging
- Working in a chaotic or high-pressure environment
- Only limited resources available for children's basic needs
- Lack of recognition or rewards for good work
- Feeling like you have little or no control over your work
- Not sure of your role/no job description
- Interpersonal relationships in the work place

Lifestyle

Burnout can be caused by a person's lifestyle. Questions to ask yourself, include:

Am I—

- Working too much, without enough time for relaxing and socializing?
- Being expected to be too many things to too many people?
- Taking on too many responsibilities, without enough help from others?
- Not getting enough sleep?
- Lacking close, supportive relationships?

View Asking for Help as Weakness

Assuming they are to be strong, counselors may view asking for help as a sign of weakness. Asking for help, however, is not a sign of weakness; it really is a sign of the commitment to the work that counseling requires. Asking for help, therefore, must be seen as a sign of commitment to the work of helping the children.

Anger

Constantly confronting injustices is painful, especially when the caregivers deal with innocent children who have no control over what is happening to them. Caregivers not only want to release rage against the children's suffering, but also against the perpetrators responsible for their victimization. Such rage, if unresolved, can cripple a person emotionally.

Unrealistic Expectations

Caregivers' unrealistic expectations can also lead to tension, especially when they can do little to "fix" the children's pain. The expectation that "I should be able to fix it" leads to feelings of helplessness. It is stressful to not be able to tell the children everything is going to be all right When caregivers have unrealistic expectations and cannot live up to them, they can become severely depressed.

Lack of Training

Those caring for and counseling children are key stabilizing elements in the children's lives. Most, however, have had little or no formal training in mental health or crisis response and intervention. Often they are unsure of the best way to help children work through their problems. Fear of making wrong choices of care or counsel can cause a lot of anxiety and stress. Caregivers can also be frustrated over not knowing the best way to respond to a need.

Inability to Detach Emotionally

Caregivers sometimes find it difficult to detach themselves from their work when it involves a lot of suffering or need. After a stressful day of dealing with the children's deep emotional and physical wounds, it is hard to lay the children's needs or their feelings aside.

Like the children, they feel it is wrong, or at least they feel guilty, to relax or participate in recreation at such times. Special efforts must be made to plan ways for workers to be able to detach emotionally.

Personality Traits

Caregivers who have perfectionistic tendencies, where nothing is ever good enough, are in serious danger of quickly having their stress turn to burnout. Rarely, if ever, is anything perfect in a child's world—especially if they are living in a crisis situation. Caregivers must make a real effort to accept things as they are. Other caregivers have a pessimistic view of themselves and the world. Some need to be in control, so they are reluctant to delegate to others.

Indicators of Being in Burnout

There also are symptoms that indicate a person likely has entered the stage of burnout. The following are crucial indicators of a person's mental and emotional health when entering the stage of burnout:

- Abusing drugs, alcohol or food
- Blaming
- Chronic lateness
- Depression
- Diminished sense of personal accomplishment
- High self-expectations
- Hopelessness
- Inability to maintain balance of empathy and objectivity
- Less ability to feel joy
- Low self-esteem

We need to think of all the symptoms of burnout as warning signs or red flags that something is wrong that needs to be addressed. If a person pays attention to these early warning signs, a major breakdown can be prevented. If a person ignores them, eventually they will experience burnout.

Need for Self-Care: Burnout Prevention

To recharge your batteries for compassionate care, you must first learn to recognize when you are wearing down and then get into the habit of doing something every day that will replenish you. That's not as easy as it may seem because real lifestyle changes take time, energy and desire. In addition, trauma counselors' natural instinct is to lay aside their own needs to help others. It is extremely important for caregivers to also monitor their own trauma reactions and to take care of their own needs. Failure to do so can result in an overload of stress and eventually burnout, which interferes with a person's ability to provide crisis intervention assistance. This can be true in the aftermath of an immediate crisis like a natural disaster, fatal car accident or a terrorist attack, or during an extended period of stress and anxiety like war. If self-care is not a priority in the counselor's strategies, either for him or her personally or the team members, emotional difficulties can become overpowering.

The risks of high levels of stress leading to burnout indicate special care is needed to prevent caregivers from experiencing serious emotional problems. If they fail in self-care, they can hurt not only themselves, but affect the quality of care the children receive. As Sandra Rankin reminds us, "Counselors who neglect their own mental, physical and spiritual self-care eventually run out of 'oxygen' and cannot effectively help their clients [the children] because all of their energy is going out to the clients and nothing is coming back in to replenish the counselors' energy."[119] Some daily replenishing helps include:

- To the extent possible, maintain normal daily routines (especially physical exercise activities, mealtime and bedtime routines). Be sure to maintain healthy eating habits and drink plenty of water.

- Connect with trusted friends or family who can help, especially in the initial stage of prevention.

- Give yourself permission to do things you find pleasurable (i.e., going shopping or out to dinner with friends).

- Avoid using alcohol and drugs to cope with the effects of being a caregiver/counselor during times of intense crisis or when the children's situations and experiences are overwhelming.

- Ask for support from family and friends in terms of reducing pressures or demands during times of helping severely traumatized children. Prayer support from others is vital, too.

- Take periodic rest breaks, at least every couple of hours. As much as possible, try to get some restful sleep, preferably without the use of sleep aids or alcohol.

- Take time at the end of each day to process or debrief the events of the day with other caregivers or colleagues.

- Keep engaged in spiritual practices that provide strength and comfort, such as prayer or small-group Bible studies that allow for interaction. This gives you an opportunity to share your needs in a way that uplifts and centers you.

- Be kind and gentle on yourself and others, as you have all shared the experience of exposure to life-changing events for the children. Everyone needs time to process the impact of these events into their lives.[120]

Prevention and Recovery Strategies

Strategies for the care of caregivers who counsel children in crisis should revolve around any plan—big or small—that alleviates high levels of stress. Some caregivers are a part of a team while others work on their own. Team leaders need to plan strategies for their team, while those working independently will have to make their own program. This is where support and accountability groups are valuable; it is not easy for counselors to not have a group to relate to or to serve as a sounding board for advice and encouragement.

Following are some components that will help build successful programs that enable caregivers to maintain their own well-being as they support the emotional needs of children in their care. Implementing these ideas will help prevent burnout and also help workers in burnout recovery.

Provide an Outlet for Emotions

Caregivers need an outlet to express their feelings of anger, frustration or fear. Just as we encourage children to express their pain to facilitate healing, so should we encourage caregivers to express theirs. Provide an emotionally safe environment in which to conduct frequent debriefing sessions. Make sure workers can feel free to express their anger, frustrations or inadequacies without any form of reprisal. Techniques used with the children for expressing feelings, may also be used with the caregivers: singing, writing, drama or other art forms.

Time together in a group can also be a forum for strategizing, discussing problems, finding solutions, sharing one another's expertise and praying together.

Support

Those serving as counselors need assurance they will be provided with the resources and supportive networks needed to become involved in the children's and the community's experience of loss, pain and grief. This requires caregivers to be provided with resources that give them a healthy "oxygen supply." A support group should be a part of the entire concept of support. Without others to learn from, vent with or lean on for support, stress is more likely to build unimpeded. Experts say finding a support system, whether through formal supervision or an informal network of other professionals to meet with for consultation and companionship, is vital in maintaining emotionally healthy caregivers.

Counselors also recommend checking out local, state, regional and national associations for networking possibilities and attending professional conferences to meet other helping professionals.

Elicit Feedback

A decline in work performance creates interpersonal difficulties on the job. Through feedback, one can clarify and set priorities regarding role demands, and encourage open communication with other team members or colleagues about mutual responsibilities. To reduce role conflicts and stress, the leader may have to consider reassigning responsibilities.

Set Boundaries

Boundaries, including a commitment to self, must be in place so there is a balance and distinction between counselors' work life and personal life. Caregivers need to know how to set limits on their energies, time, competency and resources if they are to avoid burnout. Encourage workers to set their own reasonable goals and expectations; then empower them to use their skills, knowledge and strengths as an investment in the children's lives.

Equip Workers for Holistic Care

Children who are physically ill or hungry cannot accept mental health care. Therefore, workers should be equipped with a referral list of agencies that assist with these needs (food, medical care, shelter, drug rehabilitation, etc.) if your organization cannot supply them. Caregivers can then be empowered to provide emotional and spiritual care, rather than feeling stressed out because they cannot provide the children's basic physical needs.

Make Reasonable Work Schedules

Provide counselors with a reasonable work schedule. Take into account the amount of stress involved in their work situation. Stress levels can be established by the number of children a counselor will be responsible for and by the severity of the children's trauma. The more stressful the job, the more often caregivers will need breaks.

Plan Ways to Detach from Work

Encourage workers to find ways to detach from their work in the evenings and on their days off. Taking the cares of the children or the work home each night will not allow release of daily tensions. Just as children often refuse to play when in a traumatic situation, so do those who care for them. They may feel guilty to even express humor. Yet, many caregivers state that the only way they could have stayed rational in deeply traumatic situations was to find ways to express humor and to keep laughing.

Provide Safe Work Environments

For additional emotional stability, do everything possible to provide counselors with a safe and secure counseling environment. Caregivers are more effective and efficient if they do not have to think about the environment in which they are working. This is especially true for those working in dangerous situations, such as with children on the streets or those in active war zones. Having a safe working environment also allows counselors to keep their minds on the needs of the children.

Involvement in Community

Sometimes a counselor may be working in his or her own community; other times, work will come from communities they visit for short or long-term periods. In either case, community involvement at some level should be encouraged. Within the community, caregivers may find various resources available that can provide additional support and vital networking. Also, the presence of a caregiver can have a great impact on a child's family and community.

Training

Training gives caregivers confidence and expertise in their jobs, thus eliminating a lot of stress. Every caregiver should take a basic trauma-care course. Regardless of the cause for the trauma, a child will experience loss and grief. Trauma-care principles can be adapted to any specific trauma. With trauma care as the foundation, specific aspects of training can be added on as needed. For example, do the children have addiction problems (alcohol and drugs) or have they contracted HIV/AIDS through sexual exploitation? These are specific traumas that will require specialized training over and above basic trauma-care training.

Conclusion

Although most caregivers working with children in traumatic situations are familiar with the importance of self-care, many find it a challenge to put the concept into practice in their own lives. As they face busy schedules with time needed for so many children, caregivers may tend to assume they can, or even should, handle problems and stress on their own. Research has shown that those who ignore their own needs will find their outlook on the helping profession becoming more negative, robbing them of the joys of seeing children work through their own grief and loss issues. When we are well, we are better able to connect with the children, more attentive to their needs, more creative in our work and less likely to violate boundaries.

As Henri Nouwen reminds us, "Time given to inner renewal is never wasted. In fact, it is the fuel for the journey, and more importantly, it is the discipline that will shape the very fabric of our being."[121] To experience inner renewal, caregivers need to recognize and watch for the warning signs of burnout, and immediately undo the damage by managing stress and seeking support. We need to start building our resilience to stress by taking care of our spiritual, physical and emotional health. We are called to be instruments of healing; if we do not keep our own instrument tuned, we will not be useful in promoting wellness in others.

Sixteen

CHILDREN'S TRAUMA-RECOVERY TOOLS
Phyllis Kilbourn

Feelings are important to children. How children feel about their traumatic experiences is more important than gaining knowledge of the circumstances surrounding the event. However, children find it very difficult to express their feelings without help. Many times, caregivers are at a loss in knowing how to help children express and process their feelings. This is when the use of counseling tools that incorporate a variety of verbal and nonverbal skills, or a combination of both, can be used to facilitate children's ability to communicate feelings and to help them name, express and understand those feelings. This book describes two counseling tools that will assist caregivers in their communication with traumatized children: *There Is Hope* (for one-on-one or group counseling) and *Tell Me a Story* (for group counseling). Information on obtaining electronic versions of these tools that allow for duplication is availabe at www.crisiscaretraining.org.

Introduction to *There Is Hope*

There Is Hope, an interactive trauma-recovery booklet, was first prepared for the children of Haiti after the devastating earthquake occurred in 2010, leaving total destruction in its path. With literally thousands of children traumatized by the effects of the earthquake (death of family members, loss of housing, protection and basic necessities, etc.), caregivers did not know how to begin addressing the children's fears, losses and other trauma reactions.

There Is Hope was written to help these caregivers (Sunday school teachers, parents, pastors, school personnel, and others who help children who have gone through traumatic experiences and suffered loss) provide children with opportunities to express their emotional pain through music, writing exercises, art and play activities. These activities open up doors of opportunity for supportive conversations. Hundreds of thousands of children have worked through their trauma issues with the help of this booklet. A generic version of the Haiti booklet, suitable for use with children who have been impacted by any kind of trauma, has been developed. An accompanying *Facilitator's Guide* gives page-by-page notes that guide workers in understanding and helping children with their assignments.

The booklet contains sixteen pages of assignments that help children identify their losses and work through the traumatic feelings surrounding those losses. Other trauma-related issues addressed include: identity (children are created in the image of God and are special to Him, regardless of what has happened to them), understanding the event causing the trauma, safety and protection, how feelings have changed (prior to and after the event), God's love and care, hope through knowing that Jesus has a special plan for their lives, and a concluding closure activity. As the children work through their assignments, they are given opportunities to talk about their trauma-related feelings.

Children's Experiences and Needs

Children often experience troubling emotions that may be new to them. Another feature of their trauma is the losses they have experienced. Children need help identifying their losses and understanding what these mean to them, both now and later. To bring closure to their trauma, children need to grieve their losses in a way that is meaningful to them.

The importance of having an opportunity to express emotional feelings was demonstrated by one group of Haitian children who did not receive any psychological help for several months until a caregiver started a trauma-recovery group and introduced them to *There Is Hope*. At the end of their first session using the booklets one girl remarked, "So much time has passed, yet this is the first time anyone has asked us how we felt about what happened in the earthquake." The children longed to resolve these frightful and painful feelings, but they needed help. With help, the children were able to identify their losses, and were able to process their feelings and reactions stemming from the losses.

Peer or Individual Grouping

Whether individual or group approaches are used in working through the booklet assignments depends a lot on the circumstances of the trauma and the children's resultant needs. Some caregivers prefer to have children complete these assignments in a peer group setting; while others prefer to work one-on-one with a single child. In a natural disaster, such as an earthquake, where most of the children have similar experiences and feelings ,though perhaps varying in degree of trauma, it is generally most helpful for children to process what has happened with a supportive peer group.

Other factors to consider in planning a grouping strategy include your answers to questions, such as: Does the counseling require privacy? Will our groups be all boys, only girls or both? Will the children, under their circumstances, feel free to open up and share in a group setting what could be very embarrassing incidences? Counselors also need to ask themselves, "Does the child need more individualized attention that one-on-one counseling offers?" Usually, a one-on-one approach helps caregivers delve deeper into the trauma issues affecting a child, allowing them to more quickly assess a child's trauma levels and determine if the child needs professional care.

While all of the above considerations are vital in planning the best counseling approach, the configuration of the group largely will depend on local culture and the trauma issues involved.

Methodology

Writing or drawing activities that combine both one-on-one reflection and oral communication are major methods used to invite children to join in supportive conversations about their emotional difficulties. Drawing is a natural mode of communication that children rarely resist, and that offers a way to express feelings and thoughts in a manner that is less threatening than strictly verbal means. A drawing can provide information on developmental, emotional and cognitive functioning, quicken expression of hidden traumas, and convey unclear or contradictory feelings and perceptions.

For the child who has experienced trauma or loss, it helps to externalize emotions and events too painful to speak out loud—and drawing is one of the few means of conveying the complexities of painful experiences, repressed memories, unspoken fears, anxieties or guilt. Drawings bring issues relevant to treatment to the surface, thus quickening caregivers' ability to intervene and assist troubled children.

Assignments

The assignments in the booklets are designed to give children opportunities to explore and express their feelings about the traumatic events they have experienced. The assignments also provide children with knowledge of the trauma and its impact on them. Gaining knowledge and understanding will come through supportive conversations, art work, written assignments and play activities. Once the children have identified their losses and expressed their feelings about them, the facilitator (a caregiver/counselor) can help the children come to closure on their grief issues through a concrete activity where their feelings can be released into God's hands.

Time Frame

Counseling sessions can be as difficult for children as they are for adults—sometimes even more so. No matter the purpose for the counseling, it is important to remember communication with children is not the same as it is with adults. It is important to go slowly through the assignments, exploring a single concept, such as loss, in a session. Adequate time also must be given for supportive conversations with the children. These conversations will help the children process what they are learning. Be ready for these conversations whenever they are needed, not just at the end of the session. The assignment activities are like opening the door to a child's communication system and when they are ready, they no doubt will want to talk.

Counseling sessions for children usually are conducted from thirty to thirty-five minutes. Time frames, however, must be kept flexible. Time spent in sessions and on the assignments to be covered will depend on a number of factors, including the seriousness of the situation, how the child is handling recalling issues surrounding the traumatic event, and his or her attention span. Children need time to adequately absorb and internalize what they are learning about themselves in relation to the traumatic experience.

The children's body language (wringing of hands, not making eye contact or squirming in their seats), along with signs of emotional distress, are clear signals to let you know it is time to end the session early. When this happens, quickly turn to more enjoyable activities (storytelling, music, games or a snack) before they are given permission to return to their homes. Do not let children leave if they are crying or still in distress. If this is not possible given the time, make sure someone walks home with them.

The Facilitator's Guide

Lack of training prevents many caregivers from helping children when they are experiencing trauma-produced emotional problems. Using the *Facilitator's Guide,* caregivers can quickly be taught the basics of trauma, loss, grief and recovery for children. The *Facilitator's Guide* teaches how to use the trauma-recovery booklet, *There Is Hope.* The pages on the right side of the *Facilitator's Guide* are exact copies of the children's assignment pages. The notes opposite each child's assignment page start with a written purpose that, along with the ensuing notes, explains why the session to be completed is needed and how it will help the child heal.

The notes also help the facilitator understand the key concepts to talk about with the children as they work on and complete the assignment page. The *Facilitator's Guide* also expands on the children's concepts of trauma, fear, sadness and other effects of the trauma, including changes in the children's behavior. Usually, these reactions will occur immediately following the trauma. However, sometimes a child will seem to be doing fine at the time of the trauma, and have a delayed response weeks or months later.

When training caregivers to use the children's booklet, it is an ideal time to also help trainees process and resolve any trauma issue they may have, whether past or present. Effective caregiving requires a willingness to identify with a child's hurt, vulnerability, fear, anger and sense of loss. To do this, caregivers need to be emotionally healthy. They cannot be a container for holding the children's pain, while holding on to their own.

The Facilitator's Task

Before meeting with the children, facilitators need to be sure they are able to manage their own feelings about the traumatic events affecting the children. Time must be taken to understand one's own feelings and be prepared emotionally before attempting to reassure or work with the children.

The facilitator's task is to guide the children through the assignments in their handbook (be sure there are enough booklets for each child to have his or her own). Children need help in identifying and grieving their losses. They also need help in realizing what these losses will mean to them both now and long-term. The notes in the *Facilitator's Guide* will help caregivers accomplish this task. It is important that facilitators study these pages before meeting with the children. Also, be prepared to share any additional ideas you may have to talk about with the children.

The facilitator must not be afraid to talk openly and truthfully about the events surrounding that which caused the children's trauma. The children will see through any false information and wonder why you do not trust them with the truth. Not openly talking about what has happened does not help children work through the healing process, or help them develop effective coping strategies for life's future traumas and losses. However, the child should take the lead in what to talk about. This will help the facilitator know the level of his or her understanding and feelings. Keep in mind that children need enough information to comfort them, but not so many details that the trauma increases.

Help children and families feel connected to peers and adults who can provide support and decrease isolation. Be aware of local resources to help children and families obtain additional help, if needed.

The Facilitator's Relationship with Children

To help children feel safe with you, be supportive and compassionate in talking with them. Children who have been displaced from their homes, separated from family members or who have lost loved ones are particularly feeling vulnerable. Help children share in maintaining their feelings of safety by asking them about their specific needs for comfort and self-care.

It is important to let children know you really want to understand what they are feeling or what they need. Sometimes children are upset, but they cannot tell you what will be helpful. Giving them the time and encouragement to sort out their feelings with you may enable them to eventually share their feelings. Children will need ongoing support. The more losses the child or adolescent suffers, the more difficult it will be to recover. This is especially true if they have lost a parent who was their major source of support. Children who have suffered significant losses need multiple supports.

Conclusion

Today's children are living with fear, stress, anxiety and grief caused by events like bullying and gang violence, car crashes and natural disasters, school shootings and continuing war, physical or sexual abuse and hard economic times that often lead to domestic violence. One goal of trauma work with children is to restore safety and protection to those who have experienced trauma within their homes, schools and communities. Another goal is to provide parents and youth workers with information, understanding and skills related to coping with the issues that created the trauma. The current trauma-recovery tools available to caregivers can help children become less fearful and more compassionate persons, thereby increasing their chances of living in a world of increased inner and outer peace.

PART VI:

A CONCLUDING REFLECTION

SEVENTEEN

A WALK with JESUS from CAESAREA PHILIPPI to JERUSALEM

Keith J. White

I invite you to take a walk with Jesus and His disciples. Matthew's Gospel is our guide, and the journey is from Caesarea Philippi to Jerusalem, or if you like, from Mount Hermon to Mount Moriah.

Beginning our Walk with Jesus

Caesarea Philippi was on the slopes of Mount Hermon, north of the Sea of Galilee, not far from the present-day Damascus. The pilgrimage we are embarking on with Jesus takes us from near the very north of the area in which He ministered, to near the south; from a center of pagan worship, to the heart of Jewish celebration and sacrifice. All the time, Jesus is heading for the place where the "divine cup"[122] awaits Him. And it is significant that His ministry has a new urgency and focus. He is still announcing and revealing the kingdom of heaven, but once Peter has declared that He is the Christ, the Son of the living God, Jesus shares openly and repeatedly with His followers the very heart and mystery of the gospel: that He, the Christ, must suffer and be killed before being raised to life,[123] and that the Kingdom is completely and utterly different to the kingdoms on earth, human institutions and organizations, and anything they might have come to expect.

Along the way, we will soon discover Jesus led by actions and example, not simply by words. He is on a journey of discovery about the nature of the kingdom of heaven and what it means for Him. And the way He does things, is as important as what He does. The way He says things, is as important as what He says. The process is as important as the content of the gospel.

So, let's begin our walk with Jesus. For some readers, perhaps the idea of a pilgrimage will resonate, possibly even for others it is reminiscent of the stations of the cross. And we will pause eight times in the journey to ponder eight insights into the nature of the kingdom of heaven taught by Jesus that are axiomatic in our ministry among children, young people and families.

1.   The critical importance of faith (Matthew 17: 20) and prayer (Mark 9:29)

As far as we can work it out, it was on Mount Hermon that Peter, James and John saw the transfigured Jesus with Moses and Elijah; and it was in the shadow of this snow-capped peak that a troubled father brought his epileptic son to Jesus. It is at this precise moment we join Jesus and His disciples. Jesus was coming down the mountain where the father of the boy pleaded with Him. Jesus healed the boy. The disciples, who had been unable to help, wanted to know why they could not rebuke and drive out the demon. And Jesus spoke of their lack of faith (Matthew) and the need for prayer (Mark). The two responses form an integrated truth: faith and prayer are inseparable. And they are the bedrock of our mission with children and in every setting.

It may soon dawn on us that the overwhelming importance of prayer and faith is not just something Jesus reiterates in His teaching and mentoring of His followers, but is integral to, and incarnate in, His life and ministry.

In John's Gospel, we have the privilege of eavesdropping as Jesus prays personally and intimately. Later, we will enter into His wrestling in prayer in the garden of Gethsemane.

But this prayer life was accompanied by the most profound faith in history. He has just told His followers He must suffer and die; and that He will be raised to life on the third day. Have you stopped to reflect on the faith of Jesus? I'm not sure what the writer to the Hebrews had in mind when He summoned up his great catalog of the people of faith by referring to Jesus as "the author of our faith" (Heb. 12:2), but in using a word applied to Jesus as the author of life, and of salvation, perhaps we should pause to let the significance of this moment in His ministry sink in.

Notice, before we move on, the faith of the father of the epileptic boy. We, the body of Christ, have no monopoly on faith. If we think children's or any ministry in the name of Jesus is possible without faith, this is the time to quit! Above the door of Mill Grove, my home where Ruth and I care for and support children and young people, are the words "Have faith in God." They testify to over a century of practical, down-to-earth faith: trusting God and relying on His promises. Faith and love go together. We see that beautifully clearly in 1 Corinthians 13: 4-8.

Until we can pray "Thy will be done," we are loose cannons in our interventions; until that point, faith and prayer will never be properly integrated. There is no easy answer, and no easy response to the hurting child (or parent): such a way would be a sort of "cheap grace." We will be affected, hurt, challenged to the very depths and foundations of our being, and it is here that prayer and faith alone are relevant.

As followers of Jesus, we, like Him, should seek to find the agenda of our heavenly Father in the life of a child, family or community. Our primary task is to discover the *Missio Dei* (God's Mission) and to join Him in it; not to seek to enlist His assistance for our own endeavors!

2. The necessity of changing and becoming like little children (Matthew 18:3)

Jesus has headed south and we have now arrived at Capernaum, the well-known town on the shores of Lake Galilee, where Peter's house was situated, and which once was the center of Jesus' ministry. It was the place where He had healed so many as the sun was setting and so fulfilled the prophecy of Isaiah. On this occasion, He taught it was necessary to change and become like little children in order to enter the kingdom of heaven—to let God have His way among and in us.

The meaning of this teaching is commonly misunderstood.[124] Often, people make a list of the attributes of children (i.e., they are trusting, questioning, reliant and dependent on others) and then seek to apply them to adults. We must be very careful if we do this that we do not read our adult and cultural preferences into children! A primary question concerns whether we are prepared to *change* or not. If we are not, then we are unlikely ever to enter into God's way of doing things. So, let us ask ourselves whether we are allowing Jesus to change us.

That is hard enough, but next comes the issue of *becoming like* children, and I want to admit, I am becoming steadily less sure what it means as I study its meaning with others across the world. The only clue Jesus gives us is that we should be humble. (This word comes from the Latin word, *humus*, which means earth or compost.) The little child in the midst had no status in the society of Jesus' time, and he or she had done nothing to merit a place in the kingdom of heaven. Perhaps it means we should be ready to lay aside everything we have invested in following Jesus and be prepared to start again. If you have taken up the cross, you have had to let go of all else. All status, merit or progress is meaningless. You are as marginal as a little child; you are outside the religious trading game where virtue is rewarded. Only grace can save.

So when we are in the presence of a hurting, traumatized child, seeking to help, we must start not from above or outside, but from a realization of what we have in common. It will not be a matter of simply trying to reach a child in order to bring her to the safe place we think we can provide, but prior to that, an empathy that comes from the knowledge of the necessity of identifying with the little child.

3. Welcoming/receiving/accepting children in the name of Jesus, and so welcoming Jesus Himself (Matt. 18:5)

We are still in Capernaum with the fishing boats clearly visible, as they silently weave their way backward and forward across waters of Galilee. Against this backdrop, Jesus speaks this astonishing sentence: "Whoever welcomes a little child like this in my name welcomes me."

Some years ago, I was asked a question that cut me to the quick. I had already given more than a quarter of a century to caring for children at risk in my family home, Mill Grove. The (angry) questioner challenged me: "Do you really want to be in this ministry?" I immediately knew from my instinctive defensive reaction he had touched a raw nerve. The result was a deep pondering of my calling during which I realized I had reservations, and possibly regrets, that must have affected my relationship with the children and young people I sought to help. Over time, I began to learn what it was really like to welcome children in the name of Jesus: to be open to them with my whole being. And I have come to recognize those parents, teachers and caregivers who have opened their hearts to children; who love and respect the children they are alongside.

This is the calling of our Lord and Master: full acceptance, appreciation, valuing, respect for children in His name, the name of Jesus.

The process is similar to that experienced by Jean Vanier and Henri Nouwen. In fact, Henri Nouwen's last book[125], *Adam: God's Beloved* is a brilliant description of the process involved. It shows, with an honesty and reality, our ministry is only Christlike when it is two-way; when we open ourselves up to the possibility that we are being blessed. Please do not think this welcoming is an easy or painless process!

When we are open to children and are really joyful in our ministry, then we will find we have welcomed Jesus. In a book two of us have been working on for five years or so, we are exploring whether it is in receiving or welcoming children that we become like them. If so, our work is a great privilege. (This interpretation is an antidote to a spirituality that focuses on the pilgrimage and identity of self. In such a case, ministry among children might be a way of meeting our own needs rather than theirs.)

It is sometimes a little trying, if not wearisome, to live in a place people come to see and where they often get excited. "It's so peaceful" or "so spiritual" are common comments. And the remarks seem to come in parts of the building and at times when, to those of us who live there, we find little or no trace of peace or spirituality! But the sentiments have been expressed so frequently I have been forced to ponder what they might mean. And one day, it dawned on me: the one common thread to everything that has happened at Mill Grove since 1899 is children have been welcomed in the name of Jesus. Why then? Jesus promised to slip in with them, in them, through them. If so, what visitors experience is not our efforts or personalities, but the presence of the risen Jesus! And so we are back to the insight of Rowan Williams, the former Archbishop of Canterbury: "Church is what happens when two of three encounter the risen Jesus…" Jesus is there, received and recognized.

4. Understanding how abhorrent child abuse is to God (Matthew 18: 6-9)

With barely a pause, Jesus changes moods as dramatically for example as in the final movement of Beethoven's Ninth Symphony. It could well be these words of Jesus are His most angry and condemning. And as He speaks, He surely points at Galilee: that is where the ripples of the person drowning with a millstone around his neck would forever be lodged in the imaginations of the listeners to His dire warning. It is so hard to read and hear them that we often simply omit them. Do you not shudder when you hear the numbers of church leaders in America who have been involved in child abuse? (In 1962, there was a document written by a church leader, discovered by the British newspaper *The Observer,* that insisted clergy should be secretive and silent when confronted by sexual abuse within the church).

What do you feel in your heart when you think of the children murdered in Guatemala between 1981 and 1983? Among the 100,000 Mayan peasants who were slaughtered were thousands of children. Some were smashed against rocks or thrown into rivers as their parents watched. "Adios, Nino," said one soldier as he hurled a child into the river to drown.[126] Can you conceive of how Jesus feels or "who can sound the depths of sorrow in the Father heart of God" (the title of the hymn by Graham Kendrick)?

But this is not restricted to specific acts of abuse. It includes everything, directly or indirectly, personal or institutional, that might cause children ("little ones") to sin. Have you considered the world we have allowed to be created for twenty-first century children, and the pressures on them to sin? Think of child soldiers who steal, murder and rape in the hundreds of thousands. Think of the tens of millions of child prostitutes. Think of the children of the rich who grow up to envy the possessions and wealth of others, and long to have it. Consider those who are "branded" around the world by transnational corporations and marketing machines. Think of corporate and institutional pedophilia. In all these cases, and so many more, children are being led into sin.

David Hay and Rebecca Nye write that, "The adult world into which our children are inducted is more often than not destructive to their spirituality."[127] How does God see the modern world developing around us, given His primary concern for children, little ones, the weak and the vulnerable? And where does that leave us?

I was once told by a young person living at Mill Grove: "Why do you go to church? You know everything in the Bible, and you are good, so you do not need to go!" My response was: "I go to kneel down and ask God's forgiveness for the sins I know I have committed; but also for the systems and institutions I am allowing to be created, and not challenging, that cause little ones to sin." It's a sobering thought. A mission-shaped church will always be challenging, by life example and at times advocacy, the prevailing norms wherever children are suffering or are at risk.

5. Valuing each child as an individual of inestimable worth (Matthew 18: 10-14)

The water of Galilee is still lapping near the feet of Jesus, but now it is the hills, particularly to the east, richer in colors and textures as the afternoon turns to dusk, where the listeners are focusing their attention. Do not overlook the fact that the story of the one lost sheep in Matthew's Gospel is told, while the little child placed by Jesus is still standing in the midst. It begins with a reference to the angels of children.[128]

There is also a moral: "See that you do not look down on these little ones."

Statistics are powerful and they can stir us with a sense of great injustice and suffering; but in the final analysis, it is vital to realize we are called to be good shepherds who will join in the search for the one lost sheep. The mission-shaped church is not concerned about numbers, but about individual children—each one made in the image of God. We must be ready to restructure our lives so the individual child is loved unconditionally. I have written a great deal about this important topic, including *The Growth of Love*, and *Celebrating Children*.

It is helpful to reflect on the fact that this is why we are all a part of the Christian community: because God sees each one of us as having eternal value, and sent Jesus as the Shepherd to search for us and bring us to our heavenly home on His shoulders.

"I was lost, but Jesus found me; found the sheep that went astray; threw His loving arms about me, led me back into the way" is the testimony of many Christians.

"None of the ransomed ever knew how deep were the waters crossed, or how dark was the night that the Lord went through ere He found His sheep that was lost."

6. Allowing children and their families and friends to come to Jesus (Matthew 19: 13-15)

Jesus now leaves Capernaum and Galilee, and wends His way south along the River Jordan; but on the east side known as Transjordan or Perea. He would have passed the place where He was baptized, and it is not fanciful to consider it was near such a spot this next incident occurs. John the Baptist at first resisted the request of Jesus for baptism before allowing the authority of Jesus to take precedence.

This is one of the eight elements where we probably think we can move on without much need to reflect. "Let the little children come to me." Surely we all agree on this point? What controversy could there possibly be, right? Well, the disciples, having been taught specifically by Jesus all we have just considered, actually tried to prevent people from bringing children to Jesus! And, sadly, it is not difficult to find examples of churches and Christians who have, intentionally or not, done this very thing down through the centuries.

We have tended to overestimate our own skills and importance, and to underestimate the significance of the direct relationship between children and their Savior. (This is true, for example, in a field I know about—children's Bibles. Adults have decided what they want to prevent children from reading in the Bible, and often it is the great stories of loss, suffering and separation. As a consequence, many children have not been able to relate the messiness of real life with God's presence and saving acts.)

What if people bring children to Jesus in our schools rather than church-es? What if they have some very strange ideas about baptism and the sacraments? What if they need, in our view, education and medical help? What if we are trying to raise money to renovate the church? Please do not lightly assume you and I and our ministries have been innocent in all this. But rejoice when children do find their way to Jesus; He welcomes them and blesses them beyond our comprehension.

7. Seeing children as signs of the Kingdom of Heaven (Matthew 19:14; Mark 10:13-16; Luke 18:15-17)

We are still alongside the River Jordan and the final destination of Jesus. The critical event in the unfolding revelation of His kingdom in Jerusalem is near. This is where I personally came into the whole field of Child Theology: when I preached on this verse at Westminster Chapel in London. Let me briefly mention just two of the points that dawned on me during that period. First, if children are signs of the kingdom of heaven, then we must get rid of all notions of power, territory, possession and hierarchies to enter it. This kingdom is a whole new way of living. It is an upside-down, inside-out and back-to-front world. Put simply, it works on almost exactly the opposite principles of the political kingdoms we know—from personal experience and history worldwide. God's ways are not our ways. Where He has His way, the whole feel of the place and the nature of our common life together changes.

Second, just as the child is both fully human and yet still becoming an adult, so the kingdom of heaven is both "Now" and "Not Yet." You have daily reminders of God's way of doing things whenever you see children at work and play. Is there a better sign of the Kingdom? Is this what the "Resurrection Mind" is all about, as it refuses to become fixed and finalized, remaining open to further journeying, revelation and change? This surely is a characteristic of the mission-shaped church. It is such a complete contrast with what the disciples and the mother of James and John still had in mind somewhere between the Jordan and Jericho (see Matt. 20: 20-28).

8. Understanding children's expressions in the context of God's way of doing things (Matthew 21:12 -16)

And now, at last, Jesus enters the Temple itself. He has come to His Father's house. He has come home. He has come to His own. The vast roar of the crowds has ebbed, like the withdrawing tide, and there are now just a group of young people calling out, "Hosanna to the Son of David!" as they see the signs of genuine mission in action. The authorities are as indignant as the disciples were when people brought children to Jesus. And Jesus draws their attention to Psalm 8 verse 2.

If we had time to meditate on Psalm 8, we would begin to see how the cries of newborn babies can be understood in a whole new light when we trust God's way of doing things—His purposes and intentions. In the Temple, the authorities saw the behavior of the young people, who were singing and shouting, as wholly inappropriate. Jesus saw them in a completely different way: they were doing exactly what God had intended.

As we listen carefully to everything children and young people say and try to reflect on it in the light of God's heart, we will find surprising things happening! When children shout and cry in anger, we will see sometimes this is as it should be; they have experienced abuse and injustice. When children see play as more important than formal education, perhaps that is how God sees it too. And when they do not do exactly what we think they ought to in church, is our disapproval representative of God and how He feels? Perhaps, when they are seen as placed by Jesus in the midst of our worship, it helps our worship to be more pleasing to God. At the very least, we should ponder what children and young people are saying rather than ruling it out of court straight away.

Closing Reflection

At this point, we must leave our walk with Jesus. This period in the life of Jesus is of considerable importance in understanding Christian community with children in the midst. There may be no great surprises, but perhaps we are struck by the way Jesus seems to have anticipated modern theories, policies, conventions and legislation. If we are to inspire and equip other Christians to join us in ministering to children, then it makes such a difference if we root and ground our teaching in the life and teaching of Jesus. It is, as Rowan Williams said, "always worth taking Jesus seriously."

This walk—a journey, a pilgrimage from Mount Hermon to Mount Moriah—is one Jesus calls us to join.

It was an epic one for Jesus, and to all those whose eyes and ears are open, the heart of the Kingdom and mission have been revealed; it is also momentous.

Where is the place where you now need to pause and be with the Master, so He can show you more of His will and purposes? He is in no hurry to move on. He will wait for you and with you, until you are ready to move on.

And the whole journey is framed by the cries of an epileptic boy (at the outset) and then the cries of a group of rowdy young people (at the close). Jesus heard in these shouts, an echo of the cries of suckling babes. In God's view, such raw sounds are one of the most beautiful, insightful and powerful expressions in creation.

Strange that much of this has been so hidden from the wise and learned commentators! But then Jesus had already anticipated this. I imagine Him saying, "I thank you, Father, that You have hidden these things from the wise and understanding and revealed them to babes . . . Yes, Father, for such was thy will."[129]

ENDNOTES

1. Viboch. 2005. *Childhood Loss and Behavioral Problems: Loosening the Links.*

2. Brunson, Jean. 2001. *Growing Seasons: Coordinator's Guide.* Turning Point Ministries, Inc.

3. Rando, T. 1993. *Treatment of Complicated Mourning.* Champaign, IL: Research Press.

4. Phyllis Kilbourn, Ph.D. *Offering Healing and Hope for Children in Crisis: Module 1: Trauma and Crisis Care* (Fort Mill, SC: Crisis Care Training International, 2004), 79.

5. Ibid.

6. Social Work Dictionary, 279

7. Langberg, Diane Mandt. Counseling Survivors of Sexual Abuse (Wheaton, Illinois; Tyndle Publishers, pp. 25

8. Ibid.

9. Ibid.

10. Social Work Dictionary, pp. 507

11. Kilbourn, Phyllis, ed. *Healing The Children of War* (Monrovia, California: MARC books published by World Vision, 1995), 175-196.

12. Phyllis Kilbourn, Ph.D. *Offering Healing and Hope for Children in Crisis: Module 1: Trauma and Crisis Care* (Fort Mill, SC: Crisis Care Training International, 2004), 83-88.

13. Ibid, 86-87

14. http://www.mindtools.com/Commskll/ActiveListening.htm

15. Ozer, E. J., Best, S. R., Lipsey, T. L., & Weiss, D. S. 2003. "Predictors of Posttraumatic Stress Disorder and Symptoms in Adults: A Meta-analysis," *Psychological Bulletin, 129* (1), 52-73.

16. Davies, D. R., Burlingame, G. M., & Layne, C. M. 2006. "Integrating Small-group Process Principles into Trauma-focused Group Psychotherapy: What Should a Group Trauma Therapist Know?" In L. A. Schein, H. I. Spitz, G. M. Burlingame, & P. R. Muskin (Eds.) with S. Vargo, *Psychological Effects of Catastrophic Disasters: Group Approaches to Treatment,* 385-423. New York, NY: Haworth Press.

17. Skowron, E., & Reinemann D. H. S. 2005. "Effectiveness of Psychological Interventions for Child Maltreatment: A Meta-analysis," *Psychotherapy: Theory, Research, Practice, Training, 42* (1), 52-71.

18. Cox, J., Davies, D. R., Burlingame, G. M., Campbell, J. E., Layne, C. M.,

       & Katzenbach, R. J. 2007. "Effectiveness of a Trauma/Grief-focused Group Intervention: A Qualitative Study with War-exposed Bosnian Adolescents," *International Journal of Group Psychotherapy, 57* (3), 319-45.

19. David-Ferdon, C., & Kaslow, N. J. 2008. "Evidence-based Psychosocial Treatments for Child and Adolescent Depression," *Journal of Clinical Child & Adolescent Psychology, 37* (1), 62-104.

20. Silverman, W. K., Pina, A. A., & Viswesvaran, C. 2008. "Evidence-based Psychosocial Treatments for Phobic and Anxiety Disorders in Children and Adolescents," *Journal of Clinical Child & Adolescent Psychology, 37* (1), 105-30.

21. Hoag, M. J., & Burlingame, G. M. 1997. "Evaluating the Effectiveness of Child and Adolescent Group Treatment: A Meta-analytic Review," *Journal of Clinical Child Psychology, 26* (3), 234-46.

22. Sloan, D. M., Bovin, M. J., & Schnurr, P. P. 2012. "Review of Group Treatment for PTSD," *Journal of Rehabilitation Research and Development, 49* (5), 689-702.

23. Davies, D. R., Burlingame, G. M., & Layne, C. M. 2006. "Integrating Small-group Process Principles into Trauma-focused Group Psychotherapy: What Should A Group Trauma Therapist Know?" In L. A. Schein, H. I. Spitz, G. M. Burlingame, & P. R. Muskin (Eds.) with S. Vargo, *Psychological Effects of Catastrophic Disasters: Group Approaches to Treatment,* 385-423. New York, NY: Haworth Press.

24. Yalom, I. D. 1995. *The Theory and Practice of Group Psychotherapy (4th Ed.).* New York, NY: Basic Books.

25. Ibid.

26. Ibid.

27. Burlingame, G. M., Fuhriman, A., & Johnson, J. E. 2001. "Cohesion In Group Psychotherapy," *Psychotherapy, 38* (4), 373-79.

28. Davies, D. R., Burlingame, G. M., & Layne, C. M. 2006. "Integrating Small-group Process Principles into Trauma-focused Group Psychotherapy: What Should a Group Trauma Therapist Know?" In L. A. Schein, H. I. Spitz, G. M. Burlingame, & P. R. Muskin (Eds.) with S. Vargo, *Psychological Effects of Catastrophic Disasters: Group Approaches to Treatment,* 385-423. New York, NY: Haworth Press.

29. Burlingame, G. M., McClendon, D. T., & Alonso, J. 2011. "Cohesion in Group Therapy," *Psychotherapy, 48*(1), 34-42.

30. Herman, Judith, M.D., *Trauma and Recovery: The Aftermath of Violence—from Domestic Abuse to Political Terror.* Basic Books, 1997, 217). (133)

31. Cox, J., Davies, D. R., Burlingame, G. M., Campbell, J. E., Layne, C. M., & Katzenbach, R. J. 2007. "Effectiveness of a Trauma/Grief-focused Group Intervention: A Qualitative Study with War-exposed Bosnian Adolescents," *International Journal of Group Psychotherapy,* 57(3), 319-45.

32. Burlingame, G. M., & Beecher, M. E. 2008. "New Directions and Resources In Group Psychotherapy: Introduction to the Issue," *Journal of Clinical Psychology: In*

Session, 64 (11), 1197-205.

33. Herman, Judith, M.D., *Trauma and Recovery: The Aftermath of Violence—from Domestic Abuse to Political Terror.* Basic Books, 1997, 214).

34. Yalom, I. D. 1995. *The Theory and Practice of Group Psychotherapy (4th Ed.).* New York, NY: Basic Books.

35. Duncan, B. L. 2010. *On Becoming a Better Therapist.* Washington, DC: American Psychological Association.

36. Paturel, A. 2012. "Power in Numbers: Research is Pinpointing the Factors that Make Group Therapy Successful," *Monitor on Psychology, 43* (10), 48-49.

37. Corey, M. S., Corey, G., & Corey, C. 2010, 297. *Groups: Process and Practice (8th Ed.).* Belmont, CA: Brooks/Cole, Cengage Learning.

38. Saltzman, W. R., Layne, C. M., Steinberg, A. M., & Pynoos, R. S. 2006. "Trauma/ Grief-focused Group Psychotherapy with Adolescents." In L. A. Schein, H. I. Spitz, G. M. Burlingame, & P. R. Muskin (Eds.) with S. Vargo, *Psychological Effects of Catastrophic Disasters: Group Approaches to Treatment,* 669-729. New York, NY: Haworth Press.

39. Strauss, B., Burlingame, G. M., & Bormann, B. 2008. "Using the CORE-R Battery In Group Psychotherapy," *Journal of Clinical Psychology: In Session, 64* (11), 1225-37.

40. Parton, C., & Manby, M. 2009. "The Contribution of Group Work Programmes to Early Intervention and Improving Children's Emotional Well-being," *Pastoral Care in Education, 27* (1), 5-19.

41. Burlingame, G. M., & Beecher, M. E. 2008. "New Directions and Resources In Group Psychotherapy: Introduction to the Issue," *Journal of Clinical Psychology: In Session, 64* (11), 1197-205.

42. Corey, M. S., Corey, G., & Corey, C. 2010. *Groups: Process and Practice (8th Ed.).* Belmont, CA: Brooks/Cole, Cengage Learning.

43. This is an infrequently used New Testament word coming from the word for intestines. "It literally means to pour out one's insides, one's intestines." See Rye et al., 2001:20.

44. See Rye et al., 200

45. See Rye et al., 2001: I owe this understanding of *aphiemi* to my former pastor who was raised in the Greek Orthodox Church and is fluent in Greek.

46. Ibid.

47. This concept is from Shriver, 2001:26-8.

48. See Muller-Fahrenholz, 1998:236.

49. Word meanings taken from Harper, 2001.

50. All phrases and statements, unless otherwise specified, were made by different children who were victim survivors of the civil war in Sierra Leone; many of them were also recruited to participate and commit serious violations against others.

51. This is mitigated by culture and religious beliefs, as well as the child's inherent resilience, which will come up later in this chapter.

52. "You will be more in the err..." is understood to mean: "You will be the one with the bigger fault, or more to blame."

53. The father's forgiveness was so generous and extravagant that it became an obstacle to the elder brother of the prodigal.

54. This child identified himself as Muslim.

55. Adults do need to be deliberate in apologizing if they have wronged a child.

56. Palm, Melody, Jami R. Pool, and Katie Burgmayer. (2007, 231). "Understanding the Spiritual Needs of Survivors." In *Hands that Heal: International Curriculum to Train Caregivers of Trafficking Survivors*, eds. Beth Grant and Cindy Lopez Hudlin. Faith Alliance Against Slavery and Trafficking. P. 159

57. Ibid. (218)

58. Ibid. (207)

59. Ibid. (222)

60. Heitritter, Lynn and Jeanette Vought. 1989 (55). *Helping Victims of Sexual Abuse: A Sensitive, Biblical Guide for Counselors, Victims and Families.* Minneapolis, MN: Bethany House Publishers.

61. Ibid. (53)

62. Ibid. (54)

63. Dods, Marcus. 1891. "XXI. Jesus the Good Shepherd." *The Expositor's Bible: The Gospel of St. John, Vol. I.* A.C. Armstrong and Son. Available from http://christian-bookshelf.org/dods/the_expositors_bible_the_gospel_of_st_john_vol_i/index.html

64. Maclaren, Alexander. n.d. "The Good Shepherd." *Expositions of Holy Scripture.* Available from http://christianbookshelf.org/maclaren/expositions_of_holy_scripture_i/the_good_shepherd.htm

65. Ibid.

66. Ibid.

67. Kingsley, Charles. 1887. "Sermon XXVII. The Good Shepherd." *The Good News of God.* Macmillan and Co. Available from http://christianbookshelf.org/kingsley/the_good_news_of_god/sermon_xxvii_the_good_shepherd.htm

68. Ibid.

69. Gill, John. n.d. "Luke 15." *Exposition of the Entire Bible.* Available from http://gill.biblecommenter.com/luke/15.htm

70. Henry, Matthew. n.d. "Luke 15." *Matthew Henry's Commentary on the Whole Bible.* Available from http://mhcw.biblecommenter.com/luke/15.htm.

71. Gill, John. n.d. "Luke 15." *Exposition of the Entire Bible.* Available from http://gill.biblecommenter.com/luke/15.htm

72. Ibid.

73. Maclaren, Alexander. n.d. "The Lost Sheep and the Seeking Shepherd." *Expositions of Holy Scripture*. Available from http://christianbookshelf.org/maclaren/expositions_of_holy_scripture_b/the_lost_sheep_and_the.htm

74. Henry, Matthew. n.d. "Luke 15." *Matthew Henry's Commentary on the Whole Bible*. Available from http://mhcw.biblecommenter.com/luke/15.htm.

75. Gill, John. n.d. "Luke 15." *Exposition of the Entire Bible*. Available from http://gill.biblecommenter.com/luke/15.htm

76. Ibid.

77. Jersak, Brad. 2003. *Children, Can You Hear Me?* Canada: Friesens.

78. 2012. *Time with Abba for Children*. Pastoral Care School: Pastoral Care School.

79. Ibid.

80. Ibid.

81. I am indebted in this section to ideas from William Kreidler's book, *Creative Conflict Resolution* (Glenview, Illinois: Scott, Foresman & Co., 1984) *p. 190*

82. Paul Tournier, *The Violence Within* (San Francisco: Harper & Row, 1978), pp. 113-114. *(p. 192)*

83. Elizabeth Crary, *Kids Can Cooperate: A Practical Guide to Teach Problem Solving* (Seattle: Parenting Press, 1984), pp. 40-45. *(p. 192)*

84. Kegan, R. (1982). *The Evolving Self: Problem and Process in Human Development*. Cambridge, MA: Harvard University Press.

85. Perry, B. D., Szalavitz, M., & Campbell, D. (2011). *The Boy Who was Raised as a Dog and Other Stories from a Child Psychiatrist's Notebook: What Traumatized Children Can Teach Us About Loss, Love, and Healing*. Old Saybrook, CT: Tantor Media, Inc. Audiobook

86. Grotberg, E. H. (1995). *A Guide to Promoting Resilience in Children: Strengthening the Human Spirit*. The Hague, Netherlands: The Bernard van Leer Foundation.

87. Ibid.

88. Sandage, S. J., Wibberly, K. H., & Worthington, E. L. (1995). "Christian Counselors' Resources for Multi-cultural Understanding and Counseling," *Journal of Psychology and Theology, 23*(1), 30-36.

89. Hernandez, M., Nesman, T., Mowery, D., Acevedo-Polakovich, I. D., & Callejas, L. M. (2009). "Cultural Competence: A Literature Review and Conceptual Model for Mental Health Services," *Psychiatric Services, 60*(8), 1046-50.

90. McGoldrick, M., & Giordano, J. (1996). "Overview: Ethnicity and Family Therapy." In M. McGoldrick, J. Giordano, & J. K. Pearce (Eds), *Ethnicity and Family Therapy (2nd Ed.)*, 1-27. New York: Guilford.

91. Sue, D. W., Arredondo, P., & McDavis, R. (1992). "Multicultural Counseling

Competencies and Standards: A Call to the Profession," *Journal of Counseling and Development, 70*, 477-86.

92. Griner, D., & Smith, T. B. (2006). "Culturally Adapted Mental Health Intervention: A Meta-analytic Review," *Psychotherapy: Theory, Research, Practice, Training, 43*(4), 531-48.

93. *What does the Bible say about family?* Online at http://www.gotquestions.org/Bible-family.html

94. Strongs Concordance #01129

95. Strongs Concordance #01004

96. Strongs Concordance #2009

97. Dictionary.com. Online at http://dictionary.reference.com/

98. Strongs Concordance #1696

99. Search Quotes. Online at http://www.searchquotes.com/quotation/

100. Think.Exist.com. Online at http://thinkexist.com/quotations/home/

101. Dictionary.com. Online at http://dictionary.reference.com/

102. Lifeway.com. Online at http://www.lifeway.com/ArticleView?storeId=10054&catalogId=10001&langId=-1&article=eight-characteristics-of-a-healthy-family

103. Ibid.

104. Wigger, J. Bradley; The Power of God at Home; Jossey-Bass Publishers; 2003, 16

105. Lifeway.com Online at http://www.lifeway.com/ArticleView?storeId=10054&catalogId=10001&langId=-1&article=eight-characteristics-of-a-healthy-family

106. Schneider, Thirza; *The Barnabas Letter: Children of Alcoholic Parents*; 2011; Volume 8

107. *The Only Thing Unchanged is Change*; February 12, 2009, zencaroline.blogspot.com

108. *Dysfunctional Family as a Cause of Difficult Childhood;* Buzzle.com

109. *Dysfunctional Families: Recognizing and Overcoming Their Effects;* TWU Counseling Center. Online at http://www.twu.edu/downloads/counseling/E-5_Dysfunctional_Families

110. Ibid.

111. Schneider, Thirza; *The Barnabas Letter: Children of Alcoholic Parents*; 2011; Volume 8

112. U.S. Department of Health and Human Services; Gaudin, J.M. Jr; *Child neglect: A Guide for Intervention*; Child Welfare Information Gateway; www.childwelfare.gov

113. Schneider, Thirza; *The Barnabas Letter: Children of Alcoholic Parents*; 2011; Volume 8

114. Figley, Charles R. (1995). "Compassion Fatigue as Secondary Traumatic Stress Disorder: An Overview." In Figley, Charles R (ed.). *Compassion Fatigue: Coping with Secondary Traumatic Stress Disorder in Those Who Treat the Traumatized*, 1-20. New York: Brunner/Mazel.

115. Ibid.

116. David Conrad, "Secondary Trauma." Online at *http://*secondarytrauma.org.

117. Lynne Shallcross, "Taking Care of Yourself as a Counselor," *Counseling Today*, January 2011, 1.

118. Rowland Croucher, "Stress and Burnout in Ministry." Online at http://www.church-link.com.

119. Lynne Shallcross, "Taking Care of Yourself as a Counselor," *Counseling Today*, January 2011, 1.

120. Helping Children Cope with Crisis: Care for Caregivers; ©2003, National Association of School Psychologists, 4340 East West Highway 402#, Bethesda, MD 20814

121. Charles Ringma, *Dare to Journey with Henri Nouwen* (NavPress, 2000) Reflection 1.

122. Matthew 20: 22

123. Matthew 16: 13-28

124. For over ten years, my friend Professor Haddon Willmer and I have been working on a book that seeks to understand and expound the first part of this chapter of Matthew's Gospel. It is due to be published in 2013. I owe to our conversation some of the insights of this current paper, but our joint work takes us to new places.

125. Henri Nouwen, *Adam: God's Beloved* (Maryknoll: Orbis, 2002)

126. Greg Grandin, *Empire's Workshop* (New York: Metropolitan, 2006) 90

127. David Hay and Rebecca Nye, *The Spirit of the Child* (London: HarperCollins, 1998) 21

128. The meaning of this verse, including the angels who behold the face of the Father, is explored in some detail in the forthcoming book I am writing with Dr. Haddon Willmer.

129. Matthew 11: 25 & 26

RESOURCE LIST

Adams, Marilyn M. 1991. "Forgiveness: A Christian Model," *Faith and Philosophy* 8(3).

Anderson, Pamela S. 2001. "A Feminist Ethics of Forgiveness." In A. McFadyen & M. Sarot (Eds.), *Forgiveness and Truth*: 145-55. Edinburgh: T & T Clark.

Armour, Marilyn P. & Umbreit, Mark S. 2005. "The Paradox of Forgiveness in Restorative Justice." In E.L. Worthington, Jr. (Ed.), *Handbook of Forgiveness*: 491-503. New York: Routledge.

Aschliman, Kathryn, ed. *Growing Toward Peace.* Scottdale, Pennsylvania: Herald Press, 1993.

Biggar, Nigel 2001. "Forgiveness in the Twentieth Century: A Review of the Literature," 1901-2001. In A. McFadyen & M. Sarot (Eds.), *Forgiveness and Truth*: 181-217. Edinburgh: T & T Clark.

Chircop, Lionel 1998. "Remembering the Future." In A. Falconer & J. Liechty (Eds.), *Reconciling Memories*, 2nd ed.: 20-9. Dublin: The Columba Press.

Coles, Robert 1991. *The Spiritual Life of Children.* Boston: Houghton Mifflin Company.

Crary, E. *Kids Can Cooperate: A Practical Guide* to *Teaching Problem Solving.* Seattle: Parenting Press, Inc., 1984.

Cyuma, Samuel 2005. *Conflict Reconciliation in South Africa (1990-1998) and Its Significance for the Mediating Role of the Church in Rwanda (1990-2003).* University of Wales.

Denham, Susanne, Neal, Karen, Wilson, Beverly J., Pickering, Stephanie & Boyatzis, Chris 2005. "Emotional Development and Forgiveness in Children: Emerging Evidence." In E.L. Worthington, Jr. (Ed.), *Handbook of Forgiveness*: 127-42. New York: Routledge.

Enright, Robert & North, J. (Eds.) 1998. *Exploring Forgiveness.* Madison, Wisconsin: The University of Wisconsin Press.

Enright, Robert, Freedman, Suzanne & Rique, Julio 1998. "The Psychology of Interpersonal Forgiveness." In R Enright & J North (Eds.), *Exploring Forgiveness*: 46-62. Madison: The University of Wisconsin Press.

Exline, J.J. & Baumeister, R.F. 2000. "Expressing Forgiveness and Repentance: Benefits and Barriers." In M. McCullough, K.I. Pargament & C.E. Thoresen (Eds.), *Forgiveness: Theory, Research and Practice*: 133-55. New York: Guilford Press.

Falconer, Alan D. 1998. "The Reconciling Power of Forgiveness." In A. Falconer & J. Liechty (Eds.), *Reconciling Memories*: 177-94. Dublin: The Columba Press.

Figley, C. *Helping Traumatized Families.* San Francisco: Jossey Bass Publishers, 1989.

Freudenberger, C. Dean has elaborated on these ideas in his writings on ways to deal with world hunger.

Goins, Stephanie L. 2008. *"The Place of Forgiveness in the Reintegration of Former Child Soldiers in Sierra Leone."* In H.C. Allen, Ed. *Nurturing Children's Spirituality: Christian Perspectives and Best Practices*: 289-304. Eugene, OR: Cascade Books.

Govier, Trudy 2002. *Forgiveness and Revenge.* London: Routledge.

Greenwald, D. & Harder, D.1998. "Domains of Shame: Evolutionary, Cultural and Psychotherapeutic Aspects." In P.B.A. Gilbert and Bernice Andrews (Ed.), *Shame*: 225-46. Oxford: Oxford University Press.

Hamber, Brandon E. 2003. "Does The Truth Heal? A Psychological Perspective on Political Strategies for Dealing with the Legacy of Political Violence." In N. Biggar (Ed.), *Burying the Past: Making Peace and Doing Justice after Civil Conflict,* 2nd ed.: 155-76. Washington DC: Georgetown University Press.

James, Beverly. *Treating Traumatized Children: New Insights and Creative Interventions.* Lexington, Massachusetts: Lexington Books, 1989.

Jones, Gregory 1995. *Embodying Forgiveness: A Theological Analysis.* Grand Rapids: Eerdmans Publishing Co.

Minow, Martha 1998. *Between Vengeance and Forgiveness: Facing History after Genocide and Mass Violence.* Boston: Beacon Press Books.

Kraybill, R. S. *Repairing the Breach: Ministering in Community Conflict.* Scottdale, Pennsylvania: Herald Press, 1981.

Kreidler, William J. *Creative Conflict Resolution.* Glenview, Illinois: Scott, Foresman & Co., 1984.

McGinnis, J. and K. McGinnis. *Parenting for Peace and Justice.* Maryknoll: Orbis Books, 1981.

McGinnis, K. and B. Oehlberg. *Starting Out Right: Nurturing Young Children as Peacemakers.* The Institute for Peace and Justice and Meyer Stone Books, 1990.

Morris, Herbert 1988. "Murphy on Forgiveness." *Criminal Justice Ethics,* 7(2): 15-19.

Moucarry, Chawkat 2004. *The Search for Forgiveness: Pardon and Punishment in Islam and Christianity.* Leicester: Inter-Varsity Press.

Muller-Fahrenholz, Geiko 1998. "On Shame and Hurt in the Life of Nations: A German Perspective." In A. Falconer & J. Liechty (Eds.), *Reconciling Memories,* 2nd ed.: 232-41. Dublin: The Columba Press.

Murphy, Jeffrie G. & Hampton, Jean 1988. *Forgiveness and Mercy.* Cambridge: Cambridge University Press.

Neal, Karen L. Bassett, Hideko & Denham, Susanne 2004. *Affective Processes and Children's Propensity to Forgive.* Fairfax, VA: George Mason University. Paper.

Rogers, Carl R. 1980. *A Way of Being.* Boston: Houghton Mifflin.

Rowden, Trampas J. & Davis, Sean D. "Forgiveness in Families." 2005. Online at http://foreverfamilies.byu.edu. Accessed on June 22, 2005.

Rye, Mark S., et al. 2001. "Religious Perspectives on Forgiveness." In M.E. McCullough, C.E. Thoresen & K. Pargament (Eds.), *Forgiveness: Theory, Research and Practice:* 17-40. New York: Guilford Press.

Shriver, Donald 1995. *An Ethic for Enemies: Forgiveness in Politics.* Oxford: Oxford University Press.

Shults, F. LeRon & Sandage, Steven J. 2003. *The Faces of Forgiveness: Searching for Wholeness and Salvation.* Grand Rapids: Baker Academic.

Smyth, Marie 2001. "Putting the Past in Its Place." In N. Biggar (Ed.), *Burying the Past: Making Peace and Doing Justice After Civil Conflict:* 107-30. Washington DC: Georgetown University Press.

Soyinka, Wole 1999. *The Burden of Memory, the Muse of Forgiveness.* Oxford: Oxford University Press.

Taylor, Vincent 1948. *Forgiveness and Reconciliation: A Study in New Testament Theology.* London: MacMillan & Co., Ltd.

Tournier, P. *The Violence Within* San Francisco: Harper and Roe 1978

van Deusen Hunsinger, Deborah 2001. "Forgiving Abusive Parents: Psychological and Theological Considerations." In A. McFadyen & M. Sarot (Eds.), *Forgiveness and Truth:* 71-98. Edinburgh: T & T Clark.

Van Ornum, William and J. B. Mordock. *Crisis Counseling with Children and Adolescents.* New York: Continuum, 1991

Volf, Miroslav 1996. *Exclusion and Embrace: A Theological Exploration of Identity, Otherness and Reconciliation.* Nashville: Abingdon Press.

_____ 2005. *Free of Charge: Giving and Forgiving in a Culture Stripped of Grace.* Grand Rapids, MI: Zondervan Publishing.

Watts, Fraser 2004. "Christian Theology." In F. Watts & L. Gulliford (Eds.), *Forgiveness in Context: Theology and Psychology in Creative Dialogue:* 50-68. London: T & T Clark International.

Willmer, Haddon 2001. "Jesus Christ the Forgiven: Christology, Atonement and Forgiveness." In A. McFadyen & M. Sarot (Eds.), *Forgiveness and Truth*: 15-29. Edinburgh: T & T Clark.

_____ 2007. "Forgiveness As Permission to Live." In J. Baxter (Ed.), *Wounds that Heal: Theology, Imagination and Health*: 79-98. London: SPCK.

Winter, David A. 1992. *Personal Construct Psychology in Clinical Practice*. London: Routledge.

Worthington Jr., Everett L. (Ed.) 1998. *Dimensions of Forgiveness: Psychological Research and Theological Perspectives* (1st ed.). (Vol. 1). Philadelphia: Templeton Foundation Press

This book was produced by CLC Publications. We hope it has been life-changing and has given you a fresh experience of God through the work of the Holy Spirit. CLC Publications is an outreach of CLC Ministries International, a global literature mission with work in over fifty countries. If you would like to know more about us or are interested in opportunities to serve with a faith mission, we invite you to contact us at:

CLC Ministries International
PO Box 1449
Fort Washington, PA 19034

E-mail: mail@clcusa.org
Website: www.clcpublications.com

- - - - - - - - - - - - - - - - - -

DO YOU LOVE GOOD CHRISTIAN BOOKS?
Do you have a heart for worldwide missions?

You can receive a FREE subscription to
CLC's newsletter on global literature missions
Order by e-mail at:

clcworld@clcusa.org
or mail your request to:

**PO Box 1449
Fort Washington, PA 19034**

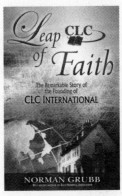

About
Crisis Care Training International
www.crisiscaretraining.org

CCTI is a ministry
of WEC International

Our Mission:

To bring the healing and hope of Christ to children and families in crisis, through training and resources.

Our Task:

Of the 2.2 billion children in the world, two-thirds (1.5 billion) are hurting. They are children at risk and children in crisis. They include street children, child soldiers, child laborers, orphans and the sexually trafficked and exploited. These are children who have been subjected to abuse, abandonment, neglect and/or exploitation.

Our task is to equip communities, local church members and caregivers with the **training and resources** necessary to bring the healing and hope of Christ to children in crisis and their families.

Our Strategy:

To accomplish our mission CCTI is:

- **Building awareness** of global children-in-crisis situations and subsequent ministry opportunities.

- **Developing resources** and training materials including a curriculum, books and a training newsletter.

- **Training and equipping** communities, local church members and caregivers to effectively and compassionately minister to children and families in crisis.

- **Creating a pool of trainers** to assist with global training needs.

- Working towards **establishing a** fully equipped and accredited **training center** available to all engaged in children-in-crisis ministry.

Contact CCTI

info@crisiscaretraining.org

www.crisiscaretraining.org

1-803-548-2811

LET ALL THE CHILDREN COME

Phyllis Kilbourn

In order to minister more effectively to children with disabilities, we first must understand the context surrounding children with disabilities and the consequences of disability on them. This book, complied by Phyliss Kilbourn, provides helpful training to those who desire to engage in more informed ministry to disabled children.

Trade Paper
Size 6 x 9, Pages 416
ISBN: 978-1-61958-067-1
ISBN (*e-book*): 978-1-61958-128-9
$14.99

BEYOND THE EDGE

100 Stories of Trusting God

WEC International (Evan Davies, general editor)

Experience the joy of sharing the gospel with people who are hearing it for the first time. Be amazed at the miraculous move of God in His people's lives. Weep over the martyrdom of missionaries for the cause of Christ See how God is using WEC international to carry out the vision of founder C.T. Studd to reach all peoples with the gospel.

Trade Paper
Size 5¹/₄ x 8, Pages 368
ISBN: 978-1-936143-94-8
ISBN (*e-book*): 978-1-61958-103-6
$14.99